Village Life in Ancient Egypt

Village Life in Ancient Egypt

Laundry Lists and Love Songs

A. G. MCDOWELL

OXFORD
UNIVERSITY PRESS

OXFORD

UNIVERSITY PRESS

Oxford University Press, Great Clarendon Street, Oxford OX2 6DP

Oxford New York

Athens Auckland Bangkok Bogotá Buenos Aires Calcutta
Cape Town Chennai Dar es Salaam Delhi Florence Hong Kong Istanbul
Karachi Kuala Lumpur Madrid Melbourne Mexico City Mumbai
Nairobi Paris São Paulo Singapore Taipei Tokyo Toronto Warsaw
and associated companies in Berlin Ibadan

Oxford is a registered trade mark of Oxford University Press

Published in the United States
by Oxford University Press Inc., New York

British Library Cataloguing in Publication Data

Data available

Library of Congress Cataloging in Publication Data
Village life in ancient Egypt: laundry lists and love songs
A.G. McDowell.
Includes bibliographical references.
1. Egypt—Social life and customs—To 332 B.C.—Sources.
2. Egyptian language—Texts. 3. Dayr al-Madinah Site (Egypt). I. Title.
DT61.M473 1999 932—dc21 98-47423

ISBN 0-19-814998-0

1 3 5 7 9 10 8 6 4 2

Typeset by Best-set Typesetter Ltd., Hong Kong
Printed in Great Britain on acid-free paper by
Bookcraft (Bath) Ltd., Midsomer Norton

For my parents

Acknowledgements

I am particularly indebted to the many people who assisted me with this book, most of whom are friends as well as colleagues and went well beyond the call of duty. This is especially true of those who generously read and commented on individual chapters, namely J. F. Borghouts, Rob Demarée, Cathleen Keller, Richard Parkinson, Gay Robins, and Deborah Sweeny. Without their help, I would have felt much less comfortable about the large parts of the book that belong rather to their areas of expertise than to my own. I am also tremendously grateful to John Baines, with whom I discussed many aspects of the work in progress and who has, as usual, been supportive and encouraging from beginning to end.

Terry Wilfong, Willem Hovestreydt, and Lynn Meskell kindly sent me copies of unpublished manuscripts, on which I drew heavily, as the reader will see from the bibliographical notes.

I am also pleased to have yet another chance to express my thanks to the Griffith Institute and its staff, whose help has been essential to almost every one of my publications. Jaromir Malek, Diana McGee, and Elizabeth Miles have been unfailingly generous with their time and assistance; while John Taylor has been a paragon of librarians, doing everything possible to get me the books I needed. I also thank Sue McKay, who submitted to my incessant use of her photocopier and office supplies with endless good humour.

The least expected and in that sense most gratifying assistance came from the Center for Studies in Law, Economics, and Public Policy at Yale Law School, which provided me with a John M. Olin Student Summer Fellowship to write the chapters on Law and Economics.

A number of institutions very kindly permitted me to reproduce illustrations from their publications, namely, the Metropolitan Museum of Art in New York, the British Museum and the Egypt Exploration Society in London, and the Institut Français d'Archéologie Orientale in Cairo. The IFAO was particularly generous in this regard. The most important contributor to the illustrations, however, was Marion Cox, who made the beautiful and clear new line drawings. I am very much obliged to her.

I am also most grateful to non-Egyptological friends whose help was as indispensable as that of any of my colleagues—to Tony Randall and Sally Crawford, who very kindly helped me to puzzle through the medical texts; to Grainne de Burca and Murray Hunt, who were characteristically generous in allowing me to use their computers and printers and in delivering the manuscript to the Press. Finally, I would like to thank my father, Robert McDowell, for reading parts of the book for legibility.

My gratitude to my parents for their support and encouragement in my work, as in all things, cannot be put into words. I dedicate this book to them.

A.McD.

Contents

List of Figures

Abbreviations

Journal titles are abbreviated as in *Lexikon der Ägyptologie*

Allam, *HOP*	Schafik Allam, *Hieratische Ostraka und Papyri aus der Ramessidenzeit.* Urkunden zum Rechtsleben im Alten Ägypten, vol. 1 (Tübingen, 1973).
Allam, *HOP* Plates	As above, plates volume.
Assman, *Hymnen und Gebete*	Jan Assman, *Ägyptische Hymnen und Gebete* (Zürich and Munich, 1975).
Bakir, *Epistolography*	'Abd el-Mohsen Bakir, *Egyptian Epistolography from the Eighteenth to the Twenty-First Dynasty.* Bd'E 48 (Cairo, 1970).
Brunner, *Altägyptische Weisheit*	Hellmut Brunner, *Altägyptische Weisheit: Lehren für das Leben* (Darmstadt, 1988).
Bruyère, *Rapport*	Bernard Bruyère, *Rapport sur les Fouilles de Deir el Médineh.*
(1922–1923)	FIFAO I,1 (Cairo, 1924)
(1923–1924)	FIFAO II,2 (Cairo, 1925)
(1924–1925)	FIFAO III,3 (Cairo, 1926)
(1926)	FIFAO IV,3 (Cairo, 1927)
(1927)	FIFAO V,2 (Cairo, 1928)
(1928)	FIFAO VI,2 (Cairo, 1929)
(1929)	FIFAO VII,2 (Cairo, 1930)
(1930)	FIFAO VIII,3 (Cairo, 1933)
(1931–1932)	FIFAO X,1 (Cairo, 1934)
(1933–1934)	FIFAO XIV (Cairo, 1937)
(1934–1935), pt. 2	FIFAO XV (Cairo, 1937)
(1934–1935), pt. 3	FIFAO XVI (Cairo, 1939)
(1935–1940)	FIFAO XX (Cairo, 1948–1952)
(1945–1946 et 1946–1947)	FIFAO XXI (1952)
(1948–1951)	FIFAO XXVI (Cairo, 1953).

Černý, *Community*	Jaroslav Černý, *A Community of Workmen at Thebes in the Ramesside Period*. Bd'E 50 (Cairo, 1973).
Černý, *LRL*	Jaroslav Černý, *Late Ramesside Letters* (Brussels, 1939).
Černý, NB	Unpublished notebooks of Jaroslav Černý, now in the Griffith Institute, Oxford.
Gardiner, *HPBM* 3rd	Alan H. Gardiner, *Hieratic Papyri in the British Museum*, 3rd ser., *Chester Beatty Gift*, vol. 1: Text and 2: Plates (London, 1935).
Gleanings	R. J. Demarée and Jac. J. Janssen (eds.), *Gleanings from Deir el-Medina* (Leiden, 1982).
Helck, *Materialien*	Wolfgang Helck, Materialien zur *Wirtschaftsgeschichte des Neuen Reiches*, parts 1–6. Akademie der Wissenschaften und der Literatur in Mainz, Abhandlungen der Geistes- und Sozialwissenschaftlichen Klasse, Jahrgang 1960–1969 (Wiesbaden, 1961–9) + Inge Hofmann, *Indices*. Abhandlungen 1969, Nr. 13 (Wiesbaden, 1970).
Hier. Pap. III	*Hieratische Papyrus aus den Königlichen Museen zu Berlin*, vol. III (Leipzig, 1911).
Janssen, *De Markt op de Oever*	Jac. J. Janssen, *De Markt op de Oever*. Rede uitgesproken bij de aanvaarding van het ambt van gewoon hoogleraar in de Egyptologie, aan de Rijksuniversiteit te Leiden (Leiden, 1980).
Janssen, *Prices*	Jac. J. Janssen, *Commodity Prices from the Ramesside Period* (Leiden, 1975).
Janssen/Janssen, *Growing up*	Rosalind M. Janssen and Jac. J. Janssen, *Growing Up in Ancient Egypt* (London, Rubicon Press, 1990).
KRI	K. A. Kitchen, *Ramesside Inscriptions, Historical and Biographical*, vols. i–viii (Oxford, 1975–90).

Lichtheim, *Ancient Egyptian Literature*	Miriam Lichtheim, *Ancient Egyptian Literature*, vols. 1 and 2 (Berkeley, Los Angeles, London, 1973–76).
LÄ	Wolfgang Helck, Eberhard Otto, and Wolfhart Westendorf (eds.), *Lexikon der Ägyptologie*, vols. i–viii (Wiesbaden, 1975–92).
McDowell, *Jurisdiction*	A. G. McDowell, *Jurisdiction in the Workmen's Community of Deir el-Medina*. Egyptologische Uitgaven, 5 (Leiden, 1990).
Peet, *The Great Tomb Robberies*	T. Eric Peet, *The Great Tomb Robberies of the Twentieth Egyptian Dynasty*, vol. 1: Text and 2: Plates (Oxford, 1930). Reprinted, 2 vols. in 1 vol. (Hildesheim and New York, 1977).
Spiegelberg, *Graffiti*	Wilhelm Spiegelberg, *Ägyptische und Andere Graffiti (Inschriften und Zeichnungen) aus der Thebanischen Nekropolis* (Heidelberg, 1921).
Valbelle, *Ouvriers*	Dominique Valbelle, *Les Ouvriers de la tombe*, Bibliothèque d'Étude, 96 (Cairo, 1985).
Village Voices	R. J. Demarée and A. Egberts (eds.), *Village Voices* (Leiden, 1992).
Wente, *Letters*	Edward F. Wente, *Letters from Ancient Egypt*, Writings from the Ancient World, 1 (Atlanta, 1990).
Wente, *LRL*	Edward Wente, *Late Ramesside Letters*. Studies in Ancient Oriental Civilization 33 (Chicago, 1967).

Major Text Collections

O Cairo 25501–25832	Jaroslav Černý, *Ostraca hiératiques (nos. 25 501–832)*, *Catalogue général des antiquités égyptiennes du Musée du Caire*, 2 vols. (Cairo, 1935).
O DeM 1–456	Jaroslav Černý, *Catalogue des ostraca hiératiques non-littéraires de Deir el-Médineh, nos. 1–456*. DFIFAO 3–7 (Cairo, 1935–51). Serge Sauneron, *Catalogue des ostraca hiératiques non-littéraires de Deir el-Médineh, nos. 550–623*.

DFIFAO 13 (Cairo, 1959).
Jaroslav Černý, *Catalogue des ostraca hiératiques non-littéraires de Deir el-Médineh, nos. 624–705.* DFIFAO 14 (Cairo, 1970).

O DeM 1001–1675   Georges Posener, *Catalogue des ostraca hiératiques littéraires de Deir el Medinéh*, 3 vols. = *DFIFAO* 1, 18, and 20 (Cairo, 1934–80), continued by A. Gasse (nos. 1676–1774), 1 vol. = *DFIFAO* 25 (Cairo, 1990).

HO   Jaroslav Černý and Alan H. Gardiner, *Hieratic Ostraca*, vol. 1 (Oxford, 1957).

O Mich   Hans Goedicke and Edward F. Wente, *Ostraka Michaelides* (Wiesbaden, 1962).

O Turin   Jesus López, *Ostraca Ieratici, N. 57001–57568, Tabelle Lignee, N. 58001–58007*. Cat. Mus. Eg. Tor., Ser. II—Collezioni, vol. 3—fasc. 1–4 (Milan, 1978–84).

P DeM   Jaroslav Černý, *Papyrus hiératiques Deir el-Medinéh*, vol. 1 [nos. i–xvii]. DFIFAO 8 (Cairo, 1978); vol. II [nos. xviii–xxxiv]. DFIFAO 22 (Cairo, 1986).

RAD   Alan H. Gardiner, *Ramesside Administrative Documents* (Oxford, 1948).

Stela Turin   Mario Tosi and Alessandro Roccati, *Stele e altre epigrafi di Deir el Medina n. 50001–n. 50262* (Turin, 1972).

Introduction

The Setting

The texts collected in this anthology belong to the New Kingdom (*c*.1570–1070 BC), a period of a different character than earlier eras of Egyptian history. At the dawn of the Eighteenth Dynasty, the native Egyptian kings ruled over only a stump of their ancient kingdom; the north of Egypt was in the hands of an alien people, the Hyksos; while, to the south, Egypt had lost Lower Nubia to the kingdom of Kush. This situation was intolerable to the last pharaoh of the Seventeenth Dynasty, Kamose, who led his countrymen in an uprising against the realms to either side. It was his son Ahmose who achieved the final victory, driving the Hyksos out of the land and pursuing them into Palestine. The years of foreign occupation had made Egypt distrustful; it was no longer enough to free Egyptian soil, but neighbouring countries must also be subjected to provide a buffer zone against future enemies. Thus Egypt acquired an empire, and now for the first time enjoyed extensive and prolonged contact with the other great civilizations of the Ancient Near East.

This widening of horizons had a powerful impact on Egyptian society. New artistic and religious ideas streamed into the country, as did new terminology, luxury goods, and technology such as the horse and chariot. Foreigners also came to settle in the Nile valley, both as immigrants and prisoners of war. On the other hand, the demands of empire and the threat of attack, most notably from the Mitanni and the Sea Peoples, led to the establishment of Egypt's first standing army. The military offered a new type of career to thousands at every level of society. Although the great majority of recruits could expect no more from the army than a small plot of land from which they and their families could extract a modest living, a few who distinguished themselves in campaigns were rewarded with promotions and considerable property. In particular, a number of the soldiers who fought alongside the founders of the Eighteenth

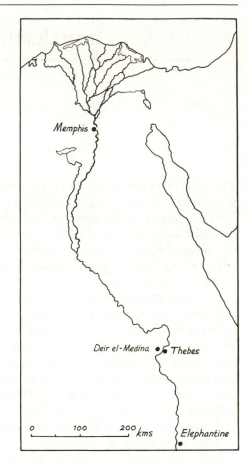

Fig. 1. Map of Egypt
showing Deir el-Medina.

Dynasty received grants of land and slaves so substantial as to make
them and their descendants people of means. Some of these new rich
moved to the growing New Kingdom cities, where they drew the
income from their estates without necessarily visiting the land from
one year to the next. These foreign contacts, new opportunities, and
growing urbanism helped to break down the rigid rules of decorum
which had governed all forms of elite culture in the Old Kingdom
and Middle Kingdoms, and contributed to the greater individuality
and variety of expression in the New Kingdom.

A separate but related development was the growth of temples.
Before the New Kingdom, the sanctuaries of gods were small and

were outranked in size and importance by the royal funerary temples. Beginning in the Eighteenth Dynasty, however, the gods shared
in the victories of their son, the pharaoh, who expressed his gratitude
for their help in the form of fields and serfs. With their vast holdings
of land, their innumerable labourers, and their many priests, the
largest temples were almost mini-states within the state. A professional priesthood was another innovation of the New Kingdom, and
a source of promising positions for the educated.

Thebes, the home town of the New Kingdom pharaohs, was
one of the great beneficiaries of these developments. Its local deity,
Amen, was raised to national importance, and the spoils of conquest
were channelled into his temples. The east bank had the two massive
temple complexes of Karnak and Luxor; the west bank, the royal
tombs and along the desert edge a row of temples dedicated jointly
to Amen and the funerary cults of the kings. Thebes now became
one of the great capitals of the ancient world; as one inhabitant wrote
of it, 'What do they say to themselves in their hearts every day, those
who are far from Thebes? They spend the day dreaming (?) of its
name.' The luxurious lifestyle of the élite at this time is illustrated in
the tombs of the nobles, who are shown surveying their vast estates,
or seated at extravagant banquets in graceful linen garments, watch-
ing the entertainment provided by musicians and dancing girls. In
the later New Kingdom, at any rate, this gilded surface appears
to have covered something of a crumbling foundation, since our
sources reveal extensive corruption, embezzlement, and power strug-
gles at every level of the administration. This need not in fact have
been anything new, however; it is the better documentation from
this period which allows us to see behind the official façade.

The temples and tombs, built of stone, are all that now remain
of this once great capital. The homes of its citizens were built of
mudbrick and have blended back into the Nile alluvium; and with a
few notable exceptions, the administrative papyri, family archives,
and private jottings that documented the lives of the literate few have
succumbed to the damp of the floodplain. All the paraphernalia of
daily life has long disappeared, apart from a small number of objects
recovered from tombs and temples. Only on the very westernmost
edge of the sprawling city did the remains of a small community
escape the general destruction. This was the village now called Deir
el-Medina, the home of the craftsmen who cut and decorated the
royal tombs in the Valley of the Kings. Built in its own desert valley,

as near as possible to the labour of its inhabitants, it lies over 50 m. above the destructive water-table. Moreover, the valley was abandoned as a settlement site at the end of the New Kingdom. The tombs built by the villagers were used for burials for a long time after, and the Ptolemies built a lovely little temple to Hathor on the site of the ancient chapel of that goddess, later converted into a church by Coptic monks who also built a monastery nearby—Deir el-Medina in fact means 'the monastery of the town'. But the houses themselves were unused; the chapels gradually buried with their dedicatory stelae still in position; and a good number of the tombs escaped the notice of the robbers. Here, where the walls have been preserved to shoulder height in places, one can still walk down the streets of three thousand years ago.

The other exceptional feature of Deir el-Medina, and the one which makes this anthology possible, is the very high rate of literacy among the inhabitants. This reached a peak in the Twentieth Dynasty, when it has been estimated that at least 40 per cent and possibly almost all the boys in the village learned to read and write—though some failed to keep up their skills in later life. Moreover, the villagers wrote not only on papyrus but also on ostraca, i.e. potsherds and pieces of limestone; the local stone flakes into smooth, white sections which offer an ideal surface for writing. Tens of thousands of documents have been recovered, both literary compositions and texts recording the day-to-day affairs of the workmen. The private texts include letters, records of economic transactions and legal disputes, testaments, magical spells, sketches, and the remains of an extensive private library, to name only a few examples. The administrative documents are equally varied. When one considers that for the rest our textual sources for Egyptian 'social' history are thinly spread and without any context to speak of, the unique value of this site becomes clear.

The Community of Workmen

The village of Deir el-Medina was a purpose-built company town, and the only people who lived there were the tomb-builders and their families. For purposes of work and administration the men were divided into two sides, the left and the right, each of which prepared the corresponding side of the royal tomb under construction. The most prominent figures in the local community were the two chief workmen, one for each side of the gang, and a scribe who was responsible for the whole. These officials, together called 'the captains', not only supervised the work in the tomb but enjoyed considerable authority within the village; they had some influence in matters of appointment and promotion, for instance, and might release workmen from their ordinary duties to carry out their own private projects. They were also paid a much higher ration than other members of the gang. The rest of the workmen all received the same standard wage and were assigned equivalent housing, although in other ways their careers varied significantly. A few performed minor administrative tasks, such as the guardians, who were responsible for the valuable materials used in the work including pigments, oil, and copper chisels. The doorkeepers ran errands for the community, and held a somewhat lower position. Foremost among those who performed the actual work were the draughtsmen, whose job was to draw the figures and hieroglyphs that decorated the royal tomb and who were therefore required to be both highly skilled and literate. They might also be asked to keep administrative records for the gang. Other skilled labourers included the sculptors who cut in low relief the figures which the draughtsmen had drawn and the painters who filled the outlines with colour. The least desirable job, on the other hand, was that of the stonecutters; it was they who actually drove the tomb into the mountain side—hard, unskilled labour. The total number of workmen fluctuated from forty or even sixty at the beginning of a reign when the new pharaoh was eager for rapid progress in his tomb down to thirty or so when the work had been completed. Ramesses IV increased the size of the gang to an unprecedented 120 men, but his successor dismissed half of these. Most workmen were recruited from within the community; sons probably served as apprentices to their fathers and learned the necessary skills from them.

The state supplied the workmen with all their needs, not only foodstuffs such as grain, fish, and vegetables (and, in good times, also pastries), but also fuel, pottery, and laundry service. Even water, which had to be brought from near the cultivation, was delivered to the village. The bulk of the workmen's wages were in the form of a monthly grain ration; they certainly received more than they could consume themselves, and the remainder could be used for barter. The grain was supplied by the government department called the

Granary, and various other Theban institutions and temples provided such commodities as garments, oil, and breads. In addition, a crew of labourers, known as service personnel, was permanently assigned to the community to produce and deliver daily requirements. In year 29 of Ramesses III, for example, a doorkeeper of the gang promised to procure extra service personnel to bring their numbers up to the following: 24 water-carriers, 20 fishermen, 14 woodcutters, 12 gardeners, 2 confectioners, 8 potters, and 8 washermen. The total of 88 men is far above that known for other periods, but the categories remain more or less the same over time. The service personnel did not live in the village.

The administrative branch responsible for the preparation of the royal burial place was called the *kher*, 'Tomb'. Rather confusingly, this same term was used for the area occupied by the entire royal necropolis, including the village of Deir el-Medina, and also for the actual grave under construction. To reduce confusion, the translation 'Necropolis' will be used when the general area or the administrative branch are meant, but 'tomb' when the word refers to the royal grave itself. Thus leading members of the gang bear titles such as 'scribe of the Necropolis' or 'chief workman of the Necropolis' and deliveries are made to the 'Enclosure of the Necropolis'.

As a branch of the administration, the Necropolis fell under the authority of the vizier, Egypt's highest secular authority after the king himself. The vizier took a direct interest in the progress of the royal tomb and visited the Valley of the Kings at frequent intervals to inspect the work. This was especially true when there were two viziers for Egypt, one stationed in the north and another at Thebes; during periods when there was only one vizier for the whole country, much of the Necropolis's official business was conducted by correspondence. Day-to-day administration was handled through the scribes of the vizier, although to a considerable extent the gang was left to carry on with the work. It is worth remembering, incidentally, that at the end of the Eighteenth Dynasty, the royal capital of Egypt moved to the northern Delta. Thebes retained its importance as a religious capital and burial place of the pharaohs, and of course as an administrative centre for the south of the country. The power in local matters of Theban officials such as the vizier and the high priest of Amen grew steadily during the Nineteenth and Twentieth Dynasties, in part as a result of the remoteness of the king. At the end of the New Kingdom, when power shifted to the high priest of

Amen, this official also took over or shared some of the vizier's responsibilities regarding the Necropolis; this transfer of power has not yet been studied in detail.

When the community at Deir el-Medina first became known to modern scholars, it was thought that the workmen belonged to the Egyptian lower classes and that their writings expressed the concerns of the poor, but it soon emerged that this was not so. Although cutting the tomb was hard and unpleasant labour, in many other respects the work conditions were very good. The Egyptian week lasted ten days, the last two of which the workmen had free from work. In addition, there were so many festivals and other interruptions to the work that the gang seems to have been in the Valley of the Kings no more than two days out of three. At the end of a long reign, when the king's tomb and those of his near relatives had been finished, the workmen might have had even less to do. This gave the more skilled members of the gang large amounts of time to work for themselves, making furniture and funerary goods for the wealthy citizens of Thebes and so supplementing their already high salaries. Although the wages in kind as described above are difficult to translate into modern equivalents, it is clear that workmen were well-off by Egyptian standards. This emerges also from records of economic transactions; all workmen were in a position to buy and sell objects such as beds and coffins, while the wealthier members of the community could afford to purchase cattle and other expensive items. The tombs of the villagers are naturally of the highest workmanship and such tombs were in themselves symbols of status and wealth. It is evident from the correspondence of some of the more prominent members of the gang that they were on terms of friendship with lower-ranking officials in the capital. All of this puts at least the officials of the gang in the top 2 per cent of the population.

Thus the community at Deir el-Medina does not represent a radically different stratum of Egyptian society from that documented by the great majority of surviving monuments, texts, and objects from the New Kingdom, but the material from the workmen's village does illustrate new facets of the Egyptian world in rich detail. This is due in particular to the sheer number of texts, and the fact that many of these are private memoranda, short-term administrative records, letters, and other ephemera—the type of document which would ordinarily not have survived. These minor records are

particularly likely to be written on ostraca, while more official documents and formal records would be drawn up on papyrus. In either
case, the scribe used a reed and ink to write in hieratic, a cursive form
of hieroglyphs, which were ordinarily reserved for inscriptions on
walls and on objects. While the ostracon itself is durable, the ink
fades rapidly when exposed to sun, wear, or moisture. Papyri, on the
other hand, become brittle with age and often either have been
found in fragments or have broken into pieces during transport to
the museum where they are now stored. Many of our texts are
therefore incomplete or contain substantial lacunae. Since the handwriting of even a well-preserved text can be difficult to read, the
transcription of these texts into hieroglyphs, the script most legible
to modern Egyptologists, is a painstaking job, and thousands of
ostraca and papyri have still never been published.

GENERAL DESCRIPTION OF THE SITE

The physical remains left by the workmen's community include not
only their houses and their tombs, as mentioned above, but also
chapels, granaries, and other structures within the valley of Deir
el-Medina but outside the village walls. Further traces of the
workmen's activities can be found throughout the necropolis area.
Along the path leading from the village to the Valley of the Kings,
for example, lie the ruins of huts where the men stayed overnight
during the week, as well as the diminutive shrines and the seats
carved into the rock-face that they built nearby for their off-duty
hours. To the south of the village, en route to the Valley of the
Queens, are caves which served as sanctuaries to Ptah and
Meresger—the latter was a goddess of the western mountains, so it
was fitting that her shrine should be in this isolated spot. And finally,
the workmen left graffiti everywhere they went; most of these merely
record the writer's name, but others are more informative. Together
these many and varied remains document the daily life and work of
the villagers to an extent which can hardly be paralleled by any other
site in Egypt and it is extraordinarily fortunate that this physical
evidence belongs to the same community that produced the tens of
thousands of documents from which the pieces gathered here have
been selected.

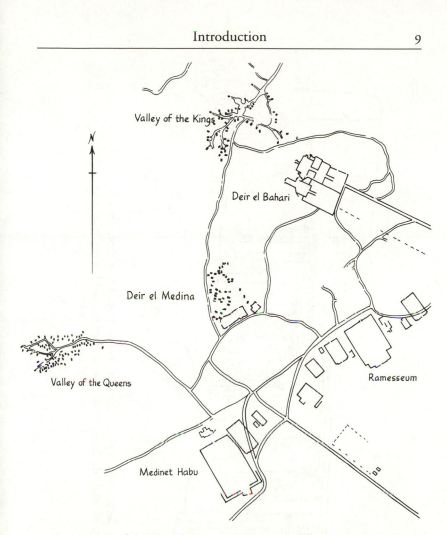

Fig. 2. Plan of the site of Deir el-Medina. (Drawn by Marion Cox.)

The Village

The walled village itself lies north–south along the middle of the valley of Deir el-Medina; in its final state it formed a trapezoid of roughly 5,600 sq. m., and contained some sixty-eight houses. One narrow road ran down the length of the village, making two sharp turns near the southern end; and several smaller roads gave access to

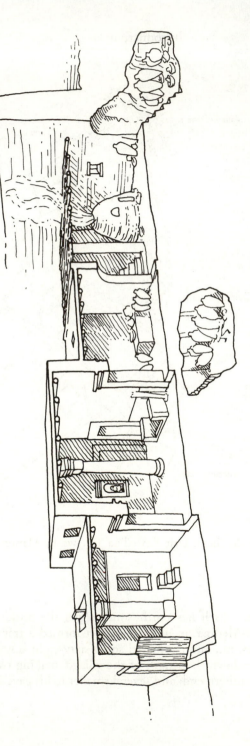

Fig. 3. Section of a typical workman's house. From left to right, the front room with altar, the living room, a smaller room, and kitchen with cellar. (Drawn by Marion Cox.)

houses on the western side of town. The stone wall which enclosed the settlement was not thick enough to protect the inhabitants against a major threat but would have kept out unwelcome strangers. A gate at the north end, opening onto the main road, was clearly the principal entrance, and a second gate gave access to the western cemetery. Whether there was also an opening to the south is not possible to say.

The houses within the walls varied considerably in size and form, in part because of the way the village developed, but also because of modifications to individual houses to meet the needs of the different occupants; the basic construction was the same in all cases, however. Walls were built of mudbrick on stone foundations, after which the whole surface was plastered with mud. The external walls were then painted white, and the internal walls of the first two rooms—the formal rooms—were whitewashed to the height of a metre or more. The front door, which opened directly onto the street, was made of wood, its doorframe of wood or limestone; the latter might be inscribed with the name of the owner. Both door and lintel might be painted red to repel demons.

This door gave access to a room about half a metre below street level, the most prominent feature of which was what the excavators called an 'enclosed bed', a solid brick structure about 0.75 m. high, 1.7 m. wide, and 0.8 m. deep, which was built against an inner wall. A small set of stairs with three, four, or five steps was built against the middle of the construction; and in most cases a low brick wall, about half a metre high, surrounded the top of the 'bed', breaking for an opening at the top of the stairs. These structures are thought to be altars dedicated to fertility and childbirth, themes which are suggested also by the paintings on the exterior which depict such scenes as the god Bes, a woman at her toilette, and a woman and infant under an arbour of convolvulus vines. Small niches hollowed in the walls probably held the stelae and the busts of ancestors which were also found in this front room. All of this suggests that this space was particularly sacred to the household cults, especially those pertaining to fertility and birth.

From here one stepped up through another red-painted door into a second room, between 14 and 26 sq. m., the floor of which was again at road level. This was the main living room, used perhaps especially by the men of the household. A wooden column on a stone base stood in the middle of the room to support the ceiling spanning this somewhat larger space; this ceiling may have been raised above the height of the surrounding rooms to let light and air into the otherwise windowless space. A low brick divan, painted white with polychrome decoration, stood along one wall and was used for seating during the day and perhaps sleeping at night. In the houses at the north-west end of the village, which were built on bedrock, a cellar was often hewn out below this bench; at least one such cellar was found to contain a large number of pottery vessels. The whitewashed walls were sometimes decorated with coloured bands or other decorations, and also contained niches, presumably for the images of local gods such as Meresger and Amenophis I which the excavators discovered in this area.

One, or sometimes two, small rooms opened off the main space; these are comparatively featureless and were perhaps bedrooms.

The kitchen was at the back of the house, and is immediately recognizable by the round brick oven which is often still in place; limestone mortars were also found sunk into the floor of this space, as were oval granite millstones and grinders. There was no ceiling, the area being open to the sky. It was often from here that the stairs went up to the roof, which is the final living space to be mentioned and one which was indispensable to the villagers. Except for the main room, which probably had clerestory windows, the houses appear to have been without windows and thus dark and airless; it is possible, too, that the streets of the village were roofed with mats, as in some modern villages of the Middle East, reducing the light still further. Then, as now, the roof was a relatively cool and airy retreat, and in larger families the extra space would also have been welcome. Recent excavations of comparable workmen's houses at Amarna have shown that there an extra room might be built on the roof, forming a small second storey, but there is no evidence for this at Deir el-Medina.

The total floorspace of a house, excluding the roof, ranged from 40 to 120 sq. m., with the average at about 70 sq. m.

A few houses were also situated outside the walls to the north of the village. Although different in design from those described above, these also have a main room with a column and divan, a kitchen, stairs, and a cellar, and in addition a stable for donkeys. There is no indication of who lived here; possibly members of the gang who either preferred not to live in the village proper or who could not be fitted in at times when there were more workmen than houses.

Cemeteries

In the Nineteenth and Twentieth Dynasties, the villagers constructed their tombs on the lower slopes of the mountain that defined the valley on the west. (The tombs of the Eighteenth Dynasty will be described below.) Space was limited, of course, and in time the mountainside became thoroughly riddled with shafts and burial chambers. Even if every workman had had the resources to construct a tomb of his own there would not have been room and it is therefore not surprising to find that these were family sepulchres, though it also happened that sons and grandsons built their own tombs, and also that one workman had two or even three tombs in his name. The sole Ramesside burial chamber found intact, that of Sen-nedjem, contained twenty bodies, only nine of which were found in coffins bearing their names. These included Sennedjem himself and his wife Iy-neferti, and several of their sons- and daughters-in-law. The rights to such a tomb were passed down from generation to generation; if there were a dispute between the heirs, this would be settled by the oracle of Amenophis I, and if the family died out, the tomb might be reassigned. However, the original inscriptions were not altered or expanded by succeeding owners despite the complex history of individual monuments, so less is known about the use of tombs over time than one might have hoped.

The superstructure of a Ramesside tomb consisted, most importantly, of a chapel. This might be a free-standing vault made of brick and surmounted by a small pyramid, or, alternatively, one or more rooms cut into the mountain side, sometimes with exterior mudbrick construction. Both types of chapels were often embellished with stelae and statues. Where the slope of the mountainside was very steep, a small terrace was built to give a level space before the tomb chapel for one or two courts, and, ideally, a pylon of brick.

From the courtyard or, in some cases, the chapel, a shaft or stairs descended to the burial chambers. These usually numbered three or four, but sometimes more; the various chambers may have

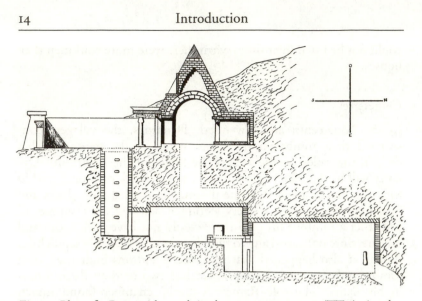

Fig. 4. Plan of a Ramesside tomb in the western cemetery (TT 5). A pylon gives access to an open courtyard before the chapel which, with its pyramid superstructure, is partially cut into the mountainside. From the courtyard, a shaft leads down to the burial chambers. (Reproduced with the kind permission of the IFAO in Cairo from J. Vandier, *Tombes de Deir el-Médineh: La Tombe de Nefer-Abou*. MIFAO 69 (Cairo, 1935), pl. 1.)

corresponded in some cases to the different branches of the family buried in the tomb.

Chapels of the Gods

The most prominent monument at Deir el-Medina today is the Ptolemaic temple of the goddess Hathor with its impressive mudbrick enclosure wall. Hathor had been a principal deity of the Deir el-Medina in Ramesside times as well and the Ptolemaic temple was built on the site of a chapel dating to the reign of Ramesses II. The remaining traces of this earlier complex suggest that it followed the pattern of the Ramesseum, even to the extent of incorporating a miniature 'palace' of the king (possibly consecrated to the royal Ka). It was unique among the chapels of Deir el-Medina in that it was constructed of stone, at least in part; and there is reason to believe that Ramesses II had contributed to the project. Certainly this king endowed the cult of Hathor in this chapel with offerings from his mortuary temple.

The only other chapel whose deity can be identified with confidence was also dedicated to Hathor; this was constructed under Seti I to the north of the site where his successor, Ramesses II, would build his own monument to the goddess. There are more than a dozen further chapels in this same area to the north of the village, some of them substantial. All were built of mudbrick and the interior walls plastered and in at least some cases painted with fine decoration, but the plaster has crumbled off taking with it the inscriptional evidence which might have allowed us to name the god or goddess who was honoured. At least one of these reticent chapels was dedicated to the deified pharaoh Amenophis I and his mother Ahmose Nefertari, whose cults in the village are exceptionally well documented. A relatively modest chapel behind the Hathor temple of Seti I appears to have been dedicated primarily to them and they were secondary honourands in the chapels of other gods as well. Although Amenophis was the most popular of the deified kings, a number of others were also the objects of long-lasting cults; indeed, of the New Kingdom monarchs up to and including Seti II, only the discredited pharaohs including Hatshepsut and the Amarna kings are not honoured on at least one monument.

In general, the plan of the chapels follows the standard Egyptian model, more or less abbreviated in individual cases. An open court, one or two covered halls (hypostyle and pronaos), and an inner sanctuary (naos) are laid out along a straight axis. The floor rises steadily from one area to the next, so that one must use a succession of gently sloping stairs to reach the sanctuary at the highest point of the building. In this dark, innermost room stood the cult image of the god—or, more often, gods, since most of the sanctuaries have three separate shrines along the rear wall. We know that the priests who served these cults were the workmen themselves, though it is not clear how individuals were selected for such tasks.

Besides the chapels to the north of the village, there was another important cluster of shrines some 150 m. away, along the path from Deir el-Medina to the Valley of the Queens. These are dedicated to Ptah, the god associated with the Valley of the Queens, and to Meresger, 'She Loves Silence', who was identified with the mountain peak which dominates the Theban necropolis. Meresger was often represented as a snake or even as group of up to eighteen snakes. The

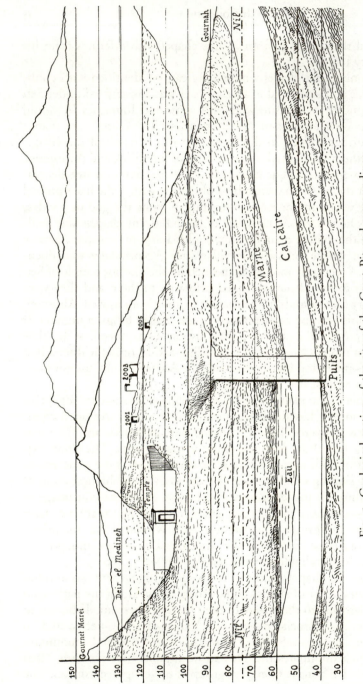

Fig. 5. Geological section of the site of the Great Pit and surroundings, showing the enormous depth reached by the workmen, well below the water table. (Reproduced with the kind permission of the IFAO in Cairo from Bruyère, *Rapport (1948–1951)*. FIFAO 26 (1953), pl. 2.)

sanctuaries of the two deities are seven natural and man-made grottos studded with stelae dedicated by members of the gang and their superiors; further stelae are cut into the rock-face itself near the entrance to the caves.

Huts on the Col

Yet another site at which the workmen left extensive remains lies along the path from Deir el-Medina over the mountain to the Valley of the Kings. At its highest point this path passes over a space of level ground before descending steeply into the Valley, and on this lofty perch the workmen built several clusters of stone huts. Each hut consisted of one or two tiny rooms, roughly rectangular in form, with a stone divan against the rear wall. The roof was made of branches and the walls were plastered; just outside the door might be a stone seat inscribed with the names and titles of the occupant. The structures were grouped tightly together, sharing as many common walls as possible, and the ruins now rather resemble a honeycomb. It is thought that, during the work week, the workmen spent the night in these mountain huts rather than return to the village. Fragments of decorated doorframes, stelae, and unfinished sculpture, as well as ostraca and graffiti on the nearby rocks, all suggest that the workmen were here for extended periods of time. So too does a chapel built up against the cliff and facing towards Karnak; since one of the graffiti nearby was left by the scribe Qen-her-khepesh-ef bearing the title 'priest of Amen-of-the-Good-Encounter', Bruyère suggested that this chapel was dedicated to this manifestation of the god. It is odd, however, that some of the expected traces of habitation are missing, such as pottery fragments, remains of cooking fires, and water emplacements.

Great Pit

Finally, it is necessary to mention the second largest monument at Deir el-Medina after the Ptolemaic temple, namely the enormous pit which lies just before the opening of the valley. This now reaches a depth of over 50 m.; a rock-cut staircase spiralling down the walls of the pit gives access to the bottom. Bruyère, the excavator, judged that the pit attained its present form in Ptolemaic times, but two documents of the Twentieth Dynasty record successive attempts to

dig down to the water-table from a location to the north of the
village; these Ramesside attempts must have been at the same spot as
the Great Pit, since there are no other very deep holes in the area.
The pit had reached a depth of 55 cubits (*c.*27 m.) at the time that the
second text was drawn up, and the intention was to continue dig-
ging. The pit never did reach the water-table, however, either in
New Kingdom or in the Ptolemaic period, if the undertaking was
indeed resumed at this later date. It is of interest to us mainly
because, when the attempt was finally abandoned, the enormous
crater was allowed to fill up with debris including many hundreds of
ostraca; it was indeed the richest source of ostraca from the area of
the village.

THE HISTORY OF OCCUPATION

The first datable remains of the workmen's community at Deir el-
Medina belong to the reign of Thutmosis I; an enclosure wall built
of bricks bearing his name surrounds the oldest part of the village.
The community of the early Eighteenth Dynasty seems to have been
relatively small compared with later times, probably because fewer
workmen were needed to decorate the simple royal tombs of the day.
Before the reign of Horemheb at the end of the Eighteenth Dynasty,
the corridors of royal tombs were left bare and decoration was
limited to the burial chamber, antechamber, and shaft. These were
painted with texts from the Book of the Netherworld called the
Amduat and with figures of the gods, all depicted in simple line
drawings and in a limited palette of black, red, and ochre, creating
the effect of a great papyrus unrolled over the tomb walls. Probably
one or two draughtsmen could have executed all the drawing; the
rest of the work would have been done by stonecutters and plasterers
who need not have been literate.

Virtually no written material is preserved from this period of the
village's history, and what little evidence we have comes from the
graves, which at this period were concentrated on the slope of the hill
to the east of the village which blocks its view of the Nile valley. They
are undecorated, but can be dated by scarabs of Hatshepsut, her
high priest of Amen Hapu-seneb, and Thutmosis III, as well as by
jar-labels and pottery types. The lowest levels of the hill slope were
occupied by the tombs of very young children and foetuses, the

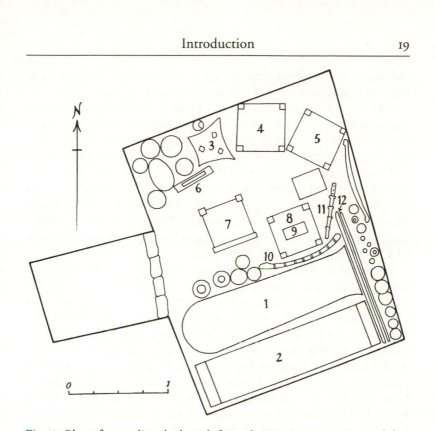

Fig. 6. Plan of an undisturbed tomb from the eastern cemetery containing the remains of a man and a woman from the time of Hatshepsut and Thutmosis III: (1) Anthropoid coffin containing the mummy of an elderly, grey-haired woman named Nebu; (2) coffin containing the mummy of an elderly, white-haired man; (3) wooden three-legged stool; (4)–(5) low stools; (6) headrest of wood; (7) low chair; (8) wooden stool with woven seat, unused; (9) statuette of a man named Sat-nem in painted sycamore wood: (10) wooden boomerang; (11) reed flute; (12) canes. (Drawn by Marion Cox after Bruyère, *Rapport (1934–1935)*, pt. 2. FIFAO 15 (1937), p. 173, fig. 96.)

middle part by those of adolescents, and the upper levels by adult burials. This group of tombs is most remarkable for the quantity of domestic furniture it contained, including an astonishing number of beds, chairs, boxes, and baskets as well as clothes, musical instruments, and food. Many of the objects show traces of use before they were interred with their owners and furnish a wealth of information about Egyptian household goods; but since they are accompanied by no inscriptions or at most by the name of the owner, we learn little about the composition of the community at this time.

On the other hand, Eighteenth-Dynasty tombs in the western cemetery were more elaborate, and a number included decorated funerary chapels. Three of these burial chambers were found virtually intact, including that of Kha, a chief of works in the Great Place and royal scribe in the reigns of Amenhotep II, Thutmosis IV, and Amenhotep III. His tomb was excavated by Schiaparelli in 1906, and his splendid funerary equipage, together with that of his wife, is now on display in Turin. It includes beautiful furniture, boxes, clothing, food, three coffins, and toiletries, from which we may conclude that Kha, at any rate, was a wealthy man.

There are few indications of what happened to the workmen during the Amarna period, when the heretic king Amenhotep IV (Akhenaton) moved the capital to Amarna. The royal family and high officials had tombs built in the cliffs to the east of their new city instead of at Thebes and a workmen's village like that of Deir el-Medina was built in the desert nearby, presumably to house the tomb-builders. It is impossible to tell whether these were the workmen from Deir el-Medina because of the dearth of inscribed material from this period at either site and especially at Amarna. Only a handful of Deir el-Medina workmen of the Eighteenth Dynasty are known by name, while only three male names have been found at the Amarna village; 'Sen-nefer' happens to occur at both, but this was a common name and tells us little. A number of funerary objects found at Deir el-Medina bear inscriptions naming the god Aten and the city Akhetaten; these may have been made at Amarna, and brought back when the workmen returned to Thebes. On the other hand, it is possible that Deir el-Medina was never entirely abandoned, and that these objects were made at the site during the Amarna period. This is certainly true, as Barry Kemp has pointed out, of a chair said to have been found at Thebes; the object itself is now lost, but according to a copy made by Burgsch, the text read 'Servant in the Place of Truth on the West of Akhetenaten, Nakhy'. 'Akhetenaten', written with the genitival *ny* was a name for Thebes before the move to Amarna and was never used for the latter. Similarly, a jar label of the Amarna period found at Deir el-Medina as well as several loose bricks stamped with the cartouche of Akhenaton (one from a house and two from a child's tomb) seem to indicate that the village was still occupied at this time.

Shortly after the Amarna period, during the reign of Horemheb, the community of workmen was completely reorganized. Our earliest textual reference is to this period: 'The major-domo of Thebes, Djehuty-mose allocated the places that are in the Necropolis to the gang of Pharaoh, l.p.h.' (See below, 'Daily Life,' no. 39). The reason for the reorganization of the gang was probably the much more elaborate design of the tomb of Horemheb, which was the first to be carved in low relief and brightly painted. This naturally required a large number of skilled artisans, and the village was expanded to the north and east to include houses for the new workmen. There are clear traces of a major fire in the village at about this time, which may have made it easier to make a clean start.

With the Nineteenth Dynasty the trickle of documentary evidence from the village becomes a flood. The western cemetery was filled with tombs during this period, so much so that there was no room left for the workmen of the next dynasty, who often had to reuse the graves of their predecessors rather than construct their own. The inscriptions in many of these tombs furnish the names and titles of the tomb owners, their parents and children, and often their friends and colleagues, and it is at this period that the workmen begin to become individuals for us. In addition, some tomb paintings depict the workmen with their families or scenes from daily life. The tomb of the sculptor Ipuy (TT 217) who lived under Ramesses II is unique in the variety and detail of its depictions of the villagers' world; it contains lively illustrations of the riverside with its market stalls, sailors, and boats moored along the shore, and of workmen constructing a shrine for the deified pharaoh Amenophis I, to name only two of the many exceptional scenes. However, most tomb paintings are more obviously religious and represent the tomb owner adoring various deities, his own funeral preparations, or the afterlife which the deceased hoped to enjoy. The one intact tomb of the period, that of Sen-nedjem, and other partially plundered tombs contained not only funerary goods but also furniture and tools. Unlike the tomb inventories of the Eighteenth Dynasty, however, those of the Ramesside period contain relatively little furniture; the pieces were also specially made for the burial and show no signs of use during the tomb owner's lifetime.

The village reached its final dimensions during this period, when about sixty-eight houses were contained within the enclosure walls. The number is only approximate because the southern end of the village is badly preserved. Meanwhile, the face of West Thebes was changed significantly with the construction of the great funeral temple of Ramesses II, the Ramesseum, at the edge of the desert nearest to Deir el-Medina. This extensive temple complex with its vast granaries became the administrative centre for West Thebes until it was overshadowed by the funerary temple of Ramesses III, Medinet Habu, in the Twentieth Dynasty. The workmen were in frequent contact with the priests, scribes and administrators based at the Ramesseum, and they were thus less isolated than the secluded site of their village might suggest. It may well be that the temple of Amenhotep III had played an equally important part in the lives of the villagers in its time, but the scarcity of texts from the Eighteenth Dynasty makes it impossible to say. Nothing now remains of Amenhotep III's complex except the two colossi which originally flanked its entrance; the stone was reused in the temple of Merneptah, which was in its turn dismantled to furnish blocks for Medinet Habu.

With the advent of the Twentieth Dynasty, the character of our sources shifts again. Except for an unexplained gap in our material for the first twenty years of Ramesses III's reign, administrative texts on both ostraca and papyri become so abundant that it is possible to write a day by day account of official activities for much of the period, and economic, legal, and other personal documents are almost as plentiful. It is not clear whether this apparent surge of written material is an accident of preservation or whether the work-men wrote more, or perhaps more workmen wrote, than previously. On the other hand, as was mentioned above, the workmen of the Twentieth Dynasty tended to use the tombs of their predecessors rather than build their own, so we can no longer draw on tomb decoration as a source of information. Moreover, very little of the preserved funerary furniture dates to this period. The dearth of imposing remains gives the impression of relative poverty, but it is clear from the texts that the workmen were buying and selling goods of considerable value; they were not necessarily less well off than before.

The reign of Ramesses III saw the construction of his immense funerary temple at Medinet Habu, which was to be the main centre of administration of West Thebes for the remainder of the New Kingdom, but for Deir el-Medina scholars his reign is perhaps better known for the strikes which occurred in its 29th year. From a detailed, day-by-day account of these strikes drawn up by the scribe of the Necropolis Amen-nakhte, we know that the workmen staged noisy demonstrations at various East Theban locations to protest shortfalls in their wages. Official records and other outside sources confirm that the rations were in arrears, a state of affairs which would recur often throughout the rest of the dynasty.

It is not clear whether the shortfalls were due to declining state resources or to difficulties with the system of distribution on which the economy was based, or perhaps to both. Near the end of the dynasty, at any rate, poverty in the Theban population together with diminishing fear of the authorities had a predictable result; the royal tombs in the Valley of the Kings were gradually plundered of their fabulous wealth. Among the thieves were the workmen of Deir el-Medina. At the beginning of the Twenty-First Dynasty the high priests of Amen, now the de facto rulers of the south of Egypt, ordered the mummies of the kings to be gathered up together with their coffins and a few remaining funerary goods and to be reburied in a common tomb. No more graves were built in the Valley of the Kings and the community of workmen was gradually disbanded.

Even before this, while royal tombs were still under construction, the gang had left its village at Deir el-Medina to find new homes at Medinet Habu and elsewhere in the region. The exact date of the move is not known, but probably fell late in the reign of Ramesses X or in the first few years of his successor. Among the incentives to leave the wadi where the workmen had lived for 450 years was the danger posed by marauding desert nomads; beginning in the time of Ramesses IX, the administrative journal of the tomb repeatedly notes that work in the tomb was suspended because of the presence of these raiders, who are variously identified as Libyans, Meshwesh, or desert dwellers. The relatively isolated village, occupied only by women, children, and the elderly while the gang was at work, was excessively vulnerable, and had to be abandoned. We know from private letters that the workmen occasionally visited the homes and tombs of their ancestors, but these were already falling into disrepair in the later years of Ramesses XI.

THE EXCAVATIONS

The first excavation at Deir el-Medina took place in 1906, but there had been considerable activity at the site for more than a century before. The zealous collectors of the nineteenth century acquired many objects from the community, probably by purchase from native dealers rather than by prospecting themselves. The locals made two particularly spectacular finds; one was the discovery in the 1840s or 1850s of a cache of papyri including the records of the great tomb robberies of the late Twentieth Dynasty. These may have come from either Medinet Habu or Deir el-Medina; they were split up and sold to various collectors. The other magnificent find was the intact tomb of Sen-nedjem, which was immediately reported to Maspero, the head of the Antiquities Service, who happened to be in Luxor at the time and who personally oversaw the clearing of the tomb. Unfortunately, the standards of documentation were not what they are today, and the tomb contents were distributed to museums as far apart as New York, Berlin, and Cairo. A number of Egyptologists also visited the site during the nineteenth century to make copies of the tomb paintings and inscriptions, including such distinguished names as Wilkinson, Lepsius, and the great Champollion himself. Their copies are the only record we have of some objects which have now disappeared.

Serious excavation began with the campaigns of Ernesto Schiaparelli for the Egyptian Museum of Turin in 1905, 1906, and 1909. Turin had already acquired a large number of objects from the village through the early nineteenth-century collector and dealer Drovetti, including a wealth of papyri, but Schiaparelli's discoveries would augment this collection beyond all expectation. In one season, 1906, he employed more than 500 workers at the site. The northern part of the valley was explored down to virgin ground; the most spectacular of the many finds was the intact Eighteenth-Dynasty tomb of the foreman Kha and his wife Meryt. This tomb and its contents were fully documented in a handsome publication, but Schiaparelli died before completing the full excavation report he intended.

From 1909 to 1912, Émile Baraize was employed by the Egyptian Antiquities Service to carry out reconstructions on the Ptolemaic temple. In the course of his work, he made many Ramesside finds in this area; these are listed at the end of an article in the journal of the Antiquities Service describing his work on the temple.

In 1913 the Berlin Museum had a short season at Deir el-Medina, which had been granted to them as part of a large concession in West Thebes. The distinguished palaeographer Georg Möller dug at four different locations in the valley between 26 February and 29 March of that year; his most important finds were more than 160 hieratic ostraca and 70 figured ostraca, 11 houses with their contents, 4 children's graves in the eastern cemetery, and 10–13 tombs in the western cemetery. A brief report of this excavation was published thirty years later by Rudolf Anthes on the basis of Möller's notes.

As one of the consequences of the First World War, the German concession at Deir el-Medina was transferred to the French, who began work there in 1917. Following several short campaigns by a number of different excavators, Bernard Bruyère took over the site for the French Institute in 1922 to begin his project of a complete and systematic investigation of all the remains left by the workmen of the Necropolis. Work continued until 1951, and reports on each season's excavations were issued with admirable rapidity. Specific tombs and groups of material from Bruyère's campaign were published and continue to be published forty years later by the French Institute, while twenty magazines full of objects still await detailed study.

Find Spots of Texts

It is most unfortunate that none of the excavators mentioned above regularly recorded the find spots of individual ostraca and papyri since this information might have helped us to reassemble private and official archives, to assign rough dates to otherwise undatable documents, and perhaps even to identify locations named in the texts. It is possible, however, to make a few general observations about the area from which different types of texts came. For example, the great mass of papyri in the Turin museum were acquired from Drovetti, who had probably purchased them from native dealers. These are mainly administrative papyri from the end of the Twentieth Dynasty, and it seems that local treasure hunters had stumbled upon the official archives of the gang from that period. Whether this was at Deir el-Medina or Medinet Habu has been a matter of some speculation; the latter is thought to be more likely since the collection contains texts from the period when the gang had moved to the safety of this temple and because an account clearly belonging to the temple archives is included among the rest. There are many papyri in Turin dating to the reigns before the gang left the village, and at least one of these was clearly drawn up at Deir el-Medina, so under this hypothesis the scribes would have taken their archives with them to the temple. This reasoning depends on the assumption that all the papyri came from a single area, of course. Not all the Turin texts are official documents; a collection of love songs (Papyrus Turin 1996) is a notable exception, for instance.

The only papyri found in situ belonged to a private archive, that of the scribe Qen-her-khepesh-ef and his descendants. They were discovered in the course of the French excavations of 1928 in the western cemetery of the village, but on the night of their discovery, before the find had been completely recorded, an unknown number of the papyri disappeared. The Chester Beatty papyri are now known to have been among the stolen texts. P. W. Pestman has reconstructed the original archive, insofar as it is now possible to do so; it contained over forty papyri and will be described below in Chapter 4 on 'Education, Learning, and Literature'.

A much greater number of ostraca were of course found in excavation. The vast majority of those published in the Cairo Catalogue were discovered during work in the Valley of the Kings by Theodore Davies and by the Carnarvon/Carter expeditions. It comes as no surprise that these are mainly administrative records pertaining to the work in the royal tomb; they include attendance lists, accounts of lamps and tools issued to the men, notes on the progress of the work, and so on.

The ostraca found in the valley of Deir el-Medina by Bruyère came especially from the area to the north of the village, though only for texts from the Great Pit was the exact find spot recorded. The administrative records concern mainly deliveries to the village of foodstuffs, wood, clothes, and other commodities for the workmen; ration distributions; visits to the village by outside dignitaries; and other activities which would have taken place here rather than at the Valley of the Kings. The vast majority of non-administrative, private, and literary texts were also found in the village or in the refuse dumps outside of the village walls, again as one might have expected. It is unclear whether the many records of legal hearings and oracular consultations found near the chapels and in the Great Pit indicate that the court sessions and oracles took place in the same area, or whether they were merely stored in archives that happened to be nearby. One need not rule out the other, of course.

Thousands of ostraca were not found in excavation at all, but were bought from local dealers. Sir Alan Gardiner reported that 'The foundation of my own collection goes back to my second visit to Egypt in 1907, when large and fine hieratic ostraca could be purchased from the Luxor dealers at 20 P.T. or about 4 shillings apiece, while good smaller ones were obtainable for 5 P.T. or less.' Gardiner bought hundreds of examples, as did others; none of these are provenanced.

The scholars who have published the finds from Deir el-Medina have done at least as much for the rediscovery of this community as the excavators. They have focused on the inscribed material, perhaps because this is at present more accessible than other genres of objects, and consequently it is through their writings that we know the workmen best. Although the study of ostraca, papyri, and stelae has been the joint work of dozens of specialists, few would disagree that the masters of the discipline were Jaroslav Černý and George Posener. Not only did the former publish thousands of non-literary texts himself and write the fundamental studies based on these texts, but his private transcriptions of unpublished documents still serve as the point of departure for current editors of this material. Posener did similar work on the literary ostraca. They did the hard work; the rest of us have the pleasure of exploring the world they opened up.

Note: in the translations of the Egyptian texts, small capitals represent text written in red ink in the original.

1

Family and Friends

Some of the most charming documents from Deir el-Medina are letters between family and friends, which are full of information about the concerns of and relations between the villagers as well as about individual styles of expression and use of language—especially by women, whose voices are seldom heard in the rest of the textual record. But even where the letters do not contain information that is directly useful to the social historian, they furnish glimpses of the personalities of the villagers that help to flesh out the drier accounts and official journals. Unfortunately, the most personal letters are also the most tantalizing, because they refer casually to people and events known to the correspondents but not to us. Some 470 letters from Deir el-Medina are preserved, of which we can present only a few; the interested reader may wish to consult Edward Wente's *Letters from Ancient Egypt*, which includes translations of 175 texts from the village.

A few words about the format of Egyptian letters may be useful. A formal letter opens with the names of the sender and the recipient, and continues with greetings in which the sender relates that he has asked various gods to provide for the health and welfare of his correspondent. The more formal the letter, and the lower the rank of the sender relative to the person addressed, the longer the greetings grow and the more gods are invoked. On the other hand, letters from a high official to someone of low rank can be extremely abrupt and very informal messages between villagers often fail to name the correspondents all together. The body of the letter may be divided into 'paragraphs' not by beginning a new line but by introducing a new subject with the words 'to the effect that' or 'furthermore' or 'another communication for my lord'. Even the beginning of the letter proper, after the greetings, may be introduced with 'another communication', in spite of the lack of any substantive communication before that point. Finally, in contrast to the florid expressions of goodwill at the beginning of an epistle, the conclusions of letters are quite abrupt. A simple 'farewell' usually brings the letter to a close.

1. A Garbled Message

Many of the letters from Deir el-Medina are very short, no more than a single line of request or instruction. In other village communities such messages would have been sent orally through the agency of any young boy who may have been at hand; but little boys are unreliable, as appears from the following letter.

Write me what you will want since the boy is too muddled to say it. Look, didn't I write you about it: a fine mat of dried grass and also a fine mat of cord?

2. Letter about a Useless Co-Worker

The author of this letter has taken on a certain Ib as a co-worker at his father's request; but Ib is no use to him at all.

The scribe Pa-baky speaks to his father the draughtsman Ma'a-nakhte-ef.

To the effect that: I heeded what you said to me, 'Let Ib work together with you!' Now look, he spends the day bringing the jar of water. There is no (other) chore for him every single day. He does not listen to your counsel which says to him, 'what have you done today?'

Look, the sun has set and he is far away ⟨with⟩ the jar of water.

3. Letters from a Neglected Friend

There were many close friendships in the village, of which the portraits of fellow workmen in many Deir el-Medina tombs are the most visible testimony. Villagers of the same age called each other 'brother' as an expression of affection, and we can recognize friendships also in the fact that the same pairs or trios appear together repeatedly in economic transactions or on stelae. Seldom, however, is friendship declared so strongly as in these reproachful letters.

A. [The scribe] Nakhte-Sobek to the workman Amen-nakhte; in life, prosperity, and health; in the praise of Amen-Re, King of gods.

To the effect that: I tell Amen, Mut, Khonsu, and all the gods of Thebes, every [god], every goddess who [re]sts in West Thebes, to grant you life, to grant you health, and to grant you a long [lifespan] and a great old age, you being in the praise of Amenophis, the lord of the [Village], your lord, who sees you every day.

Furthermore: Now what have I done? What is my offence against you? Am I not your old table-companion? Will the hour come in which you cast off your [brother]? What should I do? Please write to me about the wrong [I have done you, via the policeman Bas]; or if it is (only) to me that you do not write either good or ill, indeed, this is a bad day.

I do not ask anything from *you*. Happy is a man who is with his old table-companion. Some new [things] are good, (but) an old companion is (also) good.

When my letter reaches you, you will write to me about your health by means of the policeman Bas; report the state of your health to me today. Do not let me be told not to enter your house, and not to make [my] way inside the walls, staying away from the village. And do not [. . .] to me. I will go and enter the house, and come out again. I will enter my own place.

Amen is before you. If he lives, I will live. When I die, Amen is still before (you).

Farewell.

B. To the effect that: I tell all the gods of heaven and earth to give you life and health every day.

Furthermore: What is it with you? Write and send me the thoughts of your heart, so that I can enter into them. Really, since I was a child until today, I have been with you, but I cannot understand your character. Is it good for a man, when he says things to his companion twice, and he does not hear him, like the *hin* of oil which I requested from you, and you said to me, I will have it brought to you—but you did not bother. Send to me (about) the state of your health instead of the oil. As Amen is before you, you will find something useful in it. What you are continually doing to me is not good.

Another matter: Dunk some bread and send it [to me] quickly.
Farewell.

4. A Jokey Letter

School-boys had to write out endless model letters, practising, among
other things, the elaborate salutations which opened every official communication. As adults, they of course continued to use the same long and
pompous openings. It is no surprise that they were tempted to parody
the style in private, as in the following letter from one villager to another;
Maʿa-nakhte-ef, the recipient, was probably the prosperous carpenter
of that name, whereas the trade of sandal-maker was a relatively lowly
one.

[The scribe] Hor-Min of the guarded Necropolis [. . .] to the scribe
Maʿa-nakhte-ef.

To the effect that: I tell Amen-Re, King of Gods, to let you be
healthy, to let you live, and to let you achieve a long life and a
great old age, you being a great sandal-maker to the end of time and
being in possession of good leather and large bright hides [. . .] for
you, and having [. . .] many orders. Will you not have me thrown
out?

Farewell.

5. A Joke that Went Wrong

The sender of this letter, whose name is lost in the broken opening lines, is
trying to palliate his correspondent's anger about a joke he had made in an
earlier missive. It is in his nature to make jests, he argues; and indeed, he
goes on to illustrate what he means with yet another joke.

[*beginning lost*] I tell Amen-Re-Horakhty when he rises and sets, to
give you, l.p.h., a long life, a great and good old age, and very many
favours before Amen, your lord, every single day.

To the effect that: I have heard that you are angry; you made me
contemptible (?) through insults, on account of this joke which I
told to the Chief Taxing Master in that letter; although it was
Henut-tawy (*fem.*) who said to me, 'Tell some jokes to the Chief
Taxing Master in your letter.' You are like the story of the woman
blind in one eye who was in the house of a man for twenty years, and

he found another, and he said to her, 'I will divorce you! Why, you
are blind in one eye!' (So they say.) And she said to him, 'Is this the
discovery you have made in these twenty years that I have spent in
your house?' Thus am I, and thus is the joke I have made with
you. . . .

Love and Marriage

The evidence for wedding ceremonies in the Pharaonic period is so
scanty that there is reason to doubt whether such a rite ever took
place. There is not even a specialized word for 'to wed'; instead, a
number of expressions were used, such as 'to make N. a wife', 'to
found a house', 'to live with', and others. It would seem, therefore,
that the couple simply moved in together, after the hopeful bridegroom had obtained the consent of the girl's father. There is,
however, one unique reference to what may be the payment of a
brideprice (see below No. 22).

Although no particular legal steps were necessary to sanction a
marriage, the union did have legal consequences, particularly regarding the property of the two parties. Husband and wife each had a
claim to the property acquired in common, the man to two-thirds
and the woman to one-third; and while either party was free to end
the union, the problems of dividing up the property meant that
divorce was not so simple as marriage. The woman would not receive
her one-third if it was she who brought about the divorce, for
instance through her adultery; this is probably what lies behind
several women's oaths before the authorities that they had not
known any other men. At the same time, where the husband repu-
diated his wife, it was in her interests that this be done as formally as
possible, so that she could take steps to recover her property. The
husband, too, might prefer a public settlement, so that he would be
seen to be free of further claims from his ex-wife, particularly if he
wished to marry again.

6. A Love Charm

Although many Egyptian love charms are preserved from the Ptolemaic
period and later, this is the only such text known from Pharaonic times.
The Seven Hathors who are invoked here were goddesses also connected

with birth who determined the fate of the child and who could be called on for protection. Their cords may have been used for the protective knots which feature prominently in Egyptian magic. The threats to the gods with which the text concludes, though blasphemous to our ears, are a common feature of Egyptian magic making.

Hail to you, Re-Horakhty, father of the gods! Hail to you, Seven Hathors, who are adorned with bands of red linen! Hail to you, gods, lords of heaven and earth! Come, ⟨make⟩ So-and-so (*fem.*) born of So-and-so come after me like a cow after fodder; like a servant after her children; like a herdsman (after) his herd. If they do not cause her to come after me, I will set ⟨fire to⟩ Busiris and burn up ⟨Osiris⟩.

7. A Son-in-Law Swears to his Intentions

In this text, a concerned father asks the authorities to make his son-in-law swear an oath regarding his daughter. Unfortunately, the crucial word (*netja*) is otherwise unknown; it has been compared to a similar verb in Semitic languages meaning 'to desert' or 'divorce'. If this is correct, the husband pledges not to desert his wife on pain of a beating and the loss of any property the couple might acquire together. This settlement is unusual; ordinarily, the man would keep two-thirds and the woman one-third of their common property after a divorce. No hint is given as to why the father demanded these exceptional guarantees of his son-in-law's intentions, or at what point in the union these events took place—this may be a unique example of a legal covenant entered into at marriage.

Year 23, first month of winter, day 4. This day, Tener-Monthu said to the chief workman Khonsu and the scribe Amen-nakhte son of Ipuy, 'Make Nakhte-em-Mut take an oath of the lord, l.p.h., saying, "I will not abandon (*netja*) his (lit. "my") daughter." '

Oath of the lord, l.p.h., that he swore: 'As Amen endures, as the ruler endures, if I go back on my word and abandon (*netja*) the daughter of Tener-Monthu in the future, I will receive 100 blows and be deprived of all the property that I will acquire with her.'

(*Witnesses*):
the chief workman Khonsu
the scribe Amen-nakhte
Nefer-Hor
Kha-em-nun

8. A Case of Domestic Violence

The following appears to be a record of a court hearing at which a man was accused of beating his wife and was made to swear an oath, presumably that he would not repeat the offence. Since the ends of the crucial lines are lost, we cannot be sure that this impression is correct; it is not impossible that the woman's husband was the victim of a beating by a third party rather than the other way around. The first person pronoun is male throughout, but since the speaker mentions 'my husband' and is thus presumably female, this is not informative. At any rate, in view of the interesting possibilities raised by this case, we have included it here.

Year 20, third month of summer, day 1. Day that the workman Amen-em-ope approached the lawcourt (of)

    the chief workman Khonsu
    the scribe Wen-nefer
    the scribe Amen-nakhte
    the deputy Amen-kha
    the deputy In-her-khau
    the officer Nefer-hotep
    the officer Kha [. . .]

saying, 'As for me, my husband [. . .] Then he beat, he beat [. . .] And I caused his mother to be brought, the [. . .]'

He was found to be in the wrong, and one made [. . .] and I said to him, 'if you were [. . .] before the magistrates'.

And he took [an oath of the Lord], saying, 'As Amen lives, as [. . .] lives, [. . .] in [. . .]'

9. A Domestic Quarrel

This passage, taken from a record of various payments, favours, and services done by the workman Khnum-mose for his colleague Ruty, incidentally gives us a picture of a woman repeatedly thrown out of the house by her husband and taken in by her friends.

My son spent two years carrying his water.

A wall fell down in his storehouse and I built it up; and I used five donkey-loads of water for it, too.

I plastered three places on top of his house, and also the stairs of his tomb.

His wife spent forty days dwelling with me in my house, and I provided for her, giving her one sack of emmer and ten loaves. And he threw her out again, and she spent twenty days in the house of Menna, while I supplied

3 *oipe* of emmer

1 *inet*-garment (?)

1 *khet*-measure of *sety*-fruit.

10. Paternity Leave

The following extract, part of a journal recording who was absent from work each day and for what reason, has an interesting entry: the workman Ka-sa was given three days off when his wife gave birth. This may have been to help care for his wife or to take part in purification ceremonies.

Second month of inundation, day 23. Those who were (with) the scribe Pa-shed working for the vizier: Ipuy, Nakhte-em-Mut.

Those who were ⟨with⟩ the chief workman Khay: Khamu, Sa-Wadjyt; and Qa-ha was ill.

Those who were ⟨with⟩ the chief workman Pa-neb: Ka-sa, his wife being in childbirth and he had three days off. And Ka-sa son of Re-[mose] was ill; and Re-weben was ill.

11. Women Withdraw for Menstruation

In many cultures, women withdraw to a special place at the time of their menstruation. This practice is not well-attested for ancient Egypt until Ptolemaic and later times, when the space under the stairs of multi-storey houses was often reserved for this purpose. The only reference to the custom of withdrawal from earlier times occurs on the following ostracon from Deir el-Medina. Eight menstruating women are said to have been leaving the village on their way to the 'place of women' when some incident occurred, the description of which is lost through a gap in the text.

Year 9, fourth month of inundation, day 13. Day that the eight women came outside [to the] place of women, when they were menstruating. They got as far as the back of the house which [. . . *long gap*] the three walls.

CHILDREN AND PARENTS

12. A Widower Cares for his Children

The following account, which concerns purely personal matters, was entered on the Turin Strike Papyrus ('Work in the Royal Tomb' No. 187 below) before the main text was written down. It records payments to a doctor and to a wet-nurse by a man called Weser-hat, and also an oath by the latter that he will not be separated from his three daughters. While no background to these events is given, it is perhaps not too fanciful to conjecture that Weser-hat's wife had died in childbirth, leaving the widower to care for their three children. Note that the wet-nurse, whose duties admittedly extended over some time, is paid as much as the doctor.

Year 29, month 4 of inundation, last day (Ramesses III).
Total given to the doctor by Weser-hat:

bronze ewer	makes 4 *deben*
fine *denyt*-basket	makes 5 *deben*
sandals, two pairs	makes 4 *deben*
one staff	makes $\frac{1}{2}$ *deben* (?)
basket with lid	makes $\frac{1}{4}$ sack
fine *denyt*-basket	makes 5 *deben*
castor oil, 2 *hin*	makes $\frac{1}{2}$ sack
wooden *sheqer*-box	makes 2 *deben*
fine mat	makes $\frac{1}{4}$ sack.
Total [. . .] 22 *deben*	

(Things) that are for the wetnurse, which are in the possession of Weser-hat (but) which will be apportioned.

three necklaces of red jasper	makes 15 *deben*
one piece of log	makes 10 *deben*
sheqer-basket	makes 2 *deben*
ivory comb	makes 2 *deben*
one pair of sandal thongs and 1 *hin* of fat	makes $1\frac{1}{2}$ *deben*
TOTAL	$30\frac{1}{2}$ copper *deben*

WHAT is for him: 20 copper *deben*. WHAT is for her, [10] copper deben. TOTAL 30 copper *deben*.

Statement of Weser-hat before the lawcourt (of) the chief workman Kha, the scribe of the Necropolis Amen-nakhte, and the entire gang:
    'As Amen endures, as the Ruler, l.p.h., endures, my three daughters will not be taken from me, and I will not be taken from them.'

13. A Son Supports his Father

We have little indication of what happened to older workmen—whether they received a salary until they died or whether they were dismissed and depended on their savings and their children for support. A third possibility is suggested by the following text, namely, that a father might retire in favour of his son, who would then support his parent. The text opens with a list of items given by Weskhet-nemtet to his father including such relative luxuries as meat, oil, honey, and garments, all of which were supplied to the workmen on festival days and as special rewards. The text goes on to record that Weskhet-nemtet gave his father emmer from his rations for ten months beginning in year 1, second month of inundation, which is known from other sources to have been the time of the younger man's appointment to the gang. The amount of grain handed over monthly, $2\frac{1}{2}$ sacks, is over half the younger man's salary. Finally, Weskhet-nemtet shared with his father the services of a maidservant, as provided to the workmen by the state. In addition to the items listed here, a workman would have received fish, vegetables, firewood, and pottery; but for some reason Weskhet-nemtet fails to mention this portion of his salary.

List of everything that Weskhet-nemtet gave to his father up to year 2:

	10 large loaves
New Year	5 large loaves
Festival of Amenophis [. . .]	10 loaves, 2 mats
New Year again:	5 large loaves, $\frac{1}{2}$ sack of emmer

Given to him from the rewards which Pharaoh gave us:

	20 loaves, *shay*-cakes, 2 loaves
Again:	15 loaves, 10 pieces of cut meat
Again:	10 loaves, 5 pieces of cut meat, 2 *hin* sesame oil, 2 *hin* fat, 1 *hin* honey, 1 fine kerchief, 1 smooth-cloth tunic.

And I gave to him emmer amounting to $2\frac{1}{4}$ sacks as rations every month from year 1 until year 2, second month of inundation to third month of summer, making 10 months, each $2\frac{3}{4}$ sacks. Total, 27 sacks.

Given to him again: $1\frac{1}{2}$ sacks as rations from [. . .] Total, 25 sacks.

Given to him again: 2 sacks [given to] us by Pharaoh.

And during one year I gave [to him . . .] day of service which Pharaoh gave to us.

[. . .]

14. Bad Children Are Disinherited

Egyptian wisdom texts stress the debt that children owe to their parents and especially to their mother, for the sacrifices made on their behalf. The Maxims of Any, which was certainly read in the village, contains the following passage on the subject (7.17–8.1):

Double the provisions your mother gave you,
Support her as she supported you;
She had many burdens in you,
But she did not abandon them to me.
You were born after your months,
(But) she harnessed herself, still,
Her breast in your mouth for three years
While you flourished. Your excrement disgusted,
(But she) was not disgusted, saying: 'What shall I do?!'
She sent you to school,
When you were taught to write,
And she waited for you daily,
With bread and beer in her house.

As we shall see, many texts record support to women, presumably widowed mothers or unmarried sisters, but not all children were so mindful of their duties to their mothers. The lady Naunakhte, who had some property of her own, had it in her power to reward her good children and punish those who had neglected her. Here, in her last will and testament, she leaves her worldly goods to those of her children who deserve them. Naunakhte had been married twice, first to the scribe Qen-her-khepesh-ef, who must have been much older than her and left her property including real estate; and then to the workman Kha-em-nun, to whom she bore eight children. Note that she can dispose only of the property which she brought into the marriage and one-third of the property she and her second husband, the children's father, had accumulated together; she recognizes that even her negligent children will inherit from their father as usual.

All of the good children, except Menet-nakhte, had contributed to a small stipend for their parents which reverts back to them by the terms of the will. The lady Menet-nakhte, of course, did not share in the stipend, but Naunakhte says explicitly that she is not disinherited completely. Further on, however, she appears among the bad children who receive nothing, a contradiction which is difficult to explain.

Year 3, fourth month of inundation, day 5, in the reign of the Dual King, the Lord of the Two Lands Weser-Maʿat-Re Sekheper-en-Re, l.p.h., the Son of Re, Lord of Diadems like Atum Ramesses Amen-her-khepesh-ef Mery-Amen (Ramesses V), l.p.h., given life for ever and eternity.

This day, the lady Naunakhte made a record of her property before the following court:

the chief workman Nakhte-em-Mut

the chief workman In-her-khau

(12 *further names*)

She said: As for me, I am a free woman of the land of Pharaoh. I raised these eight servants of yours, and I outfitted them with everything that is usual for people of their character. Now look, I have become old, and look, they do not care for *me*. As for those who put their hands in my hand, to them I will give my property; (but) as for those who gave me nothing, to them I will not give of my property.

List of the men and women to whom she gave:

the workman Ma῾a-nakhte-ef

the workman Qen-her-khepesh-ef. She said: 'I will give him a bronze washing-bowl as a bonus over and above his fellows, (worth) 10 sacks of emmer.'

the workman Amen-nakhte

the lady Waset-nakhte

the lady Menet-nakhte.

As for the lady Menet-nakhte, she said regarding her, 'She will share in the division of all my property, except for the *oipe* of emmer that my three male children and the lady Waset-nakhte gave me or my *hin* of oil that they gave to me in the same fashion.'

List of her children of whom she said, 'They will not share in the division of my one-third, but only in the two-thirds (share) of their father.'

the workman Nefer-hotep

the lady Menet-nakhte

the lady Henut-senu

the lady Kha-ta-nebu

As for these four children of mine, they will ⟨not⟩ share in the division of all my property.

Now as for all the property of the scribe Qen-her-khepesh-ef, my (first) husband, and also his immovable property and the storehouse of my father, and also this *oipe* of emmer that I collected with my husband, they will not share in them.

But these eight children of mine will share in the division of the property of their father on equal terms.

SUPPORT OF WOMEN

Women in Deir el-Medina cannot be studied in isolation from the rest of the village, as a glance at the selections in chapters on family, religion, magic, literature, and law will confirm. However, women's experience was different from that of their male relatives in many respects, including the fact that they were not employed in paying jobs and so were not financially independent. The norm was for women to be supported by their husbands and fathers, although we know very little about how finances were managed within the family, except that most purchases were made by the men. On the other hand, we do have some information about women's rights over their own property, and about the position of women who did not have a husband or father to care for them.

The legal position of women with regard to their own property was equivalent to that of men. Women and men inherited equally from their parents, and any property that a woman brought into a marriage remained her own. If the marriage was dissolved by divorce or the death of her husband, she would keep this property and also one-third of the wealth the couple had acquired together (unless it was she who had broken up the marriage by committing adultery). Women could buy and sell, and use the courts or be prosecuted in them, just like the men in the village. It is unclear whether women in Deir el-Medina were able to generate any wealth themselves; at most, they might have earned a little by weaving. Nevertheless, some women did have substantial funds of their own, as we can tell from records of transactions in which they participated where sums of over half a workman's yearly salary were involved.

In general, however, women inherited little from their families, and consequently their prospects without a husband or father were not good. In some ways they were worse off than women on the cultivated land since the houses in the villages were tied to jobs in the gang, so that when a workman died his house was taken over by his successor and his relatives had to find other accommodation. It is perhaps for this reason that women inherited sheds and storehouses more often than did men, as somewhere to live if they had nothing else. For the rest, women seem to have depended on the charity of friends and family, although lists of villagers to whom luxury foods were distributed on festival days include women who may have been on their own.

On the whole, the market economy was even less important to women than to men. They produced mainly for the household, and what they could not supply themselves, they could usually get from other women by trading or borrowing. This kind of small scale exchange is largely undocumented, but there are a few of letters between women which give us a glimpse of how they relied on each other.

15. Women Help Each Other

Of the roughly 470 letters from Deir el-Medina, a significant proportion—sixty-six letters or about one in seven—are to or from women. They cover a wide range of subject matter, and indeed a number are included in this anthology as representative of various aspects of life in the village. The two reproduced here are chosen to illustrate the sort of trades and exchanges between households that were a regular though usually unrecorded feature of daily life. The women who address each other as 'sister' need not be related since this term may have been used as an expression of affection.

A. Said by Nebu-her-Maʿat-tjau ⟨to her⟩ sister Neb-iunt [in life, prosperity and health].

Furthermore: Please pay attention and give me the tunic. Go and harvest the vegetables, since they are due from you (?).

B. Said by Isis to (her) sister Nebu-em-nu, in life, prosperity and health.

Furthermore: Please pay attention and weave for me this shawl very, very quickly, before (the god) Amenophis comes, because I am completely naked. Make one [for my] backside (?) because I am naked.

(*3 lines lost at end*)

16. A Man Makes Demands on his In-Laws

In this letter, a woman asks her sister to send bread and reports that her husband has threatened to divorce her unless the couple gets more material support from her family. The husband sounds unpleasant and violent, and it is difficult to know how much weight to give his assertion that families always supplied foodstuffs to their relatives; one would not have expected a Deir el-Medina workman to depend on contributions from his wife's sister. The abrupt ending of the letter is characteristic of Egyptian correspondence.

Said by Ta-khenty-shepse to her sister Iyt. In life, prosperity and health!
   Furthermore, to the effect that: I will send this grain to you and you should have it ground for me and add emmer to it and make it into bread for me, because I am quarrelling with Mery-Ma'at. '(I'll) throw you out!' so he says, and he quarrels with my mother enquiring after grain for bread. 'Now, your mother does not do anything for you,' so he says to me, saying, 'now, you have siblings, but they do not look after you!' So he says, arguing with me daily. 'Now look, this is what you have done to me since I have lived here, although everyone supplies beer and fish daily (to) their people. In short, if you say something, you will go down to the Black Land (the cultivation).'
   It is good if you attend.

17. A Woman Goes Back to her Parents

Since the family home went with the breadwinner's job, the first problem faced by a woman who found herself without a close male relative was where to live. In the following text a father promises his daughter that she can always find a home in his storehouse if the workman Baki throws her out. It is not clear what her relationship with this Baki is; he may be her husband, so that these measures are taken in case of a possible divorce. Note the stress put on the fact that the father built this structure himself, so that it is his own private property to do with as he likes.

The workman Hor-em-wia says to the lady Tenet-djeseret, his daughter: You are my good daughter. If the workman Baki throws you out of the house, I will act. As for the house [it belongs to (?)] Pharaoh, l.p.h.; but you will dwell in the portico in my storehouse, because I am the one who built it, and no one in the land will throw you out of there.

18. Charity after a Divorce

The workman Hesy-su-neb-ef divorced his wife Hel in year 2 of Seth-nakhte, and for three years after that, the author of the following text supported her with a small monthly grain ration. This quantity, roughly equivalent to 19 litres, would not be quite enough to live on, but he did also buy a sash of hers for six times its value. Why these good deeds were recorded is not said; he may have wished to put in a claim to her inherit-ance, though that is unlikely to have been worth much.

Besides the picture it gives of how a divorced woman might survive on the charity of others, this text raises two points of interest. First, it illustrates vividly how one might set about selling an piece of property. The owner estimated the value of her sash at a quarter sack of grain, and since this is a tenth of the usual price for such an item, this one must have been of very inferior quality. Her benefactor brought it down to the riverbank, the general market-place of West Thebes, and offered it for sale. Did he place it on the ground and stand behind it, hoping some passer-by would take a fancy to it? Or did he offer it to individuals known to him as likely buyers of clothing? In any case, no one would have it, and in the end he bought it himself for much more than it was worth.

This text also adds yet one more fact to the already well-documented lives of Hesy-su-neb-ef and Hel. Hesy-su-neb-ef evidently began life as a slave, but was adopted by his master and became a member of the gang, eventually attaining the rank of deputy. He expressed his devotion to his adoptive parents by naming a son and a daughter after them and by dedicating a stela to his father. Hel, his wife, is known from P Salt 124 (No. 21 below) to have lived with Pen-dua before she married Hesy-su-neb-ef; she deceived both husbands with the notorious Pa-neb. It is not impossible that this last incident led to her divorce from Hesy-su-neb-ef, especially since Pa-neb had threatened to kill her husband's beloved father.

Year 2, third month of summer, day 24, of King Weser-Khay-Re Setep-en-Re (Sethnakhte), l.p.h.: (day) Hesy-su-neb-ef divorced the lady Hel.

I spent three years giving to her an *oipe* of emmer every single month, making 9 sacks.

And she gave me a sash, saying, 'Offer it at the riverbank (the market-place); it will be bought from me for an *oipe* of emmer.' I offered it, but people rejected it, saying, 'It is bad!' And I told her exactly that, saying, 'It has been rejected.' Then she gave it to me, and I had one sack of emmer delivered to her via Khay son of Sa-Wadjyt.

What was given to her via Nebu-em-weskhet (*fem.*): 1 *oipe*.

What was given to her via Ta-a°ot-merut, her daughter: 1 *oipe*.
Total, $1\frac{1}{2}$ sacks for the sash.

19. Women Doing Men's Jobs

Women in the Deir el-Medina had little economic independence and, like
almost all Egyptian women, were barred from positions of authority or
administrative responsibility. This is odd in that, as Gardiner pointed out,
'one of the most striking features of the Pharaonic civilization was the
confidence reposed in its womenfolk to carry on the work of their men
during the absence or indisposition of the latter' (*JEA* 37: 116). The clearest
evidence of this confidence is to be found in the Late Ramesside Letters, the
name given to a heterogeneous group of epistles, most of which are to or
from persons connected with the Necropolis in the last years of the Twentieth Dynasty. The following, a particularly good example, is a letter to the
scribe of the Necropolis Nesy-su-Amen-em-ope, who was absent from
Thebes collecting grain for the gang's rations. It was written by his wife, to
keep him informed of events at home. Among other things, she reports that
she supervised the receipt of the grain he sent and discovered a shortfall, and
passes on some of the local gossip. Note that at the end of the letter, in a
passage which is unfortunately broken, she mentions that she had received
instructions directly from the vizier.

The chantress of Amen-Re, king of gods, Henut-tawy to the scribe
Nesy-su-Amen-(em)-ope of the Necropolis; in life, prosperity and
health, in the praise of Amen-Re, king of gods. I tell Amen-Re-
Horakhty when he rises and sets, to Mut, Khonsu, and all the gods
of Thebes to give you life, prosperity and health, a long life and a
great and good old age, and very many favours before Amen-Re,
king of gods, your good lord, who looks after you every single
day. . . .
   You wrote to me, 'Receive the 80 sacks of grain from this ship of
the fisherman It-nefer,' so you said in writing. I went to receive
them, and I found he had $72\frac{1}{2}$ sacks. And I said to him, 'What is this
$72\frac{1}{2}$ sacks of grain?' so I said to him, 'although his letter says 80
sacks?' And the men said, 'What we measured for ourselves was three
complete measures of $[2]\frac{1}{2}$ sacks each, leaving $72\frac{1}{2}$ sacks of grain,' so
they said. I kept my silence at that moment, saying 'By the time you
come, Amen-United-with-Eternity will have done every bad thing
with me.' . . .

Now, the general of the army of The Place Beloved of Thoth was
sent, so they say, to take men to the Temple of Millions of Years
(Medinet Habu) under the authority of the *setem*-priest and the
major-domo, in order to give [. . .], so they say. Now One (the
Pharaoh) has given the office of prophet of the goddess Nebet to the
god's father Nesy-Amen-(em)-ope, whom Pharaoh, l.p.h., clothed
with a tunic as is fitting, so they say.

When my letter reaches the place where you are, you should [. . .]
Amen [. . .], and let someone come to me very quickly. Indeed, the
vizier has written to me saying, Let [. . . their] bread to them. And
they went [. . .] send your letter [. . .]

20. A Woman Who Did not Need a Man

The following account shows that women were not always desperate to
have a man in the house; the narrator relates that he brought all his worldly
goods to 'her' house, intending to move in with her, but 'they' threw him
out in the street. When he tried again, 'she' did the same. It is not clear why
he uses sometimes the singular and sometimes the plural. The man gives a
complete inventory of his worldly goods, which is interesting in itself; the
list has been gone over, and some items are marked with a red dot while
others have been crossed out.

List of everything I took to her house:

    ~~1 smooth-cloth sheet~~

    ~~1 sack barley~~

    ~~4 sacks emmer~~

       ~~Total, 5 sacks~~ (*these items struck out by the scribe*)

    1 smooth-cloth tunic

    2 *hin* sesame oil

    2 pairs of sandals (one remaining)

    2 *denyt*-baskets

    1 sleeping mat

    one ordinary mat

    1 jar of fat

    1 headrest

    1 runner

    ~~3 mats~~ (*struck out*)

    2 shabti boxes, 1 remaining

    1 *tjay*-box

loaves, total 165 (?)
30 loaves of the reward
30 *berey*-fish
2 sieves
2 bowls
10 jars of beer
$\frac{1}{4}$ *oipe* lubya-beans
$\frac{1}{4}$ *oipe sety*-fruit
$\frac{1}{4}$ *oipe* salt
5 bricks of natron
2 red jaspar rings
1 red jaspar eye amulet, shaped from one piece.

And they threw me out, although she had not made for me (even?) a garment for my behind.

I went again with all my property in order to live with them. Look, she acted exactly the same way again.

ADULTERY

Surprisingly, adultery does not seem to have been a punishable offence in Egypt as it was in many other ancient cultures; but there was strong disapproval of the deed on moral grounds and literary texts suggest that the deceived husband might go so far as to murder the adulterer. Charges of adultery occur in denunciations of individuals to the authorities, probably as evidence of the accused's general wickedness, or, where he was himself an official, as examples of abuse of power. The accusation is generally one of sleeping with a married woman, suggesting that the wrong was against her husband rather than the adulterer's own wife; a man's infidelity with an unmarried woman would evidently not provoke the same public censure or risk of revenge. Of course, a married man who actually wished to set up house with a new woman would be expected to divorce his wife and give back the property she had brought into the marriage as well as her share of that which they had acquired together. There are very few references to women who committed adultery, although there should have been as many of these as adulterous men. Presumably it would again be the deceived husband who would be considered the injured party, and the couple would settle the matter between them without bringing charges; the man could divorce his wife without surrendering her share of the common property.

21. Accusations against Officials

This passage forms part of a long series of charges against the chief workman Pa-neb by the workman Amen-nakhte. Amen-nakhte felt that he should have been chief workman himself and that Pa-neb had taken the job from under him by bribing the vizier. His aim was to have Pa-neb dismissed on the grounds that he was unworthy and incompetent. (See 'Law' No. 146.) The charges he brings here vary from criminal offences to evidence of bad character, and it is not clear where in this range the following accusations of adultery fall. Note that Pa-neb is said to have slept with the lady Hel when she 'was with' Pen-dua, and again when she 'was with' Hesy-su-neb-ef; the terminology strengthens our impression that marriage was a relatively informal arrangement. For Hel and Hesy-su-neb-ef, see above No. 18.

Charge concerning this: his son ran before him to the place of the doorkeepers and he took an oath of the Lord, l.p.h., saying, 'I will not shield him (?).' And he said, 'Pa-neb slept with the lady Tuy when she was the wife of the workman Qenna; he slept with the lady Hel when she was with Pen-dua; he slept with the lady Hel when she was with Hesy-su-neb-ef,' so said his son. 'And when he had slept with Hel, he slept with Webkhet, her daughter. And A'o-pekhty, his son, slept with Webkhet himself.'

22. The Wealthy Seducer

This text offers a fascinating glimpse of village personalities which resembles an episode in a novel. The poor, rather trusting servant who is the narrator of the piece has married the daughter of a workman, but the young couple had not yet set up house together. One day, on visiting his beloved, the bridegroom found that she had been seduced by Mery-Sekhmet, the son of the wealthy draughtsman Menna, known from other sources to have been a wild and irresponsible young man given to brazen lies. After initial miscarriage of justice, the officials made Mery-Sekhmet swear to stay away from the girl in future; but in defiance of authority and of his own oath he visited her again and made her pregnant. This time his own father brought him before the officials, but Mery-Sekhmet got off lightly with another oath. The text is unique in several respects and it is not impossible that it

Fig. 7. The infamous foreman Paneb, from his tomb in the village cemetery. (Drawn by Marion Cox after Bruyère, *Tombes thébaines de Deir el Médineh à décoration monochrome*. MIFAO 86 (Cairo, 1952), pl. 21.)

is a work of fiction rather than a record of a actual event; compare Menna's letter to his son, 'Literature' No. 107.

An interesting detail is the bridegroom's reference to 'bringing the bundle', which may signify the payment of some sort of bridewealth—a practice otherwise unattested in the New Kingdom.

[As for me, I am] a servant of Amen-em-one, a member of the crew. I brought the bundle to the house of Pa-yom, and I made his daughter (my) wife. Now when I had spent the night in the house of my father, I set out to go to his house, and I found the workman Mery-Sekhmet son of Menna sleeping with my wife in the fourth month of summer, day 5. I went out and I told the officials; but the officials gave me 100 blows of a stick, saying 'Really, what are you saying!' Then the chief workman In-her-khau said, 'Really, what means this giving the 100 blows ⟨to⟩ the one who carried the bundle, while another fornicates? What the officials have done is a great crime.'

Then the scribe of the Necropolis Amen-nakhte made him swear an oath of the lord, l.p.h., saying, 'As Amen endures, as the Ruler endures, if I speak with her, the wife, my nose (?) and my nostrils and my ears will be [cut off], and I will be exiled to the land of Kush.'[a]

But he went again, and made her pregnant. Then the workman Menna, his father, placed him before the officials, and the scribe Amen-nakhte made him swear an oath of the Lord, l.p.h., again, saying again, 'if I go to the place where the daughter of Pa-yom is, I will be set to breaking stone in the quarry of Elephantine.'[a] [. . .] the good thing that the officials instituted.

[a] As is usual in oaths, the scribe has substituted the pronouns 'his' and 'he' for 'my' and 'I' in the apodosis, presumably to avoid calling the penalties down on himself.

23. An Unfaithful Wife

One of the few records of an accusation of adultery against a woman is preserved on this obscure little ostracon. One side bears a letter from an unknown woman to the husband about his wife's infidelity, while the other side contains the husband's reply. Both texts are difficult to understand without any knowledge of the background to the exchange. An interesting detail in the woman's letter is the reference to the offence as the 'abomination of Monthu'; it has been suggested that this god had himself been deceived by his divine spouse so that adultery was especially repugnant to him. The essence of the man's response is not clear; he may be disclaiming any rights over the woman, saying she was not his wife or had already left him. Borghouts has suggested it expresses the husband's distress at the news of his wife's infidelity and her angry reaction when confronted.

First letter (from a woman to a man):
    I, did I not take you (aside) to say, you should look to what you will do [about] your wife! (and) to say, you are blind about her! You have kept me from deafening you. The crime is the abomination of Monthu! Look, I will make you see this continuous fornication which your [wife] committed against you.

Second letter (from a man to a woman):
    But (she) is not my wife! Is she my wife? She finished making her speech and she went outside leaving the door open.
    [. . .]

Fig. 8. The workman Hesy-su-neb-ef and his wife Hel in happier days. On this stela Hesy-su-neb-ef and family kneel in devotion to his patron, the foreman of the gang Nefer-hotep, who is shown standing in the sacred bark of Mut. The top row of worshippers include, from left to right, Hesy-su-neb-ef himself, his wife Hel, their son Nefer-hotep and daughter Web-khet, named after the foreman and his wife, and another daughter. The parents of Hel feature in the lower register; but Hesy-su-neb-ef, born a slave-boy, had no relatives in the village. (J. E. Quibell, *The Ramesseum*. Egyptian Research Account, 1896 (London, 1898), pl. x, 3.)

Composition of Households

24. A Census

This unpublished document, now in Turin, bears at least two lists of inhabitants of Deir el-Medina, house by house. The manuscript is now broken into scores of fragments, more of which are still being identified. When the text has been reassembled, it will provide unique information about the demography of the village, but even in its current fragmentary state it shines an interesting new light on the composition of Deir el-Medina households. One surprise is the relatively small size of the families sharing a house; only one of the households listed below had as many as five members, and seven houses were occupied by single men. There are naturally many ties of kinship between households, as in the first group listed below, where Djehuty-mose son of Kha-em-hedje is found to be living two doors down from his sister Tenet-pa-ip, the wife of Amen-nakhte. The two lists on the papyrus were evidently drawn up at different times and where enough survives of both to compare the occupants of a single house we recognize the natural waxing and waning of families. Pen-pa-mer son of Neb-nefer, who was included in his parent's household in the earlier list, has acquired his own house below (I (A) col. II, 7); Ta-rekh-an had been living in her husband's house before, but has now moved in with her son and daughter-in-law.

Although fragments of similar, if less detailed, lists survive from Deir el-Medina and neighbouring settlements, their function is unknown. They may have been drawn up in connection with ration distributions or with a more general purpose of monitoring residence in the village.

Recto I (A) col. II

HOUSE OF [Amen-nakhte son of Bu]-qen-tu-ef, his mother is Ta-rekh-an

His wife, Tenet-pa-ip, daughter of Kha-em-hedje, her mother is Tenet-khenu-⟨em-heb⟩

His mother Ta-rekh-an, daughter of Nefer-hotep, her mother is Khaty

His sister Kayt-mehty, daughter of Bu-ken-tu-ef, her mother is Ta-rekh-an

HOUSE OF Pa-an-kha son of Hor-mose, his mother is Nebu-em-heb

HOUSE OF Djehuty-mose son of Kha[-em-hedje, his mother is Te]net-khenu-em-heb

HOUSE OF Pen-pa-Re son of Neb-nefer [. . .]

HOUSE OF In-her-khau son of Seti [. . .]

HOUSE OF Pa-wa-Amen son of Hor [. . .]

HOUSE OF Pen-neset-tawy [. . .] son of Pa-shed [. . .]

HOUSE OF Monthu-hat-ef son of Khon [. . .]

IV (D) Recto col. II

HOUSE OF Qed-akhet-ef son of Qeny-Min, his mother is Dua-[nefer]

His wife, Merut-Mut, daughter of Nefer-Hor, her mother is [. . .]

His son, Pa-an-kher-iaut-ef son of Qed[-akhet-ef . . .]

His daughter Wen-Her, the (one of) Qed-akhet-[ef . . .]

HOUSE OF Amen-nakhte son of Khay, his mother is Henut [-Meteret]

His wife, Ta-Hefnu, daughter of Nakhte-em-Mut, her mother is [. . .]

HOUSE OF Aʿo-pa-tjau son of Sa-Wadjyt, his mother is Mer [. . .]

His wife, Wabet, daughter of Nefer-her, her mother is Dua-[. . .]

His daughter Mer-es-ger, daughter of Aʿo-pa-tjau, her mother is [. . .]

HOUSE OF Hor-nefer son of Qenna, [his] mother is [. . .]

His wife, Hut-iyt, daughter of Hay, [he]r mother is [. . .]

His son, Qenna son of Hori-nefer, [his] mother is [Hut-iyt]

V (E)

HOUSE OF Ipuy son of Nefer-Hor, her (*sic*) mother is Merut-Mut

His wife Henut-mi-Re daughter of Nakhte-(em)-Mut, her mother is Hathor

His daughter Henut-netjeru daughter of Ip[uy], her mother is Henut-mi-Re

His daughter Dua-nefret [daughter of Ipu]y her mother is H[enut-mi-Re]

His daughter Hathor daughter of Ip[uy, her mother is Henut]-mi-Re

2

Daily Life

HEALTH CARE

In Deir el-Medina, as elsewhere in Egypt, health problems were treated by means of both medicine and magic, often in combination. Medical texts such as the famous Papyrus Ebers are introduced by magic spells to be recited during treatment; while magical remedies were sometimes accompanied by fumigations and ingestions resembling those in medical texts. Nevertheless, the two disciplines do appear to have been distinguished in that, for example, remedies which are *primarily* medical do not appear in compilations with those which are primarily magical. Furthermore, the community of workmen included both a doctor and a 'scorpion charmer', one of whom prepared prescriptions while the other specialized in magical cures for scorpion bites.

Magical and medical texts differ also in their distribution within the community. Magical texts are well represented on both papyri and ostraca, suggesting that workmen were given spells by the scorpion charmer when necessary or perhaps collected them on their own. In fact, we know that in at least one case, one individual sent another a spell against poison (below, No. 87). On the other hand, medical prescriptions are represented by only one papyrus and two short ostraca. Evidently, complicated prescriptions were prepared by the doctor himself. In several of the texts below we do see villagers sending off for medical ingredients, but whether these are in accordance with a doctor's instructions or whether they represent traditional household remedies is not clear.

25. The Village Doctor

Some of the ration lists from the village record a small payment to 'the doctor' similar to that received by the guardian and the doorkeeper. He seems, therefore, to have been a member of the gang who added medical care to his other duties, for which he was compensated by the state. This seems to be confirmed by the most extensive attendance list from the village which records every day of work missed by the individual workmen over the course of an entire year, year 40 of Ramesses II; a certain Pa-hery-pedjet, though not identified as the doctor, is excused from work more often than any of the others to care for his colleagues and members of their families who were ill. (On such attendance lists, see below, No. 169.) Sometimes he is simply said to be 'with' someone, while on other occasions he is 'preparing medicine'. The medicine for 'the wife of the scribe' took him 15 days to produce (assuming he worked through the weekends, which are not covered by the list). All of this points to state aided medical care for the workmen and their families, although in 'Family' No. 12, above, we saw that a doctor received a fee from the husband of his patient, presumably for some service over and above his official responsibility.

Pa-hery-pedjet. Third month of inundation day 21 WITH A'O-PEHTY; day 22 ALSO; day 23 ALSO; day 24 ALSO. Fourth month of inundation day 7 ALSO; day 8 ALSO; day 15 ALSO; day 16 ALSO; day 17 DITTO. First month of winter day 14 OFFERING TO THE GOD.

[. . .] X + 13. Third month of winter day 25 WITH KHONSU PREPARING MEDICINE; day 26 ALSO. Third month of winter day 27 DITTO. First month of summer day 25 MAKING MEDICINE FOR THE WIFE OF THE SCRIBE; day 26 ALSO; day 27 DITTO. Second month of summer day 2 DITTO; day 3 DITTO; day 4 DITTO; day 5 DITTO; day 6 DITTO; day 7 DITTO; day 8 DITTO. Third month of summer day 3 PREPARING MEDICINE; day 17 WITH HOR-EM-WIA; day 18 WITH HOR-EM-WIA; day 21 DITTO; day 22. Fourth month of summer.

[. . .] Fourth month of summer day 5; day 6; day 7; day 8; day 24 ILL; [day] 25; day 26, ILL. First month of inundation day 1[5] ILL [. . .].

26. Filling a Prescription

In this short letter, Amen-mose writes to a priest of the Ramesseum for the ingredients of a remedy for a sick man. Amen-mose is not a doctor, however, but a scorpion-charmer/magician. It is possible that the substances requested here were required for a magical cure or else that Amen-mose used a combination of magic and medicine in his work, just as a doctor might recite a magical spell as he administered his prescription.

The scorpion charmer Amen-mose [to N.] and the temple scribe, prophet Piay of the mansion of King Weser-Maʿat-Re Setep-en-Re, l.p.h. (the Ramesseum) in the House of Amen ⟨on⟩ the West of Thebes.

To the effect that: The prophet is ill. When my letter reaches [you, you] will send him one grain,[a] one jar of syrup, one festival date-juice(?).

Farewell.

[a] i.e. a figure of a grain-bride, a fetish?

27. A Blind Workman Asks Help from his Son

Ailments of the eye were one of the most common complaints among the workmen, as they are in Egypt today. In this emotional letter to his son, the draughtsman Pay laments the loss of his eyesight and asks the younger man to send medication. Blindness would of course incapacitate a draughtsman completely. The substances Pay requests—honey, ochre, and black eye-paint—are common elements of Egyptian eye remedies. Indeed, the famous Papyrus Ebers includes a prescription virtually identical to Pay's as a cure for an affliction called *adet*, which has tentatively been identified as pterygium, a growth in the eye (Ebers no. 371): 'yellow ochre, 1; black eye-paint, 1; fermented honey, 1. Mix together and apply to the eyes.' Honey does in fact have antiseptic and anti-bacterial properties, and ochre appears in many prescriptions intended to cool and reduce swelling, so the remedy probably had a positive effect.

It is interesting to find Pay ordering these ingredients for himself. Since so many workmen suffered from eye disease, treatments are likely to have been common knowledge. It is also possible, however, that Pay was filling a prescription given him by the community doctor.

Said by the draughtsman Pay to his son, the draughtsman Pre-[em-hab]:

Do not turn your back on me—I am not well. Do not c[ease] weeping for me, because I am in the [darkness? since] my lord Amen [has turned] his back on me.

May you bring me some honey for my eyes, and also ochre which is made into bricks again,[a] and real black eye-paint. [Hurry!] Look to

it! Am I not your father? Now, I am wretched; I am searching for my
sight but it is gone.

  [a] Perhaps reconstituted from a powdered state.

28. A Request for Medicine Gone Astray

The writer of this letter has evidently been reproached by a woman for not
sending medicine when it was needed. He is clearly upset, protesting that he
had not heard about the illness in question and had never received any
request for assistance.

Aʿo-mek. As for the matters of illness about which you (*fem.*) write
me (*masc.*), what have I done against you (*pl.*)? As for the medicines
which you (*pl.*) mentioned, did you write me about them and did I
fail to give them to you (*fem.*)? As Ptah endures, and as Thoth
endures, I have not heard it from anyone; it was not told to me!
[. . .]
  (*The rest of the letter is largely illegible.*)

29. Qen-her-khepesh-ef's Medical Papyrus

There is only one extensive medical text from the village, a treatise on
complaints of the anus, rectum, and bladder from the library of the Qen-
her-khepesh-ef family. Entries consist of a heading naming the complaint
to be treated, a list of ingredients for the prescription, and instructions for
how these are to be prepared and applied. Occasionally, a description of
symptoms and their diagnosis precedes the whole. Most of the prescriptions
are for suppositories and injections.
  We can only guess why this single, very specialized document, was
acquired by a member of the Qen-her-khepesh-ef family. One possibility is
that he was the local expert in this branch of medicine. Herodotus does say
that Egyptian doctors were highly specialized, but it hardly seems likely that
each workman was a medical specialist, and we may reasonably suspect that
the owner of the text was himself a sufferer of the ailments described. This
has interesting implications for questions of self-treatment; see also the
letter from a blind workman, translated above.

ANOTHER REMEDY MADE FOR THE THROBBING OF A *BENU*[a]
  Sea-fish scales
  Galingale (*a ginger-like root*) of the oasis
  Leaves of flax
  mesta-liquid

Mix together with this (liquid). You shall make 12 pellets, and you shall apply 4 pellets to his anus (every day) so that he becomes healthy.

ANOTHER PREPARED AFTERWARDS
Have ready
    fennel (?)   1
    goose fat   1
    honey   1
Prepare in a bag of cloth. You shall make 4 pellets, placing one of them in the anus every day.

If you find he bleeds behind and if it flows (like) water,[b] you shall prepare for him:
    juniper berries
Pound and expose to the dew. Coat all the limbs with it so that he becomes healthy.[c]

If you find he bleeds behind and that it flows for 5 days, you shall prepare for him as a remedy:
    black eye paint
    ibex fat
    grains of emmer
Grind fine together. Make into 4 pellets and expose to the dew overnight. Place in the anus so that he becomes healthy.

REMEDY FOR EVERYTHING (BAD) IN THE ANUS
    carob beans   1
    northern salt   1
    natron   1
    eastern salt   1
    honey   1

ANOTHER FOR THE SAME THING
    hes of the *ima*-tree (*unknown words*)   1
    carob beans   1
    honey   1
    natron   1
Mix together. Bandage with this for 4 days.

REMEDY TO CURE PROLAPSUS IN THE ANUS[d]
    meal of lubya-beans

northern salt
goose fat
the paste of grain
honey
Mix together and apply to the anus for four days. . . .

IF IT (THE MALADY) EMERGES IN THE MANNER OF A *BENU*-ILLNESS ON
THE BLADDER, AND *SENKET* (*UNKNOWN*) IS IN HIS JOINTS WHEN HE
EXCRETES WATER BETWEEN HIS BUTTOCKS, AND HIS LIMBS ARE IN A
FEVER ON ACCOUNT OF THE ILLNESS OF HIS URINE, (AND) THE SUF-
FERING COMES AND GOES, HIS ANUS BEING HEAVY, AND THERE IS NO
END TO HIS *ŠMYT* (*UNKNOWN*);

   YOU SHALL SAY CONCERNING HIM, 'IT IS A HEAVINESS OF HIS ANUS;
AN ILLNESS THAT I CAN TREAT.'

You shall prepare as a remedy so that he becomes healthy:
   goose fat $\frac{1}{64}$
   honey $\frac{1}{64}$
   human milk $\frac{3}{64}$
Inject in the anus for four days.

   [a] A *benu* is a sore with serious complications, such as a gangrenous or cancerous
sore.
   [b] Bloody diarrhoea? This could be a symptom of haemorrhoids.
   [c] Juniper berries might serve as a purgative, which would fit the Egyptian medical
principle of treating like with like or of expelling the bad substances in the body, but
coating the limbs with juniper berries hardly seems to serve either end.
   [d] Haemorrhoids or prolapsed rectum?

30. Medical Collection on an Ostracon

Only a handful of medical texts are found on ostraca. The example translated here appears to have been a compilation of prescriptions for various
ailments. It is difficult to imagine who would have drawn up such a text and
for what purpose.

Recto
PRESCRIPTION FOR THE HEART [. . .]
Verso
OINTMENT TO CURE A RASH (?)
   leaves of acacia
   wax

smear with this for four days (in) the morning. *nedebet* (*unknown word*)

To cure a cough (?) in the whole body
  grapes
  [. . .]

Laundry

Laundry requires large amounts of water and is therefore a problem in a desert community. The state provided laundrymen for the village, each of whom did the washing for up to eight households per day. The laundry was either collected by them or delivered to the riverbank, where they washed it with natron (sodium carbonate and sodium bicarbonate), as illustrated in the tomb of Ipuy (Fig. 9). Much of the clothing recovered from the site still bears its laundry marks and the workmen occasionally kept a record of the washing they had sent out.

31. The Village Laundry List

The following is a composite list recording, house by house, the clothes handed over to various washermen. Note that each entry follows a fixed order, beginning with the most common garments, kilts and loincloths.

[. . . Work given to] the washerman Baki:
  H[ouse of . . .]:   kilts, 2; underpants, 2; tunics, [. . .];
                             sleeve, 1; [. . .]; bands, 3.
  House of Iny: kilts, [. . .]; loincloth, 1
  House of Amen-[. . .]:   kilt, 1; loincloths, 2; sleeve, 1;
                             [hand?]kerchiefs [. . .]
  House of Khonsu: kilt, 1; loincloth, 1; shawl, 1; under-
                             pants, 1; sleeve, 1; rags, [. . .]
  House of Pen-dua: kilts, 2; loincloths, [. . .]
Work given to the washerman [. . .]

32. Dropping off at the Cleaners

This short text records a large load of laundry delivered to the washermen on one day and collected on the next—presumably the combined washing of several houses, though they are not enumerated as above.

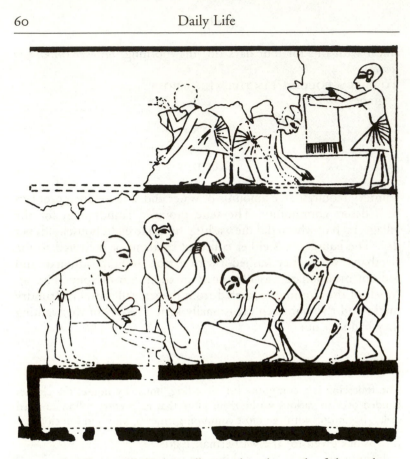

Fig. 9. Laundrymen at work, as illustrated in the tomb of the workman
Ipuy (TT 217). In the lower register, men wash clothing in tubs and, on the
left, beat them clean on a stone. Above, the wet clothes are spread out to
dry. (Reproduced with the kind permission of the Metropolitan Museum
of Art, New York, from Norman deGaris Davies, *Two Ramesside Tombs at
Thebes* (New York, 1927), pl. 28.)

Year 1, third month of winter, day 15. This day, giving clothes to the
washermen.
What came from/via him in the third month of winter, day 16.
Given to them at the riverbank to launder:

kilts	10
loincloths	8
sanitary towels	5

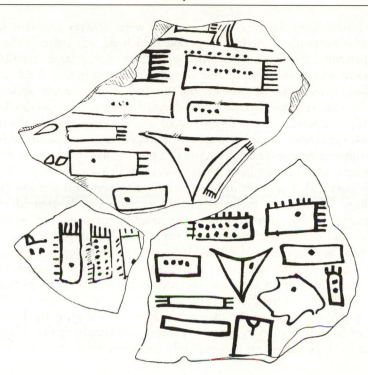

Fig. 10. Sketches of clothing on ostraca—including triangular loincloths, fringed shawls, and a tunic—with dots indicating the quantity of each item. These may represent pictorial laundry lists drawn up for, or by, persons who could not read. (Reproduced with the kind permission of the IFAO in Cairo from Bruyère, *Rapport (1934–1935)*. FIFAO 15 (1937), p. 62 fig. 32.)

WATER

One of the great drawbacks of Deir el-Medina's desert location was the complete absence of water, which had to be carried up to the valley from the floodplain by half a dozen water carriers assigned to the village. Their deliveries (or shortfalls in deliveries) are recorded in a handful of texts, from which it appears that each household received about $1\frac{1}{4}$–$1\frac{1}{2}$ sacks, or about 96–115 litres, daily. Each member of a six-person household would thus have from 15 to 20 litres for drinking and washing, but not laundry, which was done by the laundrymen at the riverbank, as we saw above.

Interestingly, the great majority of the water delivery texts date to the Nineteenth Dynasty, a period which is otherwise under-represented by the ostraca. Although there was a large, circular cistern at the entrance to the village which presumably held the village water supply at some period, this may belong to a later system from that reflected in the texts; detailed records of deliveries by individual water carriers to individual households—or shortfalls in these deliveries—would be impractical when the water was stored in a common cistern. The texts better fit a practice like that in use at the Amarna workmen's village, where water was delivered to large storage pots, called *zirs*, set into permanent emplacements outside the village. There seem to have been as many *zirs* as households at Amarna, so that each family's ration could be measured out on the spot and drawn at their convenience. Quite possibly there was a similar arrangement at Deir el-Medina in the Nineteenth Dynasty. At Deir el-Medina, however, the *zir*-emplacements would have to be at least 100 m. from the main entrance to the village, perhaps near the Enclosure of the Necropolis.

Supplying water to the men at work in the Valley of the Kings must have been an even bigger operation than supplying the village, but so far as I know, it is completely undocumented.

33. Water for Every Household

The following text from the Nineteenth Dynasty is one of the only ostraca that records the water deliveries rather than deficits. The rations are listed by household, a valuable indication that the water was intended for the village and not the Valley of the Kings. However, as Janssen pointed out, the order of the houses does not correspond to their relative positions along the streets of the village, so the water was almost certainly not delivered door to door, but to some central delivery point from which the householders could collect it. It is not clear why some households get twice as much water as others.

Col.I

[House of] Neb-imentet	$\frac{1}{4}$ sack (?)
House of Amen-nakhte son of Dydy	$\frac{1}{2}$ sack
House of Mose	$\frac{1}{2}$ sack
House of Pa-shed son of Hor-mose	$\frac{1}{2}$ sack
House of Karo	$\frac{1}{2}$ sack
[House of] Pa-shed son of Heh	$\frac{1}{4}$ sack

[House of . . .] $\frac{1}{4}$ sack
[House of Hay] son of Seba $\frac{1}{2}$ sack
[House of . . .] son of Maw-a'a $\frac{1}{2}$ sack
[House of . . .]-ope $\frac{1}{2}$ sack
[House of Ame]n-em-one $\frac{1}{4}$ sack
[House of] Djehuty-her-maket-ef $\frac{1}{4}$ sack
[House of] Huria $\frac{1}{4}$ sack

34. Delivery Shortfalls

This mid-Nineteenth Dynasty text records arrears in the water rations of
five individuals (although the first entry, Pre-hotep, was later erased by the
scribe). Note the separate ration for the watchman stationed at the Enclosure of the Necropolis.

What Nefer-hotep said in the third month of winter, day 22, water
deficit for the left side:

Pre-hotep $1\frac{1}{2}$ sacks
Neb-imentet $1\frac{1}{2}$ sacks
Kha-bekhnet   1 sack
the watchman $\frac{1}{4}$ sack
the servant woman Saroy $\frac{1}{2}$ sack
[Total], left side: $4\frac{3}{4}$ sacks

35. Attempts to Dig a Well

A. Presumably because of the difficulties of the water supply, the community attempted on several occasions to dig a well in the area in front of the
village. The first attempt, in year 15 of Ramesses III, reached a depth of
22.4 m. (43 cubits) without striking water, and the project was dropped.

Year 15, fourth month of winter, day 12. List of all the work done in
the well:

Previously: $36\frac{1}{2}$ cubits
Work subsequently: $6\frac{1}{2}$ cubits
Total: 43

B. A generation later, probably in the reign of Ramesses VI, the workmen
tried again. This time, a professional surveyor was brought in to calculate
the remaining distance to the water table, for which the sacred lake of the
Ramesseum, or perhaps the canal leading to the temple, served as a reference point. The 'Enclosure of the Necropolis' was used as an intermediate

marker. The total depth to the water table was established to be over 60 cubits, or 31.5 m.

In fact, the workmen dug 20 m. beyond the point where they expected to strike water without doing so, as we know from the enormous pit which is still one of the most striking features of the area. Over 10 m. in diameter at the opening, the well is sunk 52 m. through marly rock and solid limestone; access is via a rock-cut spiral stairway cut into its walls. When all hope of reaching water had been abandoned, the pit was used as a dump and eventually was filled to the rim with debris—including many hundreds of ostraca.

Year 2 (or 3), second month of summer, day 15. This day, the chief builder [. . .] of the estate of Amen arrived to measure (from) the well in front of [. . .] the Necropolis to the water surface (of) the lake of the Ramesseum:

From the lake to the Enclosure of the Necropolis: elevation
                                                     [. . .] cubits.
From the Necropolis to the well: 26 cubits 5 palms
Total: 60 + X
The difference makes 22 cubits 5 palms to the water surface.
So one shall dig 10 to [. . .] the water.
Total: 22 cubits 5 palms.

THE WEATHER

36. Rain

A number of graffiti record rainfalls, a rare phenomenon in Upper Egypt. The third example below probably records a visit to a pool of water left by a rainstorm.

A. Year 4 of King Ba-en-Re (Merneptah), first month of summer, day 27. This day, the water of the sky came down. The Servant in the Place of Truth, Pen-nakhte.

B. Year 2, fourth month of summer, day 4. The water came down from the water in the sky. The servant in the Place of Truth Amen-pa-Hapy (and) his brother, the scribe [. . .].

C. Year 2, fourth month of summer, day 24. (Coming) to the water of the sky:

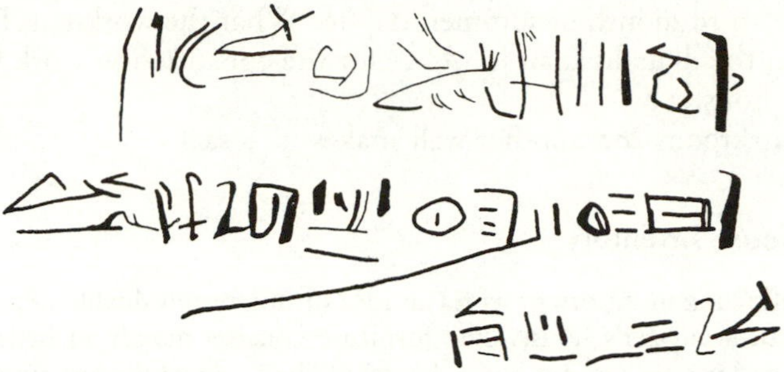

Fig. 11. Graffito written by the workman Pen-nakhte to record a rain shower in year 4 of King Merneptah. See No. 36A for translation. (Reproduced with the kind permission of the IFAO in Cairo from A. F. Sadek, *Graffiti de la Montagne Thébaine* III, 4 (Fac-similés) (Centre de documentation et d'études sur l'ancienne Egypte, Cairo, 1972), pl. CLXXXIV.

the scribe Amen-nakhte son of Ipuy;
his son Pa-nefer-em-djed;
his son Kha-em-hedje;
his son Pay-nedjem.

THE HOUSE

For texts concerning the ownership of and transfer of real property, see Chapter 5.

37. Household Repairs

Deir el-Medina was a purpose-built village and the houses followed a standard plan, but over time families altered the interiors to fit their individual needs by subdividing rooms or even whole houses. In the following extract, the workman Paneb pays a draughtsman for constructing a workroom or storeroom at the back of the house and another partition wall. Paneb was an ambitious and unscrupulous man, who would later be accused of bribing the vizier to obtain the foremanship. One is tempted to see in these renovations a sign of his aspirations to a grander lifestyle.

Year 3, third month of summer, day 16. What the workman Pa-neb gave to the draughtsman [. . .] . . . for the construction work he did in my house:

    a workroom and another wall makes $1\frac{1}{2}$ sacks

38. House Inventory

The following inventory provides an idea of the more valuable items to be found in a villager's house. The furniture consists mainly of beds, foot-stools, and various types of boxes that would have served the function of our cupboards and chests of drawers. The large amount of grain that heads the list may have been kept in the house as a form of ready cash.

In Ancient Egypt, as today, people seem to have worried about leaving their houses unoccupied. At the end of his inventory, the anonymous writer asks a female friend or relative to arrange for a house-sitter.

List of the items left behind by me in the village:
    3 sacks barley
    $1\frac{1}{2}$ sacks emmer
    26 bundles of onions
    2 beds
    sheqer-box
    2 couches for a man
    2 folding stools

Fig. 12. Figure of a woman blowing into an oven to fan the flames. The circles on the oven represent impressions made on its outer surface to prevent it from cracking during use. Many such ovens were found in situ in the back-room of the workmen's houses. (Drawing by Marian Cox after O Leipzig 1894.)

1 *pedes*-box
1 inlaid *tjay*-box
har (*unknown object*)
2 griddle-stones
1 *gatit*-box
2 footstools
2 folding stools of wood
1 sack of lubya beans (3 *oipe*)
12 bricks of natron
2 tree trunks
1 door
2 *sterti* of sawn wood
2 *hetep*-containers
1 small *hetep*-container
1 mortar
2 *medjay*

(All of) which are with Pa-shed and Sherit-Re, and all recorded.

Another matter for Sheri-Re (*fem.*): Please have Amen-em-wia stay in my house so he can watch it. Please write to me about your condition.

The Tomb

An Egyptian's greatest investment was his tomb. The workmen of Deir el-Medina, the country's top tomb-builders, naturally built their own tombs or hired their fellow villagers to do all or part of the work for them. Most of the preserved decorated tombs were constructed in the Nineteenth Dynasty, some perhaps at the expense of older monuments; in the Twentieth Dynasty, few new tombs were built and succeeding generations simply added chambers to the family sepulchre as they were needed. Surprisingly, the tomb site or even the tomb itself seems to have been state property and workmen were assigned a tomb just as they were provided with a house in the village for the duration of their employment only. A workman was assigned the tomb of his ancestors where possible, but when a family died out or moved away its tomb might be reassigned. However, various architectural elements, such as the pyramidion, were private property and could be sold or transferred through inheritance.

Building, embellishing, and maintaining the family tomb could occupy a great deal of free time, and a workman might also get time off from his labours in the Valley of the Kings for this purpose. One gets the impression that the villagers enjoyed these busman's holidays during which they could put their creative skills to use on projects of their own.

39. Tomb Improvements

The following text is one of three dealing with a dispute over the ownership of a burial chamber in the reign of Ramesses III. The problem appears to have been that shafts from two different tombs opened into the burial chamber. From the other two texts in the group we learn that the coffin and other funerary goods found inside were not inscribed, so that there was no way to decide to which tomb they belonged. In the end the chamber seems to have been assigned to Amen-em-ope, probably the author of this selection.

Amen-em-ope provides a brief history of the ownership of his tomb going back over 140 years, illustrating how a tomb might change hands from generation to generation. We are told that the reorganization of the gang under Horemheb was followed by a redistribution of property in the village. At that time Amen-em-one's ancestor, Khay, was assigned the tomb of a certain Amen-(mose). This tomb seems to have been inherited by Khay's male heirs, but at some point this line died out and the property was in danger of being abandoned. Amen-em-ope, who claimed descent from Khay through a female relative, Hel, asked the oracle of Amenophis to assign him 'a' tomb. No doubt he hoped and expected that he would be given that of his ancestor, Khay, as indeed transpired. This was therefore the second time that the property reverted to 'the state' and was reallocated to one of the workmen.

Year 7 of King Djeser-kheper-Re, l.p.h., Horemheb l.p. (*sic*): the date that Khay, my ancestor, was enrolled in the Necropolis. The major-domo of Thebes, Djehuty-mose, divided up the properties in the Necropolis for the gang of Pharaoh, l.p.h. He gave the tomb of Amen-(mose) to Khay, my ancestor, through an order. Hel, my ancestress, was his lineal descendant; he had no male heirs, and his property was becoming abandoned.

Now, later, in year 21 (of Ramesses III), second month of summer, day 1, I stood before Amenophis, l.p.h., saying to him, 'Direct (me) to a tomb among the ancestors!' He gave me the tomb of Khay through a writing and I began to work in it.

Now, later, I was building and the workman Kha-em-nun was working in his tomb. In the first month of summer, day 6,[a] he had a day off and found the opening in it, and descended into it with the police officer Nefer-hotep, while I was not there.

Now, later, in the first month of summer, day 7, the chief workman Khonsu was found sitting and drinking. Afterwards, I was standing with Hori son of Huy-nefer and the workman Bak-en-werl. I did not know where the opening of my tomb was. The scribe Amen-nakhte found the opening (?), saying, 'Come down! See the place which opens into the tomb of Kha-em-nun!'

[a] Since the date of Ramesses III's accession to the throne was first month of summer, day 26, in his reign the first month of summer, day 6 was almost a year later than the second month of summer, day 1, the date that Amenophis I assigned the tomb to the speaker.

40. Paying for the Decoration

In this text, the workman Aʿo-nakhte pays Mery-Sekhmet for paintings done in the substructure of his tomb. Mery-Sekhmet was one of the draughtsmen of the gang, so Aʿo-nakhte was able to procure the work of the pharaoh's own tomb painter for the price of some sandals, mats and baskets. The tomb owner appears to have supplied the necessary paint.

Loincloth, 1	sandals, 2 pair
loincloth	
vegetables, 3 bundles	pigment, $2\frac{1}{2}$ silver units
mat, 1	wood [. . .], 1
grain baskets, 2	
irqes-baskets, 2	
Total: $6\frac{1}{2}$ silver units	

What Aʿo-nakhte gave to Mery-Sekhmet in exchange for the painting of his burial chamber.

41. A Tomb Inventory

The authorities kept an eye on the tombs in the cemeteries of the village, as is clear from this record of an inspection by a committee including two officials from outside the village. They were unable to identify the tomb in question, which was therefore not claimed by an existing family and was presumably already very old. Valbelle points out that the tomb-furnishings listed in the inventory are typical of an Eighteenth Dynasty tomb; a number of tombs of this period were found virtually intact and their contents are comparable to this one. The lack of inscribed material in the burial chamber also points to an early date. Among the objects which one might have expected to find in a tomb but which are not listed are shabties, canopic jars, clothing and a book of the dead. The food buried with the deceased may simply not have been listed by the authorities.

Year 25, first month of summer, day 9. List of the inspection of everything found in the ruined tomb across from the burial place of the scribe Amen-nakhte (son of) Ipuy:

1 coffin of god's stone
1 sarcophagus with a linen (?) pall
1 coffin with a linen (?) pall
1 ebony folding stool with ducks' heads, mended
2 couches
1 box of papyrus
3 headrests
1 *irqes*-basket filled with rags [. . .]
2 pairs of sandals
1 scribal palette
1 bronze bowl
1 water bag
1 box (contents: 1 knife, 1 pin, 1 metal dish, 1 juglet, 1 razor case, 1 razor, 1 scraping razor)
granite vessels: 5 *menet*-jars
1 metal dish
1 pot
1 staff
food basket (with) bread
1 wooden *qeren* (*unknown object*)
1 alabaster *kebu*-jar
2 wooden *neshi*-containers of medicine
1 box (contents: 1 faience amulet, 1 alabaster *kebu*-jar, 1 pot of ointment, 10 [. . .])
1 box (contents: 1 alabaster *keb*-jar, 1 comb, 1 tweezer)
1 alabaster *nemset*-vessel
a *khar* (*unknown*)
2 pieces of scenting material
The chief workman Khonsu
the chief workman Kha (i.e. In-her-khau)

the police inspector Nefer-hotep
the police inspector Kha-em-ope
the guardian Pen-men-nefer
Kha-em-nun
Weser-hat
A'o-nakhte
Irsu
Huy-nefer
Nefer-her
the scribe Amen-nakhte.
[It was closed again and sealed] with a seal.

42. Tomb Furniture: A Pillow for the Eternal Sleep

Egyptian headrests were made of wood or stone and thus could be inscribed
with appropriate slumber-promoting texts. This example was produced for
Qen-her-khepesh-ef's tomb and invokes a good sleep in the land of the
dead.

long edge: The scribe of Thoth and of Ma'at who love him, Qen-her-
khepesh-ef son of Pa-nakhte, justified.
front: Spell (for) a good sleep in the hand of Amen, by the royal
scribe Qen-her-khepesh-ef, [justified].
rear: A good sleep inside the western district for the justified. Made
by the royal scribe Qen-her-khepesh-ef, justified.

43. A Tomb is Reassigned

The guardian Amen-em-ope is a poorly documented individual who lived
in the early part of the reign of Ramesses II. His family seems to have
disappeared from the village by the Twentieth Dynasty when his tomb was
inspected by the captains of the gang before being handed over to the
workman Menna. The coffin mentioned in this text may be that of Amen-
em-ope found in 1928 (Fig. 13).

Year 4, fourth month of winter, day 10. This day, inspecting the
tomb of the guardian Amen-em-ope by the three captains of
the [Necropolis] in order to hand [it] over [to] the workman
Menna.
   [List] of everything that was in it:

Fig. 13. Fragment of a sarcophagus belonging
to the guardian Amen-em-ope, perhaps the
same found by the officials reassigning Amen-
em-ope's tomb to the workman Menna (see
No. 43). (Reproduced with kind permission of
the IFAO in Cairo from Bruyère, *Rapport
(1928)*. FIFAO 6(2) (1929), p. 99 fig. 57, 1.)

A coffin [. . .]
(*perhaps five more lines lost*)

44. Burial

This little graffito commemorating the burial of the well-documented
scribe of the Necropolis Butehamun uses the common metaphor of death
as a landing after a journey. By the time Butehamun died in the Twenty-
first Dynasty the village had long been abandoned, but the western cemetery continued to serve as the final resting place for members of the
gang. This graffito was written in the chapel of the tomb of an Eighteenth-
Dynasty workman, Nakhte-Min; perhaps, therefore, Butehamun reused
this ancient tomb for his own burial rather than joining his ancestors in the
family vault, tentatively identified as Tomb 1338. Three of Butehamun's
coffins were purchased from dealers and are now in museums in Turin
and Brussels, but as they were not found *in situ* they shed no light on the
location of his burial.

The West is yours, ready for you. All praised-ones are hidden within
it; wrongdoers will not enter it, nor any guilty persons. The scribe
Butehamun has moored there after an old age, his body sound and
intact.
Made by the scribe of the Necropolis Ankh-ef-en-Amen.

ECONOMICS

Economic activity is the best-documented area of private life at
Deir el-Medina because the workmen kept detailed records of major
economic transactions. The community as a whole was of course on
the receiving end of the national system of redistribution; the various
branches of the state, including the Granary, the Treasury, and the
temples, supplied the workmen with all of the necessities of life, so
that in theory they were independent of the market. Not surprisingly, however, the standard government issue did not always meet
individual needs and tastes, and there was a great deal of trading
between households; moreover, the members of the gang manufactured furniture and funerary goods in their free time which found
eager buyers within the village and beyond. The many hundreds of
such transactions, as well as gifts and loans, have been studied by Jac.
J. Janssen, whose works provide a comprehensive survey of Egyptian
economic life at the village level.

Economic Exchange

In their private economic transactions, the villagers used a money-barter system of exchange. In other words, each item had a 'price' measured in grain, copper, or silver rings, but this was only for purposes of calculation; it was rare that grain or copper actually changed hands, and concrete, non-theoretical silver rings are not even known from the village. Rather, the 'prices' were used to compare the value of items on the two sides of a exchange. Thus a box worth 10 copper *deben* might be bartered for two tunics worth 5 copper *deben* each, without any real copper being involved at all.

This meant that an individual who hoped to buy a particular item, say, a bed, would have to find someone who not only had a bed to sell, but was also willing to take in exchange what the buyer had to offer. The words 'buy' and 'sell' are not strictly appropriate in this context, but in fact we often see a single, expensive item, such as an ox or a bed, traded for a collection of cheaper items, and in these cases it seems natural to think of a seller and a buyer. It did not matter so much if the commodities offered by the two parties were exactly equal in 'price' because they were more interested in an exchange satisfactory to both than in a theoretical equivalence. Moreover, the prices assigned to the various items were fairly vague, being frequently rounded to the nearest *deben*, or, for more expensive items, to the nearest multiple of 5.

45. Sale of an Ox

The following text records the sale of an ox, the type of major transaction that was most often written down. Naturally, such valuable items were traded particularly by the wealthier members of the community, and indeed in this case the seller, a chief policeman, belongs to the local elite. Hay, the buyer, cannot be identified precisely. The purchase price was assembled from a variety of items, most of which were staples that every household could use—although this is not obviously true of the almost 30 litres of fresh fat. Note that the total value of the items exchanged for the ox is 130 *deben*, 10 *deben* more than the stated value of the animal. This reflects the secondary importance of exact prices, as mentioned above.

Year 5, third month of summer, day 20. What was given to Hay by the chief policeman Neb-semen: an ox, makes 120 *deben*.
    What was given to him:

2 jars fresh fat	makes 60 *deben*
5 tunics of smooth cloth	makes 25 *deben*
1 kilt of thin cloth	makes 20 *deben*
1 hide	makes 25 *deben*

46. The Shopping List

A. This text concerns the first step of an economic transaction, the decision to acquire certain items—in this case, two heart amulets and some incense for a coffin. Pay instructs his son to find someone who is willing to sell and to offer whatever items are requested in return. Such an acquiescent approach to barter suggests that the items were urgently needed, perhaps for an imminent burial.

Said by the draughtsman Pay to his son the draughtsman Pre-em-hab: Please make arrangements to acquire the two faience hearts I mentioned to you. I shall give the price to their owner in whatever form of payment he may ask. Also make arrangements to acquire this fresh incense I mentioned to you to treat the coffin of your mother— I will give its price to its owner. Also, be sure to take this rag of a kilt and this rag of a loincloth in order to make the kilt into red bands and the loincloth into a *šhendyt*-garment. Do not neglect anything I tell you! Take care!

B. The following concise instruction, which presumably accompanied the ring mentioned in it, illustrates true target trading. The recipient would have had to hunt around until she found the owner of a tunic who would rather have a ring. Both the writer and the addressee of the letter were women, and the text is written on the scrappiest little ostracon imaginable—a fragment of a pot handle.

Another matter for Henut-wedjbu (*fem.*):
Please pay attention and seek out for me (*fem.*) one tunic in exchange for the ring; I will allow you ten days.

47. The Middleman

The attempt to buy a donkey which preceded the text below went so badly wrong that it led to a dispute before the three captains of the village. Menna, a well-to-do workman, had commissioned the water-carrier Tja°o to purchase a donkey for him. Water-carriers worked with donkeys all day and presumably knew people in Deir el-Medina and West Thebes who had animals to sell, so it was easier for Menna to employ one as an agent than to try to find a donkey himself. Interestingly, the water-carrier was paid in advance with specific goods, which, strictly speaking, would not leave him much latitude for barter. Perhaps he kept some or all of these items for himself, and negotiated with his own stock. Presumably if he found a good bargain, he could also make a little profit on the deal, although 27 *deben* was already a low price for a donkey. For whatever reason, the first two donkeys Tjaʿo offered to Menna were of such bad quality that they were rejected, and he was finally made to swear that he would deliver a decent animal or return his advance.

Year 28, fourth month of summer, day 10.

The draughtsman Menna contested with the water-carrier Tjaʿo, saying, 'I gave him 27 *deben* of copper—in the form of various valuables—saying, "Bring me a donkey!" [List of what I gave:]

1 kerchief of thin cloth	makes 12 *deben*
1 shawl of smooth cloth	makes 8 *deben*
[. . .]	
1 pair of men's sandals	makes 2 *deben*
1 sack of emmer	makes 1 *deben*
$\frac{1}{4}$ sack flour	
(total) given to him	27 copper *deben*

He brought me a donkey, but I returned it to him; and he brought me this other one, but it is not good either. Give it to him, and let him bring me a good donkey or else my money!'

It (the donkey) was given to him (Tjaʿo). He took the oath of the lord, saying, 'I will give him a donkey or the money before the first month of inundation, day [. . .].' (Before) the two chief workmen and the scribe.

48. Credit

It might of course happen that one party to an exchange did not have in hand items satisfactory to the other party, or not enough of these to make up the purchase price. In a community as small as Deir el-Medina where the inhabitants were constantly involved in transactions with one another, a natural solution to this problem was what Janssen has called an 'open credit system'. Shortfalls were noted down to be paid off at a later date or to feature as a credit to the seller in some future transaction between the same parties. Alternatively, the buyer might collect the various elements of the purchase price from family and friends knowing that they were sure to come to him for similar help in the future. Perhaps they also had debts to him which could be conveniently paid off in this way. At any one time, an inhabitant of the village would consequently be the debtor and the creditor of several others. Particularly complicated relationships or ones involving substantial sums were recorded on ostraca, as in the two examples below.

A. The following text appears to be a balancing of accounts between the workman Khnum-mose and the policeman Neb-semen. The recto lists goods given by the former to the latter through the agency of various third parties, probably on different occasions. On the verso we read that, on his part, Neb-semen had given Khnum-mose 43 *deben* worth of goods, leaving a credit of 23 *deben* to the latter.

recto
List of everything that the workman Khnum-mose gave to the chief policeman Neb-se[men son of] Ra'ia (*fem.*):

[. . .] *hin* fresh fat	[. . .]
1 wooden coffin	makes 20 *deben*
via Neb-semen	
3 tunics of smooth cloth	make 15 *deben*
2 copper *deben*	
via Pen-pa-mer:	
3 sandal-thongs	
via Pen-pa-mer:	
2 *hin* fresh fat	
via him:	
1 bed	makes 15 *deben*
via the policeman [Amen]-kha:	
2 *hin* sesame oil	
1 sheet of smooth cloth	makes 8 *deben*
via the water carrier Amen-kha:	
2 pieces *sesed* plant	makes 4 *deben*
via Neb-semen:	
2 pair sandals	
Total:	66 copper *deben*

verso
Amount of money of Khnum-mose that is with Neb-semen: 66 copper (*deben*).
What came from him: 43 copper *deben*
Its remainder: 2[3]

B. In a different form of record keeping, a certain Amen-em-one listed the various individuals who were in his debt at a given time. From this we learn that he had dealings with two of the officials of the gang, the scribes Hori-sheri and Hori, with a scribe of the Granary as well as with two chief policemen, and with one woman.

Things of Amen-em-one that are with the chief policeman Amen-em-ope:

5 copper *deben*

2 shawls of smooth cloth, makes 15 (*deben*)

Things of Amen-em-one that are with the scribe of the Granary of Pharaoh Amen-khau:

1 *menet*-jar of fresh fat

Things of Amen-em-one that are with the chief policeman Amen-wah-su:

[. . .]

Things of Amen-em-one that are with the scribe Hori-[sheri]:

1 wooden bed, makes 15 (*deben*)

What is with the scribe of the Necropolis Hori:

8 sacks of emmer

3 *hin* of sesame oil

3 *gabu*-baskets of *heqeq*-fruits

6 mats

What is with Hel, daughter of Ta-woseret:

6 *hin* of fat

8 bundles of vegetables

2 goats

1 mat

49. Gift Giving

A third form of economic exchange in the village besides redistribution and barter was reciprocal gift-giving. Again, this phenomenon has been studied by Jac. Janssen. A few texts record goods given by one person to another on special occasions such as marriage or the birth of a child (see 'Family' no. 8 above). Another group list individuals together with small quantities of foodstuffs which appear to be their contributions to a feast—a common practice in peasant societies where the host cannot otherwise assemble the necessary quantities of food. The text translated here is an example of this genre. The fact that these gifts were recorded suggests that they were not mere tokens of affection but of economic significance; the host would be expected to make his own contribution to a similar event in the future.

Hay, the deputy	5 loaves, 1 mat
Pa-tja-sa	$\frac{1}{4}$ sack emmer, 2 loaves
Monthu-pa-hapy	$\frac{1}{4}$ sack emmer, 1 loaf
Nub-em-iry (*fem.*)	5 loaves
Nes-Amen	4 loaves
Ta-weret-hery (*fem.*)	1 cask of beer, 5 loaves, 1 *ka*
Henut-waty (*fem.*)	4 loaves
Basa	5 loaves
Mut-em-opet (*fem.*)	4 loaves
Henut-waty (*fem.*), the wife of Mose	4 loaves
Ta-weret-em-heb (*fem.*)	6 loaves, 2 bundles vegetables, [. . .] emmer
Neb-nefer	10 loaves, basket [. . .], 1 bundle vegetables
Wabet (*fem.*)	7 loaves
Merut-Mut (*fem.*), she of Nefer-her	5 [loaves]
Wabet (*fem.*), daughter of Ipuy	10 cakes, 2 bundles vegetables, 1 jar of beer
[. . .]	3 loaves, 1 bundle vegetables
Pen-anket	3 loaves, 1 bundle vegetables
Hemset-her-awy-es (*fem.*)	[. . .] of inside, 5 loaves
Ta[. . .] (*fem.*)	5 loaves, 2 empty casks, $\frac{1}{4}$ sack emmer
[. . .]	

PRODUCTION FOR TRADE

Economic activity in the village was not merely a matter of barter with goods issued by the state; the workmen also manufactured commodities specifically for trade. It is difficult to assess the economic importance of such production exactly, but it would seem that skilled members of the community could earn as much from the construction, and especially the decoration, of furniture and funerary goods as they received in wages from the state. Their products included furniture for the workmen's houses and architectural elements of the houses themselves, votive objects including stelae and statutes, funerary equipment, and the wall paintings of the workmen's tombs—in fact, most of the objects of daily life recovered from the site. The texts recording this activity provide valuable information about the practical details of private industry in the New Kingdom.

At Deir el-Medina, of course, this industry was carried on within the larger context of the system of redistribution. The work was done on 'company time', in the sense that the workmen were receiving good wages even when they were not needed in the Valley of the Kings; on the other hand, they were bound to the work site and therefore had few opportunities for adding to their incomes besides crafts which could be carried on there. Some of the raw materials were 'borrowed' from the work in progress, including pigments and tools; others, such as wood, had to be obtained through barter like any other commodity in the village. Under these circumstances it would have been difficult to calculate what was a reasonable return on the craftsmen's labour or how to set prices. Nevertheless, the prices of furniture and funerary goods vary greatly—depending presumably on the ability and reputation of their creators.

50. The Carpenter's Bill

Many workmen in the gang were also skilled carpenters and even used the title 'carpenter' in their correspondence, although this did not correspond to any official position. Where the draughtsmen capitalized on their painting skills, the carpenters produced furniture, coffins, and even statutes for sale. The following is an impressive carpenter's 'bill' for objects made for one individual; the total comes to 93 *deben* (the phrase 'the excess thereof, 48' is obscure), which is more than eight months' grain ration, but the cost of the raw materials would of course have to be subtracted from this.

List of all the work that I did for the deputy Amen-nakhte:

2 chairs	makes 30 (*deben*)
1 wooden bed	makes 20 *deben*
1 coffin	makes 25 *deben*
the excess thereof, 48	
1 wooden statue	makes 15 *deben*
keskes basket	makes 3 *deben*
TOTAL:	93 copper *deben*

51. Commissions for Painting

Much of the work done by the skilled craftsmen of Deir el-Medina was highly personalized and of course made on commission. In this short letter, an unidentified writer asks the scribe Hori about some decoration the latter has in hand. Possibly this concerns the work on the royal tomb, although this would suggest that the officials of the gang had a say in the decoration. A more likely alternative is that this is a letter from a customer, who wants to know what design the scribe has composed for him.

(To) the scribe of the Necropolis Hori in life, prosperity, and health, in the praise of your noble god Amen-Re, King of Gods, your good lord, every day.

Please send me the plan you will carry out for the painting work.

52. Co-operation between Carpenters and Painters

Since the draughtsmen needed wooden objects to decorate and the carpenters had wooden objects that required decoration, there was an opportunity for co-operation between the two main groups of craftsmen in the village. The following text documents collaboration between the workman Bak-en-werl and the draughtsman Hori-sheri in the form of an exchange; the draughtsman decorated wooden objects for the carpenter in return for unfinished furniture and funerary goods.

Several of the decorated objects were ultimately intended for third parties. The three women may have been relatives of Bak-en-werl, but two of the coffins evidently went to strangers; one was for the builder Pa-aʿo-em-one and the other exchanged for a cloak in Thebes. It seems that Bak-en-werl is subcontracting part of the work on his order. Hori-sheri, on the other hand, was presumably buying unfinished objects which he would decorate and sell on.

Hori-sheri says of some of the coffins made by Bak-en-werl, 'it belonged to me as wood'. (We know the speaker is Hori-sheri and not Bak-en-werl because he refers 'his son Neb-nefer', that is, Bak-en-werl's son of that name.) The draughtsman thus himself supplied the wood for the objects he commissioned—a not uncommon arrangement. It is puzzling, however, that furniture is listed at full price, without a discount for the wood.

The decoration that is with the workman Bak-en-werl:
    funerary couch of his mother (?)   makes 12 *deben*
    the outer coffin of An (*fem.*)   makes 20 *deben*
    the small coffin of An

given to the builder Pa-aʿo-em-one	makes 10 *deben*
again, making another one for her	makes 10 *deben*
the coffin that he gave in exchange	
for the cloak in Thebes (?)	makes 10 *deben*
its inner coffin	makes 4 *deben*
the 2 doors of the tomb, painted	makes 6 *deben*
2 coffins and this inner coffin of Baket-en-Seti (*fem.*)	makes 24 *deben*

[. . .]
[. . .] that one of them [. . .] the man of [. . .] killed
92 makes 30.

verso
The carpentry work that the workman Bak-en-werl gave to the draughtsman Hori-sheri:

1 plastered, wooden *debet*-box	makes 8 *deben*
1 *afdet*-box	makes 2 *deben*
1 coffin	makes 15 *deben*
it belonged to me as wood	
1 small wooden bed	makes 15 *deben*
it belonged to me as wood	
1 wooden bed	makes 20 *deben*
it belonged to me as wood; the ebony belonged to me via his son, Neb-nefer	
1 wooden container	makes 2 *deben*
via him: 1 coffin	
1 wooden carrying pole	makes [. . .]
coiled [*keskes*]-basket	makes 4 (?)

The coffin belonged to me as [wood].
Total: 52

53. Price Setting

The following text is slightly obscure, but it appears to concern a difference of opinion about the correct price for two small statues. Ruty had given the carpenter Mery-Re $9\frac{3}{4}$ *deben* worth of goods for a male figure. On reflection, or perhaps on seeing the statue, he felt he had overpaid and the question of price was submitted to the oracle. The god valued the statue at only 8 *deben*; Ruty's credit of the 2 *deben* difference (rounded up) is duly noted. A second transaction concerning a female statue is more difficult to follow. Again Ruty paid about 12 *deben*, but whether the two parties were satisfied with this sum is unclear. In both sales, the buyer had supplied the carpenter with the necessary wood.

This was not the only occasion on which Mery-Re overcharged a customer; see below, No. 55.

recto

What Ruty gave to the carpenter Mery-Re in exchange for the statue:

1 tunic	makes 5 *deben*
5 bundles vegetables	makes $2\frac{1}{2}$ *deben*
4 mats	makes 2 *deben*
the statue as wood and also its base	makes 1 *oipe*

And the god gave the statue 8 copper *deben*.

10 copper *deben*: the excess, 2 *deben*. Likewise the [. . .]

What was given to him for the female statue:

1 cast copper bowl	makes $2\frac{1}{2}$ *deben*
and 1 *deben* for its painting	
beaten copper	1 *deben*
[. . .]	5 *deben*
1 pair sandals	
1 mat	makes [. . .] $2\frac{1}{2}$ *deben*

verso

The female statue was mine as wood. And he (i.e. the god) said: The things [given by] Qeny-Min are worth 8 *deben*.

Total money: 8 copper *deben*.

54. The Superiors Commandeer Work

Both the vizier and the captains of the gang might simply order skilled workmen to make furniture for them. This was an unauthorized diversion of state resources to private ends, since the men were taken off work in the royal tomb for these private projects, but it was common practice and undoubtedly considered one of the perks of office. In the following extract from the journal of the Necropolis, the absence of men making furniture for their chief-workman Hay are noted quite matter-of-factly.

Fourth month of winter, day 6: Sa-wadjyt was off work making a box for Hay; Khamu was off work making a statue for Hay; Kha-em-seba was off work with him. Nakhte-su, ill; Ra-hotep, ill.

Fig. 14. Riverside traders from the tomb of the workman Ipuy (TT 217). Sailors disembarking from their ship trade sacks of grain for fish and other foodstuffs. Behind the woman on the far left is a book sheltering two amphorae holding drinks of some sort. (Reproduced with the kind permission of the Metropolitan Museum of Art, New York, from Norman deGaris Davies, *Two Ramesside Tombs at Thebes* (New York, 1927), pl. 30.)

55. The Market-Place

The vast majority of recorded transactions at Deir el-Medina took place between households or through middlemen, but there are also a few references to activity at the market-place. As Janssen has shown, this was located at the riverbank, and in fact the only word the villagers had for market-place was *meryt*, 'riverbank'. An attempt to sell at the riverbank is related incidentally in No. 18 above: 'And she gave me a sash, saying, "Offer it at the riverbank; it will be bought from me for an *oipe* of emmer." I offered it, but people rejected it, saying, "It is bad!" And I told her exactly that, saying, "It has been rejected."' The speaker evidently displayed his ware to passers-by, but it aroused no interest.

The workman Amen-em-ope, who narrated the following excerpt, bought a statue of a god from an acquaintance and then took it to the marketplace to have it 'appraised' by another carpenter. The unfortunate verdict was that he had been overcharged. Nevertheless, Amen-em-ope gave the statue to the carpenter's father for a month, perhaps for its protective qualities.

What was given to him (the carpenter Mery-Re) for the image of
Seth:
   $1\frac{1}{2}$ sacks of grain
   3 bundles of vegetables
   1 pair of fowl
   1 basket with lid
   Total: 2 sacks (of grain)
   meneq-wood
I went down to the riverbank and sent for it, and I showed it to the
carpenter Sa-Wadjyt. He said, 'It is worth (only) 1 sack of grain.' I
gave it to his father, and it spent a full month with him.

THE DONKEY BUSINESS

A large number of Deir el-Medina ostraca have to do with donkeys—trading donkeys, renting donkeys, and borrowing donkeys.
They were expensive animals (25–40 *deben*) and they were rented out
for long periods of up to several months, and for both reasons, it was
useful to keep a written record of the date and terms of a sale or loan.
Moreover, transactions involving donkeys were particularly prone to
complications, not only the usual failures to pay and disagreements
about price, but also the unexpected death of the animal itself. The

records of the inevitable legal contests which followed are full of information about the practical details of the donkey business.

56. Donkey Rental

In Deir el-Medina donkey leases, the animals were owned by workmen and generally borrowed by water-carriers, or, less often, by woodcutters or policemen. Many texts name only the borrower, an indication that the record was retained by the owner who, of course, needed no reminder of his own role in the deal. The duration of the lease varied from a few days up to three months, with an average of about a month; while the price was fairly standard at $\frac{1}{2}$ oipe per day, that is $3\frac{3}{4}$ sacks of grain per month, about two-thirds of a workman's salary. This suggests that donkeys could be a substantial source of revenue to their owner. On the other hand, the borrower could not possibly have afforded to hire a donkey from his own wages and must therefore have had some other source of income about which we are ignorant. This may have been farming, since several texts mention that the donkey was used for agricultural work.

Donkey rentals are interesting from a legal point of view because they provide our only information about leasehold arrangements in the village. The houses were state-owned and could not be leased, so far as we know, so this important area of property law is otherwise undocumented.

The following is a typical record of a donkey rental, naming the dates, the price, and the borrower, but not the owner of the animal. The cost of hire, 5 *deben* = $2\frac{1}{2}$ sacks, is rather lower than usual.

Year 3, second month of winter day, 1. This day, giving the donkey for hire to the policeman Amen-kha: makes 5 copper *deben* for the month. And it spent 42 days with him. The police inspector Amen-nakhte . . . (*text interrupted*).

57. Breaking the Lease

The following text, although rather obscure, suggests that it was possible to end a lease before the contracted date. Menna seems to have rented his donkey to Raiay for 4 months, i.e. 120 days, but in fact 'seized' the animal after only 72 days. This language perhaps indicates that it was Menna who wished to have the donkey back early, but he was not dissatisfied with Raiay as a customer because two months later he gave him the donkey again. (This is the same Menna who featured in the dispute over a donkey in No. 47, above.)

At the end of the document, an interim transaction is recorded in which the donkey is said to be handed over 'for ploughing'. This is one of the indications that the water-carriers were engaged in agricultural activities in addition to their official jobs.

recto
Year 1, third month of inundation, day 3. Giving the donkey of the (work)man Menna to the water-carrier Raiay for hire up to today, although it does not amount to 4 months, total 120 days. Seizing the donkey in first month of winter, day 15. Taking it again on the third month of winter day 6 [. . .]
(*3 lines missing, damaged*)

verso
Received from him:
    straw
    5 *menet*-jars of salt
    40 handfuls of hay
    1 donkey-load of dung
    again, 2 donkey-loads of wood
Year 1, second month of winter, day 8. Giving him the donkey for ploughing.

58. Borrowing

The opening words of the following text indicate that it represents testimony in a legal dispute. Kel, a water-carrier, had borrowed a donkey he found wandering about unattended, to the outrage of its owner, Pre-hotep. It seems that Kel was unwilling to give the donkey back, offering to pay for its use or perhaps to replace it with another animal. The final lines are very broken and it is unclear what led Pre-hotep finally to take legal action. What we do learn from this case is that donkeys were left loose around the village during the day, but this did not mean that their owners relinquished their property rights in any way.

Hearing the testimony of the workman Pre-hotep, as follows: 'As for me, my donkey was handed over to my free-woman and I went up (to the Valley of the Kings) for three days. When I came back in the evening, she said to me, "I have left the donkey outside." Now when I went to lock it up in the evening, I found it in the possession of Kel, loaded with emmer. I said to him, "Who gave you that donkey?" He said, "I found it wandering about, and I took it to bring this grain job to the Enclosure of the Necropolis." I seized it, and he said to me, "Do not seize it! I will give this other [. . .] for it!" And I [. . .]

One agreed [. . .] and he gave [. . .] And I gave the donkey to his
[. . .] seized [. . .]'

59. Guarantee of Quiet Enjoyment

Like the seller of a house today, a person transferring ownership of a donkey
guaranteed that there were no outstanding claims on the property. In the
text below this was done under oath on pain of a 100 per cent fine; another
case names not only the fine but also 100 blows as the penalty if there turn
out to be other claims. It is not clear why we encounter these guarantees
only in connection with donkeys and not with other valuable commodities.
Perhaps this was because the donkeys were often sold by or through
outsiders and came from outside the village so that their histories were
difficult to trace.

[Year x +] 4, third month of winter, ⟨day⟩ 27. What the workman
Hor-em-wia gave to the policeman [. . .] in exchange for his donkey:
  1 loincloth of smooth cloth   makes 16 copper *deben*
  1 sheet   makes 10 copper *deben*
  Makes 26 deben
He (the policeman) took an oath of the lord, l.p.h., saying, 'As Amen
endures, and the ruler, l.p.h. endures, I shall not dispute about this
donkey; no one else will dispute about it. If he does, it will be against
me double.'

60. Why the Guarantee was Necessary

The need for a guarantee of quiet enjoyment is illustrated by the following
text in which an animal purchased by the workman Nefer-senut turns out
to belong to a chief policeman. The middleman who sold the donkey then
tried to get it back, presumably under pressure from the owner, but Nefer-
senut countered that he had paid the water-carrier to find him an animal
and would not return this one until he got his purchase money back. (The
purchase money, oddly enough, consisted of a male donkey and a loincloth; the sex of the animal is not stressed in the Egyptian and need not be
significant.) When the water-carrier admits the that he had indeed received
these items, the court finds for the workman.

However, after the hearing, the water-carrier persuaded the workman to
let him have the chief policeman's donkey anyway, promising to supply a
replacement. As it happened, this promise was not fulfilled until three years
later.

[. . . chief] policeman [Sobek-hotep . . .] saying, 'Give back the female donkey that was brought to you; it belongs to the chief policeman Sobek-hotep.' I [said] to him, 'Send in order to give it. Give my
male donkey and my loincloth that I gave to you (for?) the female
donkey that you brought!' [. . .] The court consulted the testimony
of the water-carrier Tjay, [saying], 'Were the male donkey and [the
loin]-cloth given to you?' And he said, '[Truly], they are in my
possession [. . . in order to buy?] the female donkey [on this] day
via the chief policeman [Sobek-hot]ep.' And the court said, 'The
workman Nefer-senut [is right]; the water-carrier Tjay is wrong.

Now after all the argument, he said, 'I will pay you any day. Give
[the] female donkey!' And I gave it [to him]. Now, three years later,
he brought me a female donkey.

61. Borrower Responsible for Deaths

The following text provides information about two important aspects of
property law. First, it gives the terms of a sub-lease of a donkey. The water-
carrier Pen-ta-Weret, who had rented a donkey from Bak-en-werl, handed
it over to Pen-niut. Bak-en-werl was not happy with this arrangement and
'disputed' it before an unnamed legal body; as a result, Pen-ta-Weret was
found liable for the rental fee. In other words, he—and not the sub-leaser—
was responsible for the animal.
  The second point is the question of who bears the loss if the donkey dies.
As we see here and in the next text, it is the leaser. This seems hard, but
certainly in long-term rentals he was in the best position to care for the
animal and to keep it in health; moreover, any other arrangement might
have tempted him to overwork the animal or scrimp on fodder. How a
water-carrier who could not afford an animal of his own managed to replace
one he had borrowed is something of a mystery. In the text below, the
donkey apparently *did* die, and as luck would have it, it was the most
expensive donkey of which we know. In the final sentence, Bak-en-werl
makes an appeal, presumably to the court, to force Pen-ta-Weret to pay.

Year 28, third month of inundation, day 9. Bak-en-werl disputed
with the watercarrier Pen-ta-Weret concerning his donkey which he
had given to Pen-niut. [. . . the court (?)] ordered Pen-ta-Weret to
pay [. . .] the hire of the donkey [to Bak]-en-werl. He took an oath
saying, 'If the donkey dies, [it] be will against me; and if it lives, it
will be against me.' The donkey was handed over to him [. . .]

As for my donkey, I paid 40 copper *deben* for it. Let him give it to
me!

62. A Loophole

If it was possible to terminate the lease early, then it seems reasonable that as soon as a rented animal appeared to be falling ill, it would quickly be returned to its owner. According to Helck's interpretation, that is what happened in the following case.

Year 31, fourth month of winter, day 17. Giving the donkey to Hori in place of his father. Fourth month of winter day 27. He was brought up. [. . .] spent the night [. . .] he died, although his hire was not [complete (?) . . .]

3

Religion

Much of the surviving evidence of Egyptian piety consists of stelae, funerary monuments, and other records that are standardized and formal and thus difficult to relate to everyday religious ideas and practice. Moreover, the cult as conducted in the major temples—those most prominent monuments of New Kingdom religion—was an affair of state, the purpose of which was to maintain the goodwill of the gods and to reaffirm the order of the world and oppose the forces of chaos. As a professional priesthood emerged to run the increasingly powerful temples, there is some doubt whether the common man was much concerned with what went on behind the temple pylons.

The evidence furnished by the workmen's community makes an important contribution to what is known about the individual Egyptian's experience of religion through both texts and monuments, and by providing both with a well-documented context. The quantity of relevant material from the site is indeed enormous, including thousands of chapels, tombs, stelae, statues, and architectural elements in the workmen's homes. Most of this material falls beyond the scope of the present book, however; the aim of this chapter is to give a sample of the textual record of piety in the village, a vast corpus in itself. Among the most interesting of these texts are the so called 'personal piety' texts on stelae that stress the worshipper's humility and reliance upon the mercy of the god and the large body of material relating to oracles consulted by private individuals.

The deities who feature most prominently in the workmen's lives were those with local cult centres. Amen-Re of Karnak, King of Gods, is not much in evidence but gods associated with the Theban

necropolis (such as Hathor, Meresger, and Amenophis I) were endowed with chapels, daily offerings, and priesthoods run by the
workmen themselves. The objects of official cults were only the
most prominent elements of the supernatural, however, which also
included minor household deities who presided over childbirth and
protected young children. The dead, too, continued to play a role in
the affairs of the living and were the objects of household cults. On
the other hand, magic and some forms of divination operated on a
more nebulous otherworldly force, not identified with any individual entity. In short, the supernatural world of the villagers was
populated by a range of beings, from the major gods to recently
deceased relatives.

The Official Cults

The official cults centred on the chapels to the north of the village.
Their most important features included regular offerings, rituals
performed inside the inner sanctuary and public festivals and processions. At Deir el-Medina, the priests who performed the required
tasks were simply workmen; particular families were probably associated with individual gods, although at least one individual is
known to have held priesthoods in the cults of both Amenophis I
and of Meresger.

   The principle sanctuary at Deir el-Medina was that of the goddess
Hathor, but more is known about the cult of deified founder of
the New Kingdom, Amenophis I. Amenophis is thought to have
established the gang of workmen, an act to which he presumably
owed his popularity; he had many sanctuaries in the area of the
necropolis, and each of his statues was regarded as a separate manifestation of the god. The workmen were most attached to their
own local version, Amenophis of the Village, but they were very
familiar with his other forms, such as Amenophis of the Garden and
Amenophis of the Forecourt. This king is depicted often in the
tombs and on the stelae of the villagers and the many festivals in his
name are mentioned in private documents and journals. The most
remarkable feature of Amenophis, however, is that he gave oracles,
and consultations of this god are sometimes recorded in lively detail.
The role which this god played in the daily lives of the workmen is
therefore easier to picture than that of any other.

63. The Ritual of Amenophis I

The daily ritual associated with a cult consisted of three main services at dawn, midday and evening. That in the morning was the most important; its purpose was to awaken the god's image, and to wash, dress and feed it at the start of a new day. The ritual itself was preceded by elaborate preparations. The priests purified themselves and replenished the libation vessels with water from the sacred well, prepared the offerings and brought them to the temple. Then, in torchlight and clouds of incense, the morning hymn was sung and the officiating priest drew back the bolts of the sanctuary. He uncovered the god, presented him with myrrh, anointed him and purified him with water, and finally withdrew, closing the doors once more, each stage of the proceedings being accompanied by hymns and spells. The services at midday and evening were similar but less elaborate.

The so-called Ritual of Amenophis I is not a special composition for this god but simply the standard daily ritual as adapted for his cult. Our two copies are both from Deir el-Medina and may have been used there or in the mortuary temple of the king, which was situated elsewhere. The following spells correspond to the preparatory stages of the ritual in which the offering meat is roasted over a fire and a libation is poured at its presentation; and to closing stages in which the priest wipes away his footprints and shuts the doors of the sanctuary.

As is usual in magical and religious manuals, the objects and acts of the Amenophis ritual are associated with the world of myth either directly or through word-play. In the third spell below, for instance, the cuts of meat offered to the god are simply identified with body parts of the gods Horus and Seth; while, in the second spell, the word for the fat offering, *adj*, suggests one of the names of the god Horus, 'The One Who is Whole', which is also *adj*. The gods named in the ritual are especially those associated with the story of Osiris, god of the underworld whose death and resurrection set the pattern that all deceased persons hoped to follow. As here, the deceased is himself called 'Osiris'. Osiris' son Horus, his brother Seth and their roles in his story also feature prominently in the spells. These gods were not the objects of significant cults in the village, but belonged to a corpus of myths, spells and rituals largely separate from the everyday religious routine of the villagers.

(Preparing the offering)

SPELL FOR PUTTING INCENSE ON THE FIRE for the Osiris King Djeserkare Son of Re Amenophis: Take to yourself the Eye of Horus, so that its scent may come to you.

SPELL FOR PLACING FAT (*ADJ*) ON THE FIRE: May provisions upon provisions come, after Horus has stood up to make whole (*sadj*) his two eyes in this his name of 'The One Who is Whole' (*adj*); after Thoth has come to you and turned back (*hesi*), in this his name of 'The Praised One' (*hesi*).

SPELL OF MEAT ON THE FIRE: The breast (is) the Eye of Horus; the haunch (is) the testicles of Seth. As Horus is content on account of his eyes, and Seth is content on account of his testicles, so King Djeserkare Son of Re Amenophis is content on account of these choice meats.

SPELL FOR THE ROASTING SPIT FOR THE OSIRIS the King, Lord of the Thrones of the Two Lands, Djeserkare Son of Re Amenophis ⟨and for⟩ the Ennead of Horus: You spit with your finger.

SPELL FOR THE FAN (to fan the flames): O! the Osiris King Djeserkare and the Ennead of Horus. May your hearts be placed in your bodies for you!

SPELL FOR A LIBATION WITH BEER: The Eye of Horus is refreshed for him; the testicles of Seth are refreshed for him. As Horus is content on account of his eyes, and Seth is content (on account of) his testicles, so King Djeserkare is content on account of his choice meats.

(*Closing the sanctuary*)

SPELL FOR REMOVING THE FOOTPRINT with (a broom of) *heden*: May Thoth come and may he rescue the Eye of Horus from its enemy. No male opponent or female opponent shall enter this temple.

SPELL FOR FASTENING THE DOOR: Closing the door by Ptah; fastening the door by Thoth, the deputy of Re. Closing the door, fastening the door with a doorbolt.

64. A New Cult Statue for Ramesses VI

The following description of a cult-statue of Ramesses VI is an extract from a copy of a letter to the king, possibly from the scribe Amen-nakhte. The statue was to be installed in the 'Residence' of Ramesses II which formed part of the Hathor temple in Deir el-Medina, where it would join statues of other kings going back to Ramesses II himself. In the second part of the letter, not translated here, the author asks the king to provide a man to perform the offerings—'an infirm of the army of the soldiers of the south who are at ease (?)'—and to release him from any corvée labour that was exacted from ordinary Egyptians. The establishment of royal statue cults such as this one was a common practice in the New Kingdom and later; the donor would continue to enjoy the income from the land making up the endowment in the form of a reversion of offerings while enjoying various advantages such as lower taxation and freedom from corvée labour for the field workers.

The description of the statue of Ramesses VI is particularly welcome because very few actual cult images have survived since they were made of costly materials and were easily accessible to later generations who eventually appropriated them. The present statue does not appear to have been exceptionally rich—the body was of wood, though the kilt was gilded and the crown was of lapis lazuli, while the uraeus and sandals were of a decorative copper alloy—but it would have represented a very substantial expenditure for a member of the gang.

The beautiful statue whose name is 'The Dual King, Lord of the Two Lands Ramesses VI, Beloved like Amen', of good *nib*-wood and persea-wood, the torso coloured and all of its limbs of faience like real red jasper, and his kilt of hammered (?) yellow gold; its crown of lapis lazuli, adorned with serpents of every colour; the uraeus on his head of sixfold alloy inlaid with real stones; its sandals of sixfold alloy; its right arm bearing a *mekes*-symbol cut with a cartouche in the great name of his majesty; his left arm furnished with a sceptre of Amen-Re, Lord of the Thrones of the Two Lands; its horns curved [. . .] therein; the uraeus which is on his head of sixfold alloy; which will be installed in the House of Ramesses II, the great god, [beside the House of Hathor], Mistress of the West, like the statues my ancestors had made for King Ramesses II, the great god, and also [King Merneptah], the great god, and also every king who donned the White Crown and whose statue rests here. Three offerings are conducted for them daily, at every rising of the sun over the mountain, and Pre-Horakhty will grant that Pharaoh celebrates millions of jubilees while he is king of Egypt, his statue receiving incense and libations for its god's offerings before it exactly like the lords of this great and holy place.

65. The Priests

The local cults were celebrated by workmen who served as priests in their spare time and by the women of the village who bore the title 'songstress' of this or that god. In some cases the priesthood of a god ran in one particular family, but the only evidence for how priests were actually selected is provided by the following question to the oracle found in the Valley of the Kings.

Shall one appoint Seti as prophet?

66. Local Festivals: Festivals of Amenophis I

Unlike the rituals described above, festivals were public events. In some cases, the image of the god would be placed in a portable shrine and carried out of its sanctuary to less restricted areas of the temple such as the forecourts and roof, or through the pylons to the outside. The various offerings, processions, sacred dramas, singing of hymns, and other rites and ceremonies could stretch over periods as long as fourteen days, and the great festivals of major Theban gods were accompanied by the lavish distribution of food to the population. Valbelle has collected all the known festivals from the village; there were several dozen in all, though not all were celebrated in any given period.

Many festivals of Amenophis I are known by name, but it is seldom clear what aspect of the king they honour or exactly how they were celebrated. The calendar dates of the festivities recorded in these two texts are so close that they may belong to celebrations, in different years, of a particularly important festival lasting over several days. There is some reason to believe that Amenophis either died or was buried in the third month of winter and that this is the event commemorated. The first text below concerns a procession of Amenophis I which went as far as the Valley of the Kings; here the god ordered curd to be distributed to the workmen as a gift. The second text mentions four days of festivities attended by 120 persons connected with the Necropolis.

A. Year 1, third month of winter, day 21. This day, King Amenophis, l.p.h., went up and he reached the Valley (of the Kings) with the gang running before him. He had the storehouse opened and four pots of curd taken out, and he gave them [. . . as] favours ⟨to⟩ the gang.
By the scribe Yot-nefer.

B. Year 7, third month of winter, day 29. The Great Festival of King Amenophis, l.p.h., the Lord of the Village was being held. The gang rejoiced before him for four solid days of drinking together with their children and their wives. There were sixty of inside (the village) and sixty of outside.

67. Great Festivals: The Festival of the Valley

The Festival of the Valley was the occasion on which the statue of Amen-Re left his temple at Karnak to visit the gods of West Thebes. From the Nineteenth Dynasty onwards he was accompanied by the statues of the gods Mut, Khonsu, and Amaunet, as well as those of deceased kings and possibly also of prominent commoners. The procession visited the Hathor sanctuary at Deir el-Bahri and then the royal funerary temples, ending with the funerary temple of the reigning king. Private persons celebrated with offerings and a festival meal in the presence of their deceased relatives at the family tomb.

Year 5, second month of summer, day 1: crossing over to West Thebes by Amen-Re, King [of Gods], to pour water for the dual kings.
[. . .] month of summer, day 10: crossing over to Thebes by the 3 (?) [. . .]

68. Preparations for the Festival

Major festivals required considerable organization, not the least part of which was gathering together the garlands, incense and offerings required for the various ceremonies. Several letters concern such preparations.

A. (*opening lost*)
To the effect that: I have sent to you by the policeman Pa-sar:
  2 cakes of $\frac{1}{10}$ *oipe* of grain
  5 *deben* incense
  again, 5 *deben* incense
(on?) the day of your offering to Amen at the Festival of the Valley. They do not give me anything that you send to me.

B. What was brought to you via the washerman Ka: 1 large loaf. Send me a skin and some paint and some incense; and send us greenery and flowers [on] day 18, because they will pour a libation on day 19.

69. Music for the Cult

Much of the music which accompanied religious events was provided by the women of the community. Many women bore the title 'Songstress of Hathor' or some other god, and in illustrations of religious processions they are shown playing sistra and tambourines, singing, and dancing. To judge from the following terse letter, however, men might also participate in the singing; and this evidently involved an occasional squabble.

Now do not say, 'I will do the singing; I will not allow you to do the singing.' Pa-sen organizes the singing for Meresger.

70. Stelae

For what reason the individual felt moved to express his devotion to any particular deity of the plethora in a hymn or on a stela it is usually impossible to tell.

This is a commission for a design for a stela of a sort very common at Deir el-Medina, on which the worshipper is shown adoring his god. The ostracon on which the text is written is itself in the shape of a stela, perhaps to show the artist the format that was required.

Please send it to me very quickly, today! Look to it!!

A figure of Monthu seated on a throne and a figure of the scribe Pen-ta-Weret kissing the earth before him and adoring him, in draft.

71. The Mercy of Meresger

One of the most striking goddesses at Deir el-Medina was Meresger, 'She loves silence'. This was the goddess of the Theban Necropolis who was identified with the mountain peak that rises over the Valley of the Kings, but was also depicted as a snake or as a combination of snake and woman. Her principle sanctuary was a cave near the Valley of the Queens, as was appropriate for such an earthbound ('chthonic') deity; but stelae dedicated to Meresger also dot the mountain peak itself.

This is an excellent example of the genre of personal piety stelae. The author claims to have done wrong and aroused the fury of Meresger, the Peak. His punishment was swift and sharp; it is described as a sort of suffocation and his state is compared to that of a woman in labour gasping for breath. (The brick he mentions is that on which Egyptian women sat when they were giving birth.) But the goddess is also merciful and having once shown Nefer-abu her power, she returns to soothe and comfort him.

Giving praise to the Peak of the West; kissing the earth to her Ka. I give praise; hear my invocation. I am righteous on earth. Made by the servant in the Place of Truth Nefer-abu, justified, an ignorant man, without sense.

I did not know good from bad when I made the transgression against the Peak, and she punished me, I being in her hand night and day. I sat on a brick like a pregnant woman while I called out for breath without its coming to me. I humbled myself to the Peak of the West, great of power, to every god and every goddess. Behold, I

Fig. 15. Stela dedicated to the goddesses Meresger, in the form of a woman with the head of a snake, and the goddess Taweret, depicted as a hippopotamus. Each is identified in the vertical text in front of her. The stela was dedicated by the deputy Hay of the time of Ramesses III. (Drawn by Marion Cox after Mario Tosi and Alessandro Roccati, *Stele e altre epigrafi di Deir el Medina n. 50001–n. 50262* (Turin, 1972), p. 289.)

will say it to the great and the small in the gang; Beware of the Peak, because a lion is in her. The Peak, she strikes with the strike of a fierce lion when she is after the one who transgresses against her. I called out to my mistress (and) found her coming to me as a sweet wind, and she was merciful to me, after she let me see her hand. She returned to me in peace, and she made me forget the sickness that was in my heart. So the Peak of the West is merciful when one calls to her.

Spoken by Nefer-abu. He says, Behold, may the ears of all those who are alive on earth take heed: Beware of the Peak of the West!

72. Living near to God

One of the most important divinities at Deir el-Medina was Hathor, goddess of love and of the desert, who often took the shape of a cow. Hers was the principal sanctuary, although this was entirely destroyed when the Ptolemaic temple to Hathor was built on the same site. Many of the village women bore the title 'songstress of Hathor', but relatively few further details of her cult are preserved.

Qen-her-khepesh-ef, who dedicated the following stela, describes an intense communion with Hathor quite unparalleled in our sources. He says that he was born in a cave sanctuary near Deir el-Bahri. It is difficult to take this assertion literally, but the cave in question, above the temple of Hatshepsut, was evidently a centre of healing and Hathor was a goddess of fertility, so it may be that his parents had visited the cave to promote conception. Qen-her-khepesh-ef also claims to have eaten the priestly loaves. The focus then shifts to the sanctuaries of Meresger and Ptah in the mountainside near the Valley of the Queens, where the stela was probably erected. Here, Qen-her-khepesh-ef says, he drank from the sacred water and slept in the sanctuary; this last brings to mind the practice of incubation, that is, of spending the night in a temple in the hope of receiving revelation in a dream. Incubation was popular in Ptolemaic times, when indeed it seems to have been practised in Deir el-Bahri itself; it is not definitely attested earlier, although the gods were believed to appear to mortals in their sleep. This may be the first reference to the practice. It is therefore interesting to note that Qen-her-khepesh-ef was the son of Naunakhte, who had inherited from her first husband, the scribe Qen-her-khepesh-ef, the famous handbook for the interpretation of dreams (below, No. 81).

Giving praise to the Ka of Hathor, Mistress of the West, Lady of Heaven, Mistress of all the Gods. Kissing the earth to your name. I am a *ba*-soul in the presence of his Lord; I was born in your temenos of the cave beside Deir el-Bahri, in the neighbourhood of the *Menset*-temple (of Amenophis I and Ahmose Nefertari). It was beside the great *akhu*-spirits that I ate from the offering bread of the lector priest. I strolled in the Valley of the Queens; I spent the night in your temenos and drank the water that issued from the mountain (?) in the temenos of *Menet*; it waters the rushes and the lotuses in the temenos of Ptah. My body spent the night in the shadow of your face; I slept (in) your temenos. I made stelae in the temple beside the lords of Deir el-Bahri.

For the Ka of the one who is excellent and correct, who fashions the images of all the gods, the servant in the Place of Truth, Qen-her-khepesh-ef, justified for ever. His father, the servant in the Place of Truth, Kha-em-nun; his sister (i.e. wife), the lady Ta-nofret; his son, Amen-nakhte; his son [. . .] Ka-(em)-per-Ptah.

73. Manifestations of God

Perhaps the most direct and palpable experience of the divine was a phenomenon described by the phrase 'a manifestation of god has come about', the significance of which has been discussed by Borghouts. In all cases, an individual has offended in some way against a god, for example by swearing a false oath in his name. As a result a 'manifestation of god comes about', which induces the guilty party to make a confession and perhaps to ask for mercy. The form of the manifestation is seldom specified. The workman Nefer-abu, who swore falsely by the god Ptah, was made by that god to 'see darkness by day'; this evidently means he was blinded, perhaps only temporarily. The same man had transgressed against Meresger, as he describes in No. 71 above, and was punished with suffering like that of a woman in labour, although there the term 'manifestation' does not occur. It seems likely that, to the guilty mind, any misfortune could suggest itself as divine censure. For some of those affected, public confession with its consequences may have been sufficient atonement; others erected a stela stressing their humility.

See also No. 144 in 'Law' below.

A. The stela bearing the following text was dedicated by the workman Huy to the moon, a form of the god Thoth. Huy testifies that the moon had punished him for taking his name in vain in the matter of a certain scoop which had perhaps been lost or stolen and he proclaims the god's power to the creatures of the sea and the sky.

By the servant of the Moon, Huy. He says, I am the man who falsely said 'As true as . . .' to the Moon concerning the scoop, and he caused me to see the greatness of his strength before the entire land. I will recount your manifestation to the fish in the river and to the birds in the sky, and they will say to their children's children, 'Beware of the Moon, the merciful, who knew how to avert this.'

B. The following account of a manifestation occurs within testimony before the court; the workman Nakhte-Min reports that a woman called Ta-nehesy stole a cake from him on a festival day of the goddess Ta-Weret but was later induced to confess her misconduct by a manifestation. Borghouts suggests that the cake was an offering to the goddess and that the purpose of Nakhte-Min's testimony was to make it a matter of public record that he was not responsible for the disappearance of the cake.

Testimony of Nakhte-Min to the court:

As for me, I was sitting in my chapel at the Birth of Ta-Weret, and Ta-nehesy stole a cake from me. Now after ten days, she came to say to me, 'A manifestation has come about.'

(*The text then turns to an apparently unrelated matter.*)

74. Manipulating the Power of a God

Borghouts suggests that the *Weret* under discussion in the following enigmatic little letter is in fact a figure or statue of the goddess Ta-Weret (see below). The writer fears that whoever stole his Weret might use it to work a manifestation of the god Seth against him; Ta-Weret and Seth are related by their common interest in birth, by the hippopotamus form they each can take, and by the fact recorded by Plutarch that Ta-Weret was at one time Seth's concubine. This text illustrates another facet of the manifestation of a god—the possibility that a third party might use it as a magical force for his own purposes.

Please make me a *Weret*, because the one you made for me before was stolen, so it (or she) may work a manifestation of Seth against me!

MINOR GODS: BES AND TA-WERET

Bes and Ta-Weret have in common their particular association with the home, and especially with childbirth, with the protection of children, and with sleep. Ta-Weret, whose name means 'The Great One' or 'The Big One', was depicted as a composite of pregnant hippopotamus, crocodile, and lioness. Birth, marriage, and nourishment were her domain, and she is sometimes associated with Hathor. A number of cult statues of Ta-Weret are mentioned in the Deir el-Medina sources—'Ta-Weret of the dom palms', 'Ta-Weret among the acacias', 'Ta-Weret of the clear water', and others—and there was almost certainly a temple of her in the village, but outside the village the only known New Kingdom temple of the goddess is that mentioned in the land survey known as the Wilbour Papyrus. This may be because chapels of Ta-Weret were usually found in settlement sites, few of which are well preserved. Many stelae and other cult objects in her name were found in the workmen's village, but most are fairly standard in form and tell us little about her nature. The text quoted below is one of the most informative.

Bes had an equally outlandish appearance; he is represented as a dancing dwarf with a lion's mane and ears, a wide grin, and tongue hanging out. His grotesque appearance may have been intended to frighten off dangerous demons and snakes, for which purpose he also carried knives. Although Bes features in depictions of royal rituals, it is not clear whether he had an official cult and he is certainly best known as a household god. He was widely depicted on domestic goods such as the beds, headrests, toiletries, and mirrors as well as on wall paintings in the home, but he is not the subject of any texts, so far as I know.

75. Praise for Ta-Weret

The following text was inscribed on one of a pair of small doors (36 cm. high) which originally belonged to a shrine, perhaps a niche in the wall of a house. The doors were purchased from a dealer in Luxor, but there can be no doubt that they came from Deir el-Medina given the names mentioned in the text (the dedicator, Amen-wah-su, was a village scribe of the Nineteenth Dynasty). The chief interest of the text lies in the epithets of Ta-Weret, which clearly associated her with a happy home and family life.

Giving praise to Ta-Weret, Lady of Heaven, mistress of all the gods, lady of nourishment, mistress of provisions, lady of marriage, mistress of the dowry, lady of the wind, mistress of the North wind, rich in property, lady of affluence:
  in order that she might give a long life, endurance upon earth, and joy, while my house is richly provided with nourishment such as she

gives, while my eyes see her beauty, as something presented to the *ka* of the truly silent one, the beautiful of character, the kindly one, beloved of god, the stone mason of Amen in the work of the temple of Luxor, the *wab*-priest of Amen in the landing place of *Hut-Waret* (*unknown*), Mose, justified. His beloved son, the servant of Amen, Amen-wah-su.

THE DEAD

76. An 'Able Spirit of Re' Stela

The *akh*-spirits were the blessed dead, those who had attained a seat in the sun-bark of the god Re to which all the deceased aspired. They had magical powers which protected them from the dangers of the afterlife and which they could also use for or against the dead and the living. One became an *akh* (pl. *akhu*) through one's own knowledge of spells and magic, though funerary rites and especially through the intervention of the gods, particularly Re.

Although everyone would wish for himself and his relatives to become *akhu*, the attitude of the living towards existing spirits was mixed. Over fifty stelae from Deir el-Medina testify to the existence of household cults devoted to deceased relatives who had become *akhu*; the text given below is from one such stelae. But the spirits could be dangerous if offended, and the offerings to the *akhu* were propitiatory as well as reverential. The Maxims of Any advise the reader to

> Satisfy the *akh*; do what he desires,
> and abstain for him from his abomination,
> that you may be safe from his many harms.
> Every misfortune is his.
> The head of cattle is taken from the field?
> It is he who did it.
> Any damage (to) the threshing floor in the fields?
> 'It is an *akh*!' they say again.
> Uproar in the house? Hearts are discouraged?
> All of these are his doing.

(Many extracts from the Instructions of Any were found in Deir el-Medina, but not, as it happens, this particular passage.) Eventually *akhu* developed into the word for 'demon' in the Coptic period. There is no reason to believe, however, that the following text from a stela belonging to a household cult was dedicated with sentiments other than piety and affection.

Fig. 16. Stela dedicated to 'the Osiris, the able spirit of Re, Sheri-Re',
discovered in one of the houses of the village. Sheri-Re holds a lotus flower
in her right hand and stretches out her left towards an altar with offerings
of loaves and vegetables. (Reproduced with kind permission of R. J.
Demarée from R. J. Demarée, *The 3ḫ iḳr n Rˁ-Stelae*. Egyptologische
Uitgaven 3 (Leiden, 1983), pl. XI.)

For a spell to promote the deceased's transfiguration into an *akh*, see
below, No. 114.

A boon that the king gives (to) Re-Horakhty that he might grant
spirituality in heaven and power on earth to the Ka of the able spirit
of Re, Pa-nakhte-em-waset, justified.

77. A Letter to a Deceased Wife

Some of the most vivid testimonies to the Egyptian belief that the dead not only exist but can be a powerful force in the world of the living are letters from individuals to their deceased relatives. These are generally prompted by some misfortune thought to be caused by the deceased himself or by some other dead person whom he can influence, for instance, by taking him to court in the beyond. The following letter from the scribe Butehamun to his dead wife, Ikhtay, was written on a limestone ostracon, much rubbed and undecipherable in parts. It follows the traditional tripartite format of letters to the dead; first, Ikhtay is reminded of Butehamun's affection for her, then some injury to Butehamun is recorded, and finally, there is a request that Ikhtay intercede for him. Unfortunately, the centre section of this example is virtually unintelligible and thus the nature of Butehamun's distress is unclear.

The extract below is the final section of Butehamun's letter in which he asks Ikhtay to petition the Lords of Eternity on his behalf. This passage vividly conveys Butehamun's sense of the inevitability of death together with its unknowability, while his doubts that his words will reach his wife in the Beyond contrast strikingly with the hopefulness expressed by the act of writing at all. The ostracon was almost certainly left at Ikhtay's tomb as the most promising point of contact with the other world.

Said by the scribe Butehamun
of the Necropolis to the songstress of Amen Ikhtay.
Pre has gone,
his ennead following him,
and the kings of old likewise.
All the people in one body
follow their companions.
There is not one of them who will remain,
and we will all follow you.
If one can hear me
(in) the place where you are,
tell the Lords of Eternity,
'Let (me) petition for my brother,'
so that I may make [. . .] in [their] hearts,
whether they are great or small.
It is you who will speak with a good speech in the necropolis.
Indeed, I did not commit an abomination against you
while you were on earth,
and I hold to my behaviour.
Swear to god in every manner,

saying 'What I have said will be done!'
I will not oppose your will in any utterance
until I reach you.
[May you act] for me (in) every good manner,
if one can hear.

ORACLES

Consultation of oracles is first definitely attested in the New Kingdom, though there is some evidence that the practice was very much
older. In the most elaborate form of consultation, an image of the
god was placed upon a litter and carried by priests who were themselves workmen; a 'yes' answer was expressed by moving forwards, a
'no' answer by moving backwards. Although the villagers' faith in
the oracle suggests that it was not manipulated by the priests, the
mechanics of the procedure are not known. There may also have
been other, simpler ways of consulting the god, though these are
poorly documented. For example, the inner hall of one of the chapels
dedicated to Amenophis I and Ahmose Nefertari was connected to a
tomb directly underneath by a rectangular opening, while a stone
slab hid the aperture. It has been suggested that this feature was
somehow used in oracles.

Any sort of question could be put to the god, such as the health
of a distant relative or the soundness of a business transaction. The
god's answer in such minor matters is seldom preserved because
they were affairs of the moment and there was no need to keep an
account. Only consultations concerning legal disputes were recorded
in full, since the winner of the case might wish to be able to cite dates
and witnesses in the future. Most of what we know about oracles at
this period is therefore drawn from legal texts. (See also pp. 172–175.)

78. Questions Addressed to Oracles

Many ostraca bear short questions to the oracle. No further information is
provided, and we can only speculate about the history behind the individual
inquiries. Most could be answered with a negative or an affirmative, but
some form pairs of opposites between which the god would presumably
have chosen (e.g. g and h below). The technique described above could have
been used to answer any of the following, but it is also possible that some
simpler method was employed, inasmuch as many of the questions seem
too trivial to put to the god in the course of a procession.

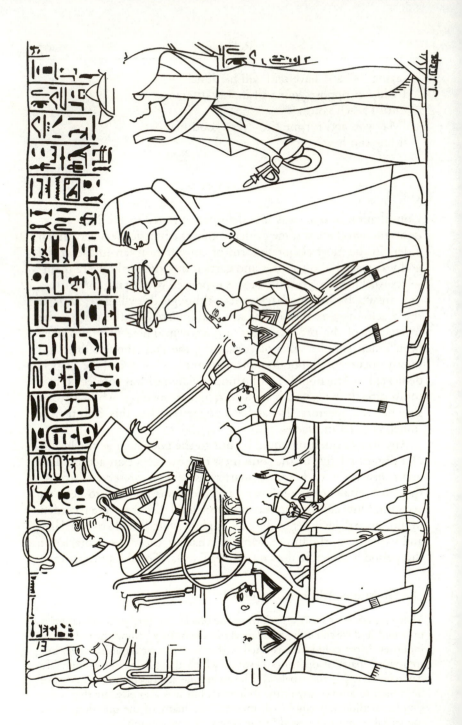

(*a*) Remove him from the post of deputy of the gang.
(*b*) My good lord! He really said this!
(*c*) My good lord! Shall we be given rations?
(*d*) As to the cattle that the woman is claiming, does she have a share in them?
(*e*) As to the dreams that one sees, are they good?
(*f*) He will give the donkey.
(*g*) Shall I burn it?
(*h*) Shall I not burn it?
(*i*) Will the place be given to Menna as she intends?
(*j*) No!

79. Request for an Oracle

Some petitioners questioned and challenged the oracle with striking self-assurance, but few matched the author of the following letter to an unnamed divinity. The papyrus was purchased in Cairo and its original provenance is unknown; it may have been drawn up in the late Twentieth Dynasty at Medinet Habu. It was during this period that the workmen moved from their village to the temple, and since a scribe of the Necropolis features in the text, there is some justification for counting it among the writings of the community. The writer hoped to consult the god about some garments for which he was responsible. The problem is not made very clear, but he seems to owe kilts to the vizier which he could not supply. There is a reference to a similar incident in which the oracle had ruled on a question about kilts for Isis (either a woman or the goddess of that name), but the writer complains that now the god was concealed in his sanctuary where he could not be approached; this letter was sent via a priest to tell the god to come out in the open or at least to send some message.

Fig. 17. (*opposite*) In this scene from the tomb of the workman Kha-bekhnet (TT 2), the tomb owner presents offerings to the god Amenophis during a procession. Eight workmen carry the statue of the god on its lion throne while two others wave fans before the deified pharaoh. A priest in a leopard skin cloak walks along side. It was in the course of such processions that the god could be consulted on legal matters and the like. (Reproduced with the kind permission of the IFAO in Cairo from Jaroslav Černý, 'Le Culte d'Amenophis Ier chez les ouvriers de la nécropole thébaine', *BIFAO* 27 (1927), 159–203. Fig. 13 on p. 187.)

I was looking for you to tell you some matters of mine, but you happened to be hidden in your sanctuary and there was no one admitted to send it to you. Now, when I was waiting, I found Hori, this scribe of Medinet Habu, and he told me, 'I am admitted.' So I am sending him to you.

Look, you will cast off mystery today and come out in the course of a procession, so that you may judge the matters of the five kilts of the temple of Horemheb and these further two kilts of the scribe of the Necropolis. The vizier will not take the clothes, saying, 'until you make up their number . . . !'

Now as for one like you, being in the place of mysteries and hiding, he sends out his voice; but you do not send me either good or bad (messages). Behold, you caused there to be eleven (kilts?) for Isis, your [. . .] when you looked into it (?); while (now) it happens that your voice does not come out like the Netherworld of a million years.

Farewell.

80. Striking a Bargain with the God

The easy familiarity with the deity reflected in the last text is again evident in the following extract. The author promises Amen-Re specific offerings if his prayer is granted.

Said by Hor-nefer to his god Amen-Re, Lord of the Thrones of the Two Lands:

If I see that you bring it about that I get (it), I will make a jar of imported date-beer for you, and also a jar of beer, and so will my man, [and also . . .]-loaves and white bread.

81. Dreams

Sleep is a liminal state in which those of this world may be brought into contact with beings of another sphere, such as gods and the dead. The latter can communicate with the sleeper through dreams, which, if properly decoded, may reveal useful information or forecast the future.

The 'Dream Book' is a key for the interpretation of dreams. It consists of eleven preserved columns of visions each followed by a very brief interpretation. The dreams considered good omens open the list, while those that were bad omens make up the end; and the words 'if a man sees himself in a dream' are written in large characters down the margin to be read before

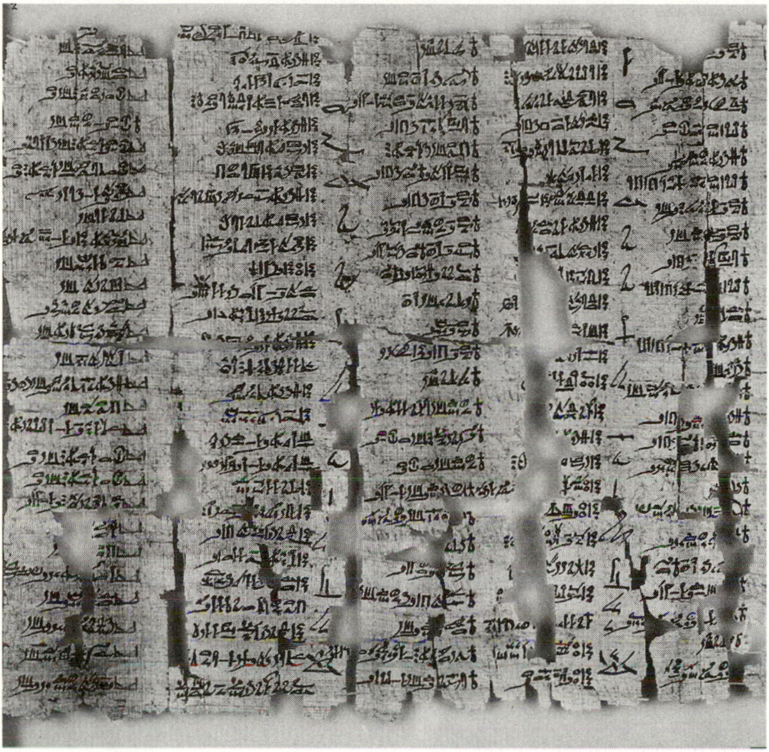

Fig. 18. Qen-her-khepesh-ef's dreambook (Chester Beatty III). Written vertically in widely spaced, large signs to the right of the interpretations are the words, 'If a man sees himself in a dream', which apply to the entire page. The first column to the left of this lists images that might appear to the sleeper, and the second column contains the interpretations, each preceded by the sign ♿, 'good', or ◡, 'bad'. (Photo kindly supplied by the British Museum, London.)

each entry. The principles behind the interpretation are often unclear but seem to resemble those of magic, such as 'like affects like' and 'one thing suggests its opposite'.

The copy of the dream book from Deir el-Medina belonged to the library of the scribe Qen-her-khepesh-ef and his descendants; according to the colophon it was 'made', which in this case surely means 'copied by', the scribe Amen-nakhte the son of Kha-em-nun, i.e. Qen-her-khepesh-ef's grandson. The language is pure classical Egyptian, however, so the text may go back to a Middle Kingdom original.

Auspicious dreams:
IF A MAN SEES HIMSELF IN A DREAM:

sitting in a garden in the sun	good: it means pleasure
demolishing a wall	good: it means purification from evil
[eating] excrement	good: consuming his property in his house
mating with a cow	good: spending a happy day in his house
eating crocodile-[meat]	good: [becoming] an official among his people
offering water (?)	good: it means prosperity
drowning in the river	good: it means purification from every evil
sleeping on the ground	good: consuming his property
seeing carobs (?)	good: finding a happy life
[seeing] the moon shining	good: pardoning him by his god
veiling himself [. . .]	good: his enemies flee before him
falling [. . .]	good: it means prosperity
sawing wood	good: his enemies are dead
burying an old man	good: it means prosperity
cultivating vegetables	good: it means finding victuals

Inauspicious dreams:
IF A MAN SEES HIMSELF IN A DREAM:

seizing one of his lower legs	BAD: a report about him by those who are yonder (i.e. the dead)
seeing himself in a mirror	BAD: it means another wife
god has dispelled his weeping for him	BAD: it means fighting
while he sees himself suffering (in) his side	BAD: extracting his property from him
eating hot meat	BAD: it means not being found innocent
shod with white sandals	BAD: it means roaming the earth
eating what he abominates	BAD: it means a man eating what he abominates in ignorance
copulating with a woman	BAD: it means mourning
he is bitten by a dog	BAD: he is touched by magic

he is bitten by a snake	BAD: it means the arising of words against him
measuring barley	BAD: it means the arising of words against him
writing on a papyrus	BAD: reckoning his wrongs by his god
stirring up his house	BAD: [it means] being ill
suffering through another's spell (?)	BAD: it means mourning
being a steersman in a ship	BAD: every time he is judged, he will not be found innocent
his bed catching fire	BAD: it means driving away his wife

82. Calendar of Lucky and Unlucky Days

The Cairo Calendar, from which the following short extract is taken, belongs to a well-attested genre of handbooks offering predictions and injunctions for each day of the year. In its most elaborate form, these indicate not only for each day, but for each part of the day (morning, afternoon and evening), whether it was auspicious or inauspicious. This might be followed by an explanation in terms of a mythological event or by advice about activities to be undertaken or avoided on that day. Drenkhan has collected the actual dates of important events such as journeys, court sessions, and royal coronations, and shown that these are unaffected by the predictions for those dates. She suggests that the calendars were used as horoscopes are today; the reader would not in fact change his plan for the day but might feel more or less comfortable about them.

The papyrus quoted here was purchased in Cairo from a dealer who said it came from Luxor; in the editor's opinion, the original provenance was Deir el-Medina (a column on the *verso* (v. XX) records the dimensions of various corridors and chambers in the tomb of Ramesses II). The handwriting suggests that the text was copied in the Nineteenth Dynasty, although the grammar and vocabulary are Middle Egyptian. It opens with an introduction claiming that the god Thoth himself compiled the contents.

HERE BEGINS THE BEGINNING OF INFINITY AND THE END OF ETER-NITY, MADE by the gods of the shrine and the assembly of the ennead, AND COMPILED BY THE MAJESTY of Thoth in the Great House in the presence of the Lord of All, WHICH WAS FOUND IN THE LIBRARY IN

THE REAR-HOUSE of the ennead. HOUSE of Re, HOUSE of Osiris, HOUSE of Horus.[a]

FIRST MONTH OF INUNDATION, DAY 1: good good good.
Birth of Re-Horakhty, purification throughout the entire land with the water of the beginning of the inundation which comes forth as Nun (the primeval waters)—'young', he is called. Thus all the gods and goddesses are in great festivity on this day; everyone's doing likewise.

FIRST MONTH OF INUNDATION, DAY 2: good good good.
If you saw anything, it will be good on this day: it is the day of coming forth before Re by the ennead, their hearts being pleased when they see his youthfulness, after they have slain the enemy on behalf of their lord and overthrown Apophis in all of his places, falling on his back in the midst of the flood.

FIRST MONTH OF INUNDATION, DAY 3: good good BAD.
Anyone born on this day will die of a crocodile: it is the day of making *ipy* (*unknown word*) in the river of the gods of the underworld.

FIRST MONTH OF INUNDATION, DAY 4: good good BAD.
Do not do anything there on this day: it is the day of going forth by Hathor with the executioners to direct the river body. Thus, the movements of the gods are in a headwind. Do not navigate a boat on this day.

FIRST MONTH OF INUNDATION, DAY 5: good good good.
If you saw anything on this day, it will be good on this day. It will be good, since the gods are content in the heaven on account of the navigation of the great bark.

FIRST MONTH OF INUNDATION, DAY 6: BAD BAD good.
Anyone born on this day will die through the agency of a bull.

[a] The significance of the group 'House of Re, House of Osiris, House of Horus' is unknown.

83. The Wise Woman

The *rechet*, or Wise Woman, is an intriguing but poorly attested figure; what little evidence we possess suggests that she was a woman with powers of divination and healing. In the text below, the scribe Qen-her-khepesh-ef asks someone to consult the Wise Woman about two boys who died in

suspicious circumstances, and also more generally about his own life and
that of the boys' mother.

Qen-her-khepesh-ef speaks to Iner-[wau] (*fem.*): Now, what means
your not going to the Wise Woman about the two boys who died in
your charge? Consult the Wise Woman about the death the two boys
suffered: was it their fate or was it their lot? And consult (about)
them for me, and also see about my own life and the life of their
mother. As for any god who will be (mentioned) to you afterwards,
you will write to me about his name [and you will do the wo]rk of
one who knows [her duty (?)].

MAGIC

Magic achieves its effects by acting on an impersonal, supernatural
force by means such as the power of the word and the principle that
like affects like; its instruments are the spell and the accompanying
action, along with paraphernalia. The performer transfers himself to
the spiritual world in which magic is most potent by ritual purification and often also by equating himself with a god and his case to
events in myth. The principles of magic are similar to those under-
lying the cult, but the former aims to manipulate while the latter
seeks also to communicate with, explain, and serve the supernatural
beings. Magic was not seen as evil, however; it is explicitly stated that
the gods gave magic to man 'to ward off the stroke of an event'. In
Deir el-Medina, a scorpion-charmer, evidently a magician of some
sort, drew rations for his special services.

Very many magical spells have been preserved from Deir el-
Medina, as from elsewhere, and the few translated here by no means
cover the full range. Most spells are defensive, against various dis-
eases, dangerous animals, and other threats, but see also the love
charm translated above under 'Family and Friends' (No. 6). No spell
would be complete without its associated magical action, and the
first selection below includes instructions for the latter.

84. A Spell Against Nightmares

This spell is to be pronounced by the person who has just suffered a
nightmare; it is preserved on the same papyrus as the 'Dream Book' (No. 81
above) and indeed follows directly on the section dealing with unfavourable

dreams. The speaker equates himself to the infant Horus and asks the help of his mother Isis, who orders the nightmare to be destroyed and invokes a good dream to take its place. The performer claims that as the god Re is victorious over his foes, so he too is now victorious over his enemies. Instructions for the magical actions which should accompany the spell round off the text.

WORDS TO BE SPOKEN BY A MAN WHEN HE DREAMS IN HIS (OWN) PLACE

Come to me, come to me, mother Isis! Behold, I see that which is far from me in my city!

I am here, my son Horus! Come out with what you have seen so that your dumbness ceases and your dreams retreat. May fire come out against the thing that frightened you! Behold, I have come to see you, that I might drive out your evil, that I might destroy every harm.

Hail to you, good dream! May night be seen as day; may every evil harm done by Seth the son of Nut be driven out. As Re is justified over his enemies, so I am justified over my enemies.

THIS SPELL IS SPOKEN by a man when he dreams in his (own) place. Cakes should be given to him in (his) presence together with some fresh vegetables moistened with beer and myrrh. The man's face should be rubbed with them.

To drive out every evil dream that he has seen.

85. A Spell Against an Enemy

In this spell against an enemy, the performer identifies himself with a fly who can penetrate and escape from anywhere—into his enemy's bed and out again to the floor, and into his very belly causing him to be contorted with pain. On the other hand, the performer claims he is Horus and thus invincible.

You will stop, whoever comes! I am
the one who enters the sleeping place (?) and comes forth (upon)
    the ground;
a man who fights.
You will stop! Where are you with regard to me?
I will enter your belly as a fly,
and I will see your belly from the inside.
I will turn your face into the back of your head;

the front of your foot into your heel.
Your speech is no use;
it will not be heard.
Your body will be weak
and your knee will be feeble.
You will stop! I am Horus, the son of Isis,
I will leave on my feet.

86. The Scorpion-Charmer

The scorpion-charmer was a member of the gang who specialized in curing scorpion stings and snake bites by magical means such as the preparation of amulets, recitation of spells, and magical acts. He received extra wages for his services. The following extract consists of instructions for the use of a magical spell with an assurance that this is used by scorpion-charmers everywhere.

The scorpion-charmer features again in Chapter 5 (No. 138) where he submits a question to the oracle on behalf of a petitioner.

TO BE RECITED OVER A FIGURE OF ISIS DRAWN ON A STRIP OF FINE LINEN IN WHICH *NESUT*-LEAVES HAVE BEEN PUT; RUB (?) THE UPPER PART THEREWITH. IT IS A TRUE ANTIDOTE TO POISON. They (these spells?) are in the hand of the scorpion-charmer everywhere.

87. Sharing a Magical Spell

Magical spells are among the very few literary texts, apart from student copies of the classics, that occur regularly on ostraca as well as papyrus. Perhaps it was useful to have a spell in portable form to take to the Valley of the Kings or wherever it was needed. One could even imagine a workman being given a spell on an ostracon by a colleague or professional magician for a particular emergency. The following extract confirms that spells were passed on from one individual to another. Here the scribe Pa-hem-netjer, not a member of the community, brings a spell against poison to the scribe of the Necropolis Pa-nefer-em-djed, demonstrating that such magic was practiced by lay people and not only by professional scorpion-charmers.

Year 3, third month of inundation, day 28. This day, (coming) by the scribe Pa-hem-netjer to give the spell for catching the poison to the scribe Pa-nefer-em-djed of the Necropolis in the house of Ab-imentet.

88. A Myth

Myths were important to Egyptian religion from earliest times but few narratives are preserved from before the New Kingdom. The Story of Horus and Seth from this period is the longest native account of the adventures of major deities (the great myth of Osiris is best known from the account by Plutarch, a Greek). Many episodes from myths also feature in magical spells, where the situation of the subject is identified with that of a god who overcame his difficulties successfully. The adventures of Isis, who guarded her infant son Horus against numerous threats, are related particularly often in spells to protect young children. The following spell against scorpion bites includes another story about this cunning Isis, namely of how she tricked her aged father Re into revealing his most secret name so that she could pass this—and the kingship—on to her son Horus. The ritual element of the cure included reciting the spell over drawings of Re, Isis, and Horus on the hand of the patient; he then licked off the figures to ingest the magic power.

Now, Isis was a wise woman. She was more cunning than millions of men; she was more clever than millions of gods; she was more shrewd than millions of *akhu*-spirits. There was nothing of which she was ignorant in heaven and earth, like Re who supplies the needs of earth. The goddess plotted in her heart to know the name of the noble god.

Now, Re entered every day at the head of the crew (of the sun-boat), established on the throne of the Horizon. The divine elder's mouth drooped; he let his spittle dribble to the earth. ⟨His⟩ saliva had fallen on the ground. Isis gathered it in her hand together with the earth that was on it, and she fashioned it into a noble serpent which she made in a pointed shape. It did not move, though alive before her, and she released it at the crossroads that the great god passed in order to enjoy himself throughout his Two Lands.

The noble god appeared outside, the gods of the palace behind him while he strolled as (he did) every day. It stung ⟨him⟩, the noble serpent; living fire broke out in himself. It even raged among the pine-trees.

The divine god sent out his voice; the cry of his majesty reached heaven. His ennead said, 'What is it? What is it?' The gods said, 'What? What?' But he could not find his voice to answer it. His lips were quivering and all his limbs were trembling. The poison took hold of him and his flesh as the flood takes hold of (all) around it.

. . . (*The god calls for help*) . . .

Isis came with her magic power. Her utterance possesses the breath of life, her speech dispels suffering, her words revive the one whose throat is constricted. She said, 'What is it, what is it, divine father? What? A serpent has brought weakness upon you? One of your children has raised his head against you? Then I will overthrow him with my potent magic; I will make him retreat to see your darkness.'

The holy god, he opened his mouth: 'As for me, I went on the road, strolling in the Two Lands and the Desert. My heart desired to see what I had created. A serpent stung me without my seeing it. It is not fire, it is not water; (but) I am colder than water, I am hotter than fire. All my limbs are covered in sweat; I tremble, my eye is not fixed, and I do not see. Heaven rains on me in the summer season.'

Isis said to Re . . . 'Tell me your name, my divine father. A man lives when one recites in his name.'

'I am the one who made the earth, who built the mountains, and who created what is on it. I am the one who made water, so that the Great Swimmer came into existence. I am the one who made the bull for the cow, so that passion came into existence . . . I am Khepri in the morning, Re in the afternoon, and Atum in the evening.'

But the poison was not repulsed from its course; the great god was not healed.

SAID BY Isis [. . .] to Re: 'Your name was not among those you mentioned to me. Tell it to me, so that the poison will come out. A man lives when his name is pronounced.'

The poison burned [. . .] with a burning; it was (more) powerful (than) a flame. The majesty of Re said, 'Give me your ears, my daughter Isis, that my name may come forth from my belly to your belly. The most divine among the gods has hidden it so that my place might be spacious in the Bark of Millions. If it should happen that for the first time (it) leaves my heart, tell it to (your) son Horus, after you have bound him with a divine oath and set god before his eyes (?).' The great god announced his name to Isis, Great of Magic.

Depart, scorpion![a] Come out from Re! Eye of Horus, leave the god! Flame of the mouth, I am the one who made you; I am the one who sent you. Come out upon the ground, powerful poison!

Behold, the great god has revealed his name. Re lives, the poison having died. So-and-so born of so-and-so lives, the poison having died, through the speech of Isis the Great, mistress of the gods, Re's own name (?).

---

[a] These words are spoken by Isis on behalf of her father Re, and at the same time by the healer on behalf of his patient.

THE AFTERLIFE

No aspect of Ancient Egypt is so well documented as beliefs about death and the afterlife. The written material from Deir el-Medina is quite traditional; a selection of relevant texts follows below.

89. Shabti of Setau

The Field of Rushes where the deceased hoped to spend the rest of eternity was an idealized Egypt, an agricultural society in which he would live in comfort on his estates surrounded by family and friends. The grain would not grow by itself, however; someone would have to work the land, and there would also be obligations of corvée labour for the State. In the world of the living, high officials and priests were ordinarily exempt from this onerous duty, but in the next even the king might be obliged to work for the gods. To protect himself from such heavy labour, the tomb-owner had shabtis, small figures in the shape of a mummy which would answer to his name if he were called upon to work the fields, repair the dikes, or serve in some other way. The shabti carried a hoe and a basket for its work, and was inscribed with a spell corresponding to chapter 6 of the Book of the Dead. Ideally, the tomb-owner would have 365 such servants, one for each day of the year, with overseers and scribes to supervise them.

The following text is from a shabti belonging to the workman Setau, buried at the end of the Eighteenth Dynasty. Note that the text names Aten as the god to whom offerings are made, suggesting that it was inscribed in the Amarna period.

The servant in the Place of Truth Setau, justified, says: Oh, this shabti! If one counts off, if one reckons Setau, justified, to do any work which is done there (i.e. in the hereafter)—now indeed an obligation has been set up for him there, as a man at his duties, to cultivate the fields, to irrigate the riparian lands, to transport the sand of the West to the East—if you are called at any time, 'Here I am!', ⟨you⟩ shall say there, for the Ka of Setau, justified.

May you be given wine and milk that come forth upon the offering table before Aten, for the Ka of Setau.

90. The Book of the Dead

The Book of the Dead is a collection of spells to help the deceased in his transition from this world to the next and to protect him against the dangers of the Netherworld; its ancient title was in fact the Book of Coming Forth by Day. Many of the spells go back to the Coffin Texts of the Middle Kingdom. The Book is not a continuous narrative and the arrangement of the spells is not standardized, rather, the prospective dead person selected the elements to be included in his personal copy and the order in which they would appear. The text was usually written on papyrus, illustrated with vignettes, and placed in or next to the coffin, though spells and vignettes might also be depicted on the walls of the tomb. It draws on the many different ideas about the afterlife that existed at the time, some of them irreconcilable to our eyes. The spell below (109a) seeks to obtain for the speaker a place in the bark of the sun-god Re as it travels through the underworld to re-emerge in the east at dawn; but it also describes the Field of Rushes, mentioned in the previous section, where the grain is said to grow to impossible heights and is harvested by spirits 4 m. tall.

Spell for knowing the Eastern Souls. Words spoken by the great chief Kha, justified: I know that northern gate of the sky, the southern part of which is the pool of *kharu*-geese, while its northern part is the water of the *ro*-geese, the place where Re navigates by the winds and by the oar. I am in charge of the rigging in the god's ship; I am a tireless oarsman in the bark of Re.

I know those twin sycamores of turquoise between which Re comes forth, which grew at Shu's sowing, at this gate of the Lord of the East through which Re comes forth. I know the Field of Rushes. Its wall is of copper; its barley is 7 cubits, the ears being 2 cubits and the stalk 6 cubits; its emmer is 2 cubits, its stalk being 8 cubits. The *akhu*-spirits, every one of them 8 cubits tall, are those who reap it beside the Eastern Souls. I know the Eastern Souls; they are Re-Horakhty, the calf who is before the god; they are the morning star.

91. Pyramidion of Tut-er-bay and his Son Pa-ser

From the Old Kingdom onwards, lower levels of society gradually adopted funerary practices which had originally been restricted to royalty. This is

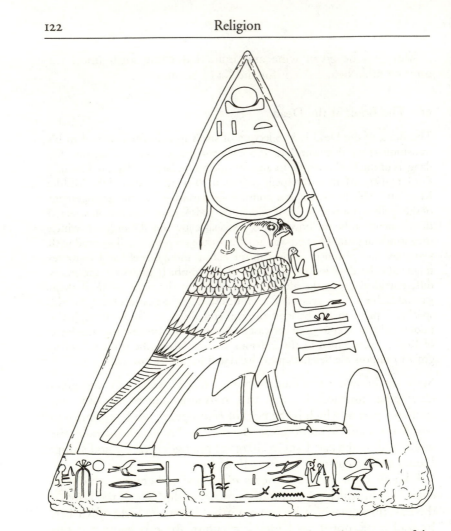

Fig. 19. South face of a pyramidion belonging to the scribe Ra-mose of the Nineteenth Dynasty. The figure represents the god Re Horakhty, who is called here 'the great god, lord of heaven'. (Drawn by Marion Cox after Turin no. 1603, Annamaria Fornari and Mario Tosi, *Nella Sede della Verita* (Milan, 1987), 159.)

well illustrated by the incorporation of small pyramids into the tombs of workmen at Deir el-Medina, at a time when the Pharaohs themselves had abandoned these for less conspicuous tombs in the Valley of the Kings. The villagers' pyramids were constructed of brick with a stone top, called a pyramidion; in the inscriptions on the latter, the tomb-owner praises the sun-god in his manifestations of Re in the morning, Khepri in the daytime, and Atum in the evening.

East Face
upper register: Re at his rising.
main text: Praising [Re] when he rises in the [East]ern horizon of the sky by the servant in the Place of Truth Tut-er-bay, justified. His son, who causes his name to live, the servant in the Place of Truth Pa-ser.

He says, 'Hail to you, Re, at your rising!'

South Face
upper register: Khepri in his bark, the great god.
main text: Praising Re Horakhty, the great god who illuminates the two lands, Khepri in his bark, lord of forms, sacred in [. . .] May they cause my limbs to flourish on the [. . .] of seeing his beauty daily. His father, the servant in the Place of Truth, Tut-er-bay, justified, the honoured one.

West Face
upper register: Re, the great god, who loves life (?) in truth (?).
main text: Praising Re at the offering of every day by the Osiris, the servant [in the Place of Truth] Pa-ser, justified. 'Hail to you [. . .] everything that you have created in every place of yours. When you are with me, may you let me praise the divine face [. . .] for the Ka of his son Pa-ser.'

North Face
upper register: Re at his setting.
main text: Praising Re when he sets in the Western horizon of the sky by the Osiris, the servant in the Place of Truth, Tut-er-bay, justified. He says, 'Hail to you, Atum who is in the West, who illuminates the underworld for the spirits.'

Invocation offerings for the sun[folk].

92. The Song of the Harper

Harper's songs contain some of the most interesting reflections on life and death in Egyptian literature. They are inscribed on tomb walls, ostensibly as entertainment at a banquet which is sometimes depicted. The theme is death, which is inevitable but about which we know nothing. Some songs are frankly sceptical about the other world and efforts to prolong one's

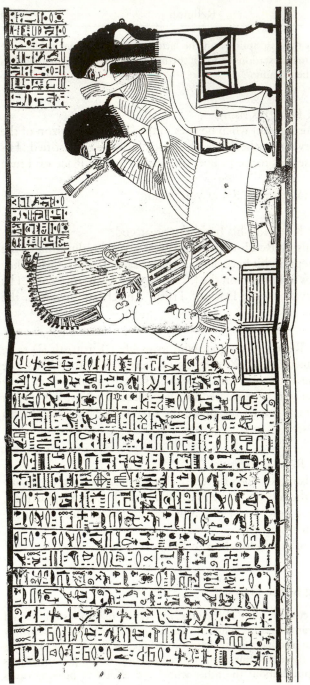

Fig. 20. A blind harper sings to the chief workman In-her-khau and his wife Wab in this detail from their tomb. The text to the harper's song is written behind him (for translation see No. 92). (Reproduced with the kind permission of the IFAO in Cairo from Bruyère, *Rapport (1930)*, FIFAO 7 (Cairo, 1933), pl. 23.)

existence after death and thus urge the listener to enjoy life while he can with wine and song. Here the contrast between the song's cynicism about the afterlife and its place in the tomb is particularly striking. Others, however, describe this world as transitory and the next as a place of rest and peace, suggesting that we should focus on the latter. The single example of a harper's song from Deir el-Medina takes a more cheerful view; while it is optimistic about life beyond the grave, it nevertheless exhorts the listener to enjoy the good things of this world while there is still time.

Spoken by the singer of the Osiris, the chief workman in the Place of Truth, In-her-khau, justified.

I say,
I am this noble, this man, (in) very truth,
through a happy destiny,
made by the god himself.
The physical form passes away
since the time of the god,
and new generations come in its (*lit.* their) place;
the souls and noble *akhu*-spirits who are in the Netherworld,
and the mummies likewise.
They who built temples and tombs, too,
they are men who rest in their pyramids.
Make for yourself a temple in the necropolis,
so that your name will endure in it!
Your works of the necropolis shall be reckoned,
your place of the West shall be excellent.
The waters flow north, the northwind goes south,
and every man will (go) at his (appointed) hour.
Make holiday, Osiris, chief workman In-her-khau, justified!
Do not let your heart grow weary, not at all!, (you) and your
    beloved;
Do not vex your heart in the season of your existence.
Make holiday to the utmost!
Put ointment and perfumed oils gathered beside you,
and garlands of lotus and mandragora flowers to your breast.
The one who sits beside you is the woman of your heart.
Do not let your heart be angry on account of anything that has
    happened.
Set song before you, do not recall evil,
the abomination of god.
Concentrate on delights.

Oh righteous one, oh truly just man!
tranquil, kindly, content, and calm,
who is joyful and speaks no evil,
give drunkenness to your heart daily,
until that day comes in which there is a landing.

4

Education, Learning, and Literature

INTRODUCTION

The literary texts from Deir el-Medina include works of which no other copies are known and also give these and more familiar literary texts a well-documented setting from which it is possible to reconstruct something of the use and ownership of *belles lettres* by the villagers. No other Egyptian community offers us this opportunity. This chapter will focus on literary and scholarly works in their context, that is, on works used for educational purposes, works collected by individuals to be read for pleasure, and above all, works composed by the villagers themselves.

The category of literature and learning itself is, of course, somewhat artificial and many of the relevant texts are to be found in other sections of this anthology; for example, medical texts belonged to private libraries and formed part of the interests of the well-lettered man but are incorporated in Chapter 2 on 'Daily Life' because of their significance for questions of health. Similarly, hymns are both literary compositions and religious statements; some are included in Chapter 4, 'Religion', while others, signed by their authors, are presented below. A complete picture of the villager's intellectual life naturally includes all of these texts.

Another problem regarding text selection arises from the fact that many of the best-known literary works of Middle and Late Egyptian are represented in the village. Since these 'classics' have been translated many times and are incorporated in every collection of Egyptian literature, they are not included here; instead, this chapter focuses on lesser-known works and especially on texts known only from the village and no other source. Such an approach gives a somewhat impoverished impression of the literary experience of the workmen because it omits over half the texts that they read and collected, but it also underscores their contribution to what is known of Egyptian literature. None of the texts translated below would be known if not for the Deir el-Medina workmen; while among the important local texts omitted here because they are widely published are the *Tale of Horus and Seth* and the *Turin Love Songs*.

A category of special interest among the literary texts are those composed by the workmen themselves. Unfortunately these are difficult to identify with confidence because the words 'made by N'. at the end of a text were used to indicate both authors and mere copyists. Only one work was incontestably a local composition, namely the *Instruction of Amen-nakhte* (No. 102, below). Nevertheless, for working purposes it is assumed below that if a literary work is unique and is said to be 'made by' one of the villagers, then it was he who composed it.

EDUCATION

School

Perhaps the largest single category of texts on ostraca is that of student exercises, mostly extracts from Egyptian literary texts of the Middle Kingdom, the 'classical period' of Egyptian literature. These have long been thought to be the product of a local elementary school of the sort well documented in literary and autobiographical texts, such as, for instance, *The Blinding of Truth* (see No. 108). Indeed, the ostraca from Deir el-Medina have in the past been used as one of the chief sources of information about teaching methods. They have been thought to demonstrate that students learned to write in full sentences rather than sign by sign; and also that they first learned to read from texts in the already ancient Middle Egyptian language, which was as remote from their own vernacular as Chaucer would be to a modern school child.

Other evidence, however, points to these texts as the work of advanced students—that is, products of the secondary education curriculum. First, there is the fact that we never hear of a school at Deir el-Medina; the one reference to such an institution occurs in a letter of the late Twentieth Dynasty, after the gang had left the village and moved to Medinet Habu. Second, some fifteen texts are signed by their student copyists, who identify themselves as 'assistants' or 'apprentices' working under the direction of an established member of the gang. On workdays they no doubt helped their mentors with the work in the Valley of the Kings, mastering the trade, while on free days they gradually acquired the learning expected of Egyptians of the official class. Where they had acquired the basic skills of reading and writing we cannot say.

93. Colophons

The signatures at the end of student exercises, called 'colophons' provide what little information we have about the identity of students and teachers in Deir el-Medina, and the relationships between them. In several cases, fathers taught their own sons, or a grandson was trained by his grandfather; sometimes, however, a father who was himself literate sent his son to someone of higher rank for his advanced instruction. About half the known tutors were draughtsmen, the others being scribes and chief workmen. These higher-ranking members of the gang were the most educated and were perhaps also more likely to have been granted assistants. The students, on the other hand, included not only the future office-holders of the gang, but also people who would never rise above the rank of stonecutter, and possibly also one woman.

A. To a Copy of the *Instruction of a Man for his Son*

This colophon to a copy of the Middle Kingdom wisdom text, the *Instruction of a Man for his Son*, is dedicated to the draughtsman Mery-Sekhmet of the early part of the reign of Ramesses II. Mery-Sekhmet seems to have been a mentor to several future draughtsmen, who are called his 'sons' on monuments although they were not members of his family. Nefer-senut, the pupil here, is probably Nefer-senut the son of Ka-sa; we know that he was still very young when his father died because he is shown in the latter's tomb as a small boy weeping over his father's mummy. Perhaps Mery-Sekhmet took over the education of the child after the death of his father.

IT HAS COME WELL AND [IN] PEACE FOR THE DRAUGHTSMAN MERY-SEKHMET, HIS BELOVED ASSISTANT NEFER-SENUT.

B. To the *Satire on the Trades*

Although the Neb-nefer of this colophon to the *Satire on the Trades* calls himself 'scribe', he is probably the chief workman Neb-nefer, here tutoring his son and successor, Nefer-hotep. A local official such as a chief workman would of course prefer to have his own son as his apprentice so that the latter would be in position to take over the job after the father's retirement.

It has come well and in peace [. . .] scribe Neb-nefer, his assistant Nefer-hotep.

94. A Call to Lessons

The following little ostracon illustrates how a meeting between tutor and student might be arranged. The first line is from the instructor Piay to his pupil informing him that his next assignment, the third chapter of the text he was studying, was ready for him. The student returned the ostracon with his eager promises to do so written on the verso; Piay then sent back the shard a third time with instructions to bring yesterday's exercise, presumably to be examined.

recto
The scribe Piay speaks to the scribe Amen-mose as follows: 'A third (chapter) is ready for you.'

verso
Amen-mose: 'I will do it! See, I will do it, I will do it!'
Piay: 'Bring your chapter and come!'

95. The Curriculum

The curriculum of at least some advanced students *outside* Deir el-Medina is preserved in the Late Egyptian Miscellanies, a group of texts on papyrus written by apprentices in minor government offices; these texts appear originally to have been composed in Memphis and Thebes, although none of them were found in excavation. The students who copied the Miscellanies were instructed in the Middle Egyptian classics and also Late Egyptian hymns, official letters and reports, all strung together on the same papyrus in no particular order.

   In the workmen's village, comparable exercises were generally written on ostraca, although a few copies on papyrus have survived. Again, the curriculum included both classical texts and compositions in the vernacular. Of these, the Middle Egyptian literary texts on ostraca are easy to identify as students exercises by the colophons mentioned above and the dates inserted to mark the end of a day's work. Student exercises in Late Egyptian are less distinctive, since the anthology of texts which characterizes the papyri is broken up into individual texts on ostraca. Only where an ostracon matches

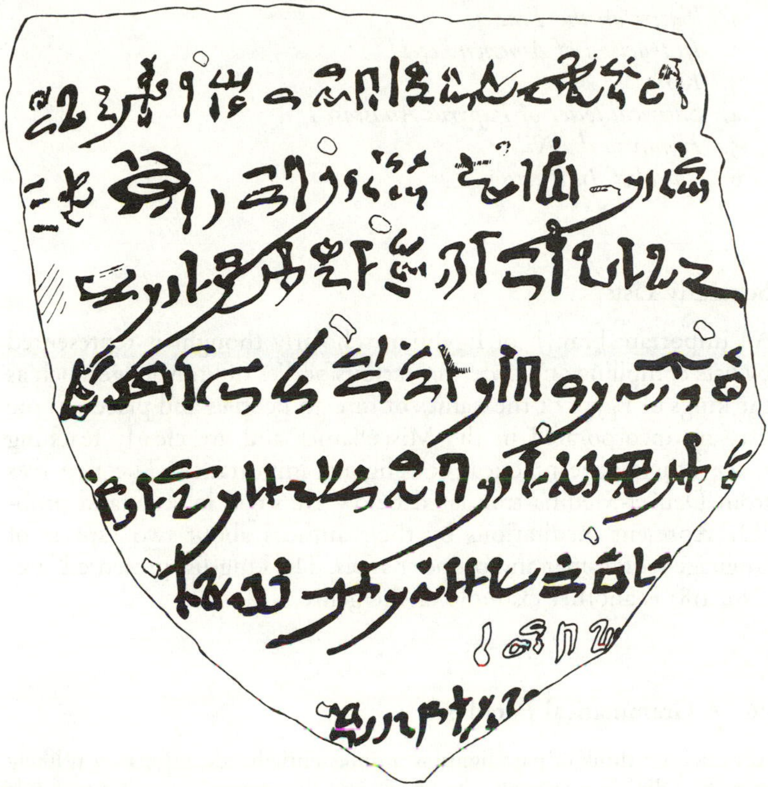

Fig. 21. A student copy of the Satire on the Trades (O Glasgow D. 1925.77). Verse points, a type of punctuation, are written above the line in red ink. The date, also in red, is written in the second line from the bottom. (A.G. McDowell, *Hieratic Ostraca in the Hunterian Museum, Glasgow* (Oxford, 1993), pl. 16. Red is indicated in this reproduction by outlined, as opposed to inked-in, characters.)

an extract from the Late Egyptian Miscellanies themselves can we be certain it is a student copy; this happens often enough to show that the curriculum in the village was in many respects identical to that in use in the capital cities.

The thousands of student copies of Middle Egyptian literary texts have been used by Annie Gasse to draw up a list of the most widely-copied works in order of popularity:

1. *'Satire on the Trades'*
2. *Instruction of Amenemhet I*
3. *Kemyt*
4. *Satirical letter of Papyrus Anastasi I*
5. *Hymn to the Nile*
6. *'Loyalist' Instruction*

Scholarly Lists

An important branch of Egyptian scholarly thought is represented by lists compiling and ordering various bodies of knowledge, such as the kings of Egypt or the names of foreign peoples and places. Some lists are incorporated in the Miscellanies and are clearly teaching tools; others have practical or religious importance. The two lists from Deir el-Medina translated below are small in scale and probably represent meditations by their authors about two aspects of language—grammar and proper names. The king-list presented later (No. 118) is another example of the genre.

96. A Grammatical Paradigm

Although we think of paradigms as quintessentially educational, it is likely that the following example was an exercise in categorization by an adult scribe. The writer did not consider his little project too be of any great importance; it is written along the edge of an ostracon which is otherwise filled by a list of wooden objects, some of them quite obscure.

The combination *iw* + subject is the standard opening of one type of sentence in Late Egyptian; there is no exact equivalent in English, but 'I am, you are, etc.' gives an approximate sense.

iw.i	I am
iw.f	he is
iw.k	you are
iw.n	we are
iw.w	they are (a late New Kingdom form)
iw.sn	they are (an earlier form)
iw.t	you (*fem.*) are
[. . .]	

97. A Name List

A number of texts simply contain a list of names arranged according to their first element. None of the names in the following such list are actually known from the village and many are not known at all; the list therefore appears to be quite theoretical. There is no direct evidence that Egypt had an alphabet at this early date or any similar means of ordering words as words and not as representing things. The name lists may be a first step in this direction of thought.

Shemsu-nefer	(The good attendant)
Shemsu-su-em-reshut	(Who attends him joyfully)
Shemsu-su-em-heb	(Who attends him at the festival)
Shemsu-su-em-hesy	(Who attends him in favour)
Hesy-men	(The favoured one endures)
Hesy-her-imentet	(Favoured in the West)
Hesy-Maʿaty	(Whom the just one favours)
Hesy-ab-su	(Who is favoured by the one who desired him [i.e., his father])
Maʿaty-her-maʿau	(The just one is in the breeze)
Maʿaty-men	(The just one endures)

LITERATURE

The literary life of the workmen is unevenly represented in the surviving texts because ostraca are not well suited to literary works; they are too small, or, if large enough (like the copies of the Ghost Story inscribed on large pots) too unwieldy for comfortable reading. The largest category of literary ostraca is, accordingly, student exercises as discussed above, preserving endless copies of the half a dozen classics which made up the standard curriculum. As Annie Gasse has pointed out, we have remarkably few Middle Egyptian texts beyond this group, and even less fiction in Late Egyptian, the contemporary language. The remaining literary ostraca include a relatively few hymns and a modest number of magical spells—the latter perhaps written up as 'prescriptions' for individual cases. In general, the texts workmen would have wanted to read, or even store conveniently, were written on papyrus and have not survived in any numbers, a notable exception being the archive of the Qen-her-khepesh-ef.

98. A Private Library

The library collected by the scribe Qen-her-khepesh-ef and his descendants over more than a century was discovered in the course of the French excavations of 1928. The papyri were found in the necropolis of Deir el-Medina in a narrow space between a pyramid and a chapel where they had been left by their last ancient owner. During the night after their discovery, however, a substantial number of the papyri were stolen, to appear on the antiquities market soon afterwards. The total extent of the archive can therefore not be determined, but P. W. Pestman has identified on internal evidence at least forty papyri which belonged to it, including the Chester Beatty papyri (now in Dublin and in the British Museum), the Naunakhte papyri (in the Ashmolean Museum, Oxford and in Cairo), P DeM I–XVII (in Cairo), and perhaps also Geneva P MAH 15274. This group is our main source of information about the range of documents owned by private persons as well as of the history of text ownership.

It is interesting to compare this range of texts with that found on ostraca. The most common literary texts on ostraca are the Middle Egyptian classics in the form of student exercises; but the only example of this genre in the archive is the *Satire on the Trades*. This suggests that the owners did not read the classics for pleasure. Qen-her-khepesh-ef's family did, however, collect stories in Late Egyptian, a genre which is poorly represented on ostraca. Of course, it must be remembered that the Qen-her-khepesh-ef family collection reflects the personal taste of its owners. Other villagers may well have collected Middle Egyptian literature; indeed, 'Menna's Letter' (No. 107 below) quotes two Middle Kingdom classics of which no copy has survived in the village, although they were clearly known to Menna.

Catalogue of texts in the Qen-her-khepesh-ef family archive

1. New Kingdom Literature

Tales

Tale of Horus and Seth	Ch.B. I
Tale of the Blinding of Truth	Ch.B. II

Poetry

The Chester Beatty Love Songs	Ch.B. I
Poem on the Battle of Kadesh	Ch.B. III

Instruction text

Maxims of Any (extracts)	Ch.B. V
Miscellany texts	Ch.B. IV, V, XVIII
Satirical letter of Pap Anastasi I	Ch.B. XVII

2. Middle Egyptian Literature

Satire on the Trades	Ch.B. XIX

3. *Religious texts*

Hymn to the Nile	Ch.B. V
Other hymns	Ch.B. IV, XI
Ritual of Amenophis I	Ch.B. IX
Book of invocations	Ch.B. VIII–IX
Book of protection	Ch.B. IX

4. *Medical texts*

Treatise on ailments of the anus	Ch.B. VI

5. *Magical texts/self-help texts*

Spells	Ch.B. V–VII, XI–XIII, XVI; P DeM 1; Geneva P. MAH 15274
Magico-religious	Ch.B. VIII
Magico-medical	Ch.B. XV
Book of aphrodisiacs	Ch.B. X
Spell incorporating the myth of Isis and Re	Ch.B. XI
Dream book	Ch.B. III

6. *Non-literary documents*

official letters	Ch.B. III
private letters	P DeM III–XVI, XVIII
private accounts	P DeM II, VII, XIII, XVII
wills and testaments	Naunakhte I–V
official records	Ch.B. XVI, Geneva P MAH 15274

99. The Amen-nakhte Family Archive

Although we have few other literary texts on papyrus, we can be confident that further collections once existed. For example, we happen to know that the descendants of the scribe Amen-nakhte owned papyri which they kept in the village even after the villagers had moved to Medinet Habu. One of these descendants, Djehuty mose, mentions them in a letter to his son Butehamun. At the time of writing, the villagers had moved to Medinet Habu, but the family continued to store their documents near the abandoned village. The sense of the extract below is not crystal clear—we do not know whether the documents in the chamber of the stairs (if that is the correct translation) were the same as those that were exposed to the rain—but we can at least be confident that some of the family papyri were deposited in the tomb of Amen-nakhte. This recalls the Qen-her-khepesh-ef family archive, which was also found in a hiding place next to a pyramid tomb.

The Amen-nakhte family archive has not been recovered. Perhaps the later members of the family eventually moved the texts out of the village.

Now, you wanted to question that I was concerned about the matter of the documents that were lying in the chamber of the stairs (?). As for the documents onto which it rained in the chamber of Hori-sheri, my ancestor, you brought them outside, and we found that (they) were not erased. I said to you, 'I will unbind them again.' You brought them down, and we deposited them in the tomb of Amen-nakhte, my ancestor. You wanted me to be concerned!

100. Collecting Texts

Although the Book of the Dead was bought and sold as part of the funerary equipment, perhaps even by individuals who could not read, there is no evidence from Deir el-Medina that copies of other written works were available on the market. An individual interested in having a particular text would presumably find someone who owned a copy and transcribe that for himself. This is probably the situation reflected in the following letter:

To the scribe Nefer-hotep in l.p.h, in the favour of your noble god, Amen-Re, King of Gods, who makes you happy every day.

Further: If you have not written on the papyrus roll, send it to me. I am eager for it. See, I have found this bookroll in the possession of this man! Or else write to me about what you are going to do.

Fare you well in the presence of Amen.

INSTRUCTION TEXTS

101. P Chester Beatty IV

The *verso* of Papyrus Chester Beatty IV from the Qen-her-khepesh-ef family archive bears a pastiche of moral maxims, a model letter, and a disparaging description of the soldier's life. Much of this material is fairly routine, but sandwiched among the conventional moral maxims are several unique and strikingly original passages on the value of education and scholarship. The miscellany-type context of the excerpts suggests that they were intended for students, although the contents are more sophisticated than most student exercises.

A. The Love of Learning

The following tribute to learning is unique; it differs from eulogies of the scribal profession found in the Miscellanies or the Instruction Texts in that it celebrates authorship, the creation of texts, rather than mere writing skills and knowledge of the classical literature. Moreover, where the Miscellanies hold out to students the incentives of easy work and good pay, the extract translated below stresses the fame that comes to an author after death, that is, it appeals to the great Egyptian aspiration for immortality.

The extract is rounded off by a list of celebrated authors which perhaps reflects the works familiar to an educated person. Several of these writers are not represented in the student exercises and would presumably have been encountered in advanced 'private reading'. For example, Ptah-hotep, the author of an early instruction text is known from a few ostraca that, judging from their rarity, did not belong to the basic curriculum. This is a further indication that some workmen read Middle Egyptian classics for pleasure and not merely for training.

BUT NOW, IF YOU HAVE DONE THESE THINGS, YOU ARE versed in writings. As for the learned scribes from the time that came after the gods—those who foretold the things to come—their names endure for ever, although they have gone, having completed their lifetimes, and all their relatives are forgotten.

THEY DID NOT MAKE FOR THEMSELVES pyramids of copper with stelae of iron. They were not able to leave an heir in the form of children [who would] pronounce their names, but they made for themselves an heir of the writings and instructions they had made.

THEY APPOINTED FOR THEMSELVES [the book as a lector] priest, the writing board as a beloved son. Instruction texts are their pyramids; the reed-brush is their child; a stone surface (their) wife. Both great and small are made his children, for the scribe, he is their chief.

GATES AND CHAPELS WERE MADE FOR (THEM); they have crumbled. Their mortuary priest is [gone] while their stelae are covered with dirt and their graves forgotten. But their name is pronounced on account of their writings which they made when they were (alive). The memory of what they did will be good for ever and eternity.

BE A SCRIBE! PUT IT IN YOUR HEART, so that your name will fare thus. A papyrus roll is more useful than an engraved stela, than a con-structed chapel wall.[a] These (i.e. papyrus rolls) act as chapels and pyramids for the sake of pronouncing their name. Certainly, (one's) name in the mouth of men is a useful thing in the necropolis!

A MAN HAS PERISHED and his corpse is dirt; all his relatives have crumbled to dust. The book is what causes him to be remembered in the mouth of the reciter. A papyrus roll is more useful than a constructed house, than tomb-chapels in the West; better than a constructed mansion, or than a stela in the temple.

IS THERE ONE HERE LIKE HORDEDEF? Is there another like Imhotep? There have been none among our relatives like Neferty or Khety, the foremost of them. I shall let you know the name of Ptahemdjedhuty and Khakheperreseneb. Is there another like Ptahhotep or Kaires, either?

THOSE SAGES WHO FORETOLD THE FUTURE, that which came forth from their mouth happened. One benefited from (it) as a saying written in his books. The children of others are given to them as heirs, like their own children. They concealed their magic from all men, (but) it is read in their instructions. Departure caused their name to be forgotten; writings are what cause them to be remembered!

   [a] i.e. the literary memorial is more lasting than the solid one.

B. Can Wisdom be Taught?

In this further extract from Chester Beatty IV the author advances a theoretical protest on the part of his reader that a human nature is fixed and cannot be improved through teaching, only to reject it utterly. The same question of whether wisdom can be taught is explored more fully in the epilogue of another New Kingdom instruction text, the *Maxims of Any*, where father and son dispute the issue at some length. It is not quite clear whether the author of our text presents any grounds for his view that education can alter nature; possibly he argues that an individual life span is too short to build up the experience that makes one wise—one must rely on the accumulated wisdom of the ancestors. On the other hand, the remark about the shortness of life may belong to the imaginary objection to the teaching—life is too short for change.

I have spread out an instruction for you; I have shown [you] the path of life; I have set you on a painless road, ⟨in⟩ a palisade which protects against the crocodile; a good and pleasant light, a shade without heat. May you carry it out (i.e. the instruction), so that your name will be recognized when you reach the Other Side.

   Beware lest you say, 'Every man is according to his character, ignorant and wise alike; destiny and fortune are graven on the character in the writing of god himself.' Every man lives his lifetime in the space of an hour. Teaching is good—there is no tiring of it—so that the son may answer with the sayings of his father. I have made you know the truth in your heart. (But) do what is correct in your view.

102. *Instruction of Amen-nakhte*

It is very rare indeed that we know anything about the authors of Egyptian literary works, but a number of compositions from the village are explicitly said to be by members of the gang—in some cases well-documented villagers. The question is whether these attributions are to be taken literally or whether the supposed author was in fact a mere copyist of someone else's work.

The following composition is one of those that can confidently be attributed to a local author, the scribe of the Necropolis Amen-nakhte. His name appears in the opening line of all six extant copies—not at the end, where a copyist would sign his work—and one example also mentions his assistant, Hor-Min, the son of Amen-nakhte's colleague Hori. If the other five works signed by Amen-nakhte were also his own compositions, he was the most prolific of the known writers in the village (see Nos. 106, 112, and 113, below). In contrast, Amen-nakhte left behind almost no physical monuments and his tomb cannot be identified, although he was one of the most powerful men in the village. It is as though he had taken to heart the Instruction of P. Chester Beatty IV (above No. 101), 'a papyrus roll is more useful than a constructed house, than tomb-chapels in the West . . . or than a stela in the temple'. The copy below was probably drawn up by a student as it ends with a date and this may be true of all six copies, which are all on ostraca; Amen-nahkte's composition may therefore be said to have entered the literary canon in the village.

The Instruction is a literary exercise, a flowery exhortation to heed his words of wisdom. The few actual guidelines offered at the end of the text advise Hor-Min to be concise, to be patient, and not to speak until he is spoken to—all elements of conventional Egyptian wisdom.

Beginning of the educational instruction,
sayings for the path of life,
made by the scribe Amen-nakhte
(for) his assistant Hor-Min.
He says: You are a man who listens to words
so as to separate good from bad;
Pay attention and hear my words,
do not disregard what I say!

Sweet, sweet it is to find a man
who is skilled in every pursuit.
Let your heart be like a great dike,
beside which the water is raging.
Accept my statement in all its import;
do not be reluctant to observe (it).
Look with your (own) two eyes to every profession
and to everything executed in writing;
then you will know the way and that it is excellent,
the pronouncement I made to you.
Do not neglect (my) words
or my character.
A long report is out of place.
Let your heart be patient in its haste.
May you speak after you are (*lit.* he is) called.
Then you will be a scribe and you will pass through the House of
    Life.[a]
Become like a chest of writings!
[. . . month] of winter [day . . .]

[a] A temple institution combining the functions of a school and a scriptorium.

103. Instruction of Hori

Hori's instruction, like Amen-nakhte's is basically an exhortation to become a scribe, but where Amen-nakhte announces the excellence of the
scribal profession in general terms, Hori stresses the tangible and immediate benefits of learning. He points to the student's father to illustrate the
advantages of a good education, namely, respect from the man in the
street, a long life, and a good income. Neither the student nor his father are
identified in the text. It seems unlikely that Hori is addressing his own son
and that the father described in the third person is none other than himself.
If Hori's pupil is indeed the son of someone else, then this instruction text
is unique in holding up a specific third person as a role model to be
emulated. Bickel and Mathieu suggest that Hori was teaching his namesake
Hori-sheri (i.e. Hori Junior), the son of the scribe of the Necropolis Amen-
nakhte; as mentioned above, Amen-nakhte was a much admired author as
well as an important official and fits Hori's portrait of a distinguished and
prosperous scribe to a tee.

The text is not provided with verse-points, but the scribe begun each new
verse on a new line, as in a modern poem. (The same is true of No. 105
'Thou Shalt Not', below.)

Fig. 22. Drawing of a scribe or draughtsman wearing a curled wig and an elegant pleated tunic of which only the sleeve is visible (O DeM 2057). The skilled artist who drew this piece was representing himself or a colleague, and the figure is in marked in contrast to that of a simple stonecutter in Fig. 25. (Reproduced with the kind permission of the IFAO in Cairo from J. Vandier d'Abbadie, *Catalogue des ostraca figurés de Deir el Médineh*. DFIFAO II (Cairo, 1937), pl. LXVI.)

Beginning of the educational instructions made by the scribe Hori,
    saying:
Set your heart to writing very, very greatly;
(it is) an excellent office for the one who executes it.
Your father possesses the hieroglyphs,
and he is shown respect in the street.
He does well possessing it, his years are (plentiful) like sand;
he is well-provided during his day on earth
until he reaches the Other Side.
Be a scribe, that you might become like him;

so that the strength of your w[ealth] may be plentiful for you.
[. . .]
Your name will become like his name;
you will receive [. . .] of your father, without [. . .]
You will be happy on earth.

104. The Fate of the Unmindful Son

The following little text prevents a variant on a common theme of student exercises, namely that the pupil who refuses to learn will end up in some sort of manual labour, the miseries of which are described in humorous detail. The opening line evidently appealed to the father-teachers of the village, and the text is known from eight copies. On the other hand, the fate of towing ships held out as a warning must have seemed rather far-fetched to the young villagers who grew up in the desert.

Come, let me tell you the miserable occupations of the maladroit fool who does not listen to the instruction of his father to become an excellent scribe: He is in the boat and he is handed over to the cable on his head and to the water. He has become one with the crocodiles and the hippopotami. Every man is dragging for himself; [. . .] arrives [. . .]

105. Thou Shalt Not . . .

Although the following instruction takes the form of a series of injunctions, each paired with an explanation or elaboration, its outlook is sanguine rather than negative. Because the future is uncertain, one should not waste effort on planning for tomorrow; but neither should one boast about youth or strength which could disappear in an instant. The reader is urged to help the people near him from whom he may someday need help in return, and to play down their imperfections and minor transgressions. Hard work, generosity, modesty, and forbearance are the themes of this sanguine text.

Do not be afraid today about tomorrow before it has come; yesterday is not like today in the hands of god.
Do not ridicule an old man or an old woman when they are bent double with age; beware lest they [place a curse] on your old age.
Do not satisfy another woman while your mother has nothing; it shall be heard by [. . .]

Do not straighten what is crooked—may you do what is loved; every man is drawn to his own character as to his limbs.[a]

Do not boast of your strength while you are young; your tomorrow may be found to be bitter fruit on [your] lips.

Do not take a great bite of the property of the king, lest [. . .] swallow you yourself.

[. . .] the palace, l.p.h., instructs [. . .]

Do not spare your limbs when you are young; food will come through the hands and provisions through the legs.

Do not boast of property which is not yours; next it will be stealing and transgressing commands.

Do not raise up (magnify) a crime which has become a small thing; a mast lying down looks like a foot.

Do not raise up a small crime, lest it grow large; a shipwright can raise it up like a mast.

Do not prepare a plan for tomorrow when it has not yet come; it is today until tomorrow comes.

Do not ignore your neighbours on days when they are in need, so that they will serve you in your [need].

Do not celebrate without your neighbours, so they will attend to mourning you on the day of burial.

Do not boast of grain at the time of ploughing; one shall see on the threshing floor [. . .]

Do not be unyielding in fighting with your neighbours; your supporters [. . .]

[. . .] vigilant to know [. . .]

[a] Perhaps, do not try to correct people's flaws because they like themselves as they are.

SATIRICAL LETTERS

The following two compositions belong to a well-established literary genre of the reproachful letter from a scribe to his errant apprentice or colleague, usually in a highly exaggerated, humorous tone. The most famous example of the genre is Papyrus Anastasi I, which takes advantage of the format to list innumerable words and toponyms that the incompetent scribe does not know—and which the copyist therefore learns. The two examples from Deir el-Medina are preserved in only a single copy each, so they may have been written for pleasure rather than used as school texts.

106. Amen-nakhte's Letter

That this letter is a literary composition and not a real communication is clear from the verse-points and the signature of the scribe Amen-nakhte son of Ipuy. As Bickel and Mathieu point out, the unusual expression 'Look with your (own) two eyes' occurs also in the *Instruction of Amen-nakhte*, an indication that the letter was indeed composed by and not merely copied by the same scribe.

> Oh, you who are greater than me,
> you who are confident
> and say, 'I am a somebody!'
> your heart is a monument of 30 cubits,
> (but) your body is like a cord.[a]
> What joy it is to you that your name is called,
> and you fly off in haste;
> (but) you make the journey of a mill-stone,
> you go around like a transport ship.
> It is only when he makes a bad name for himself
> that one such as you is famed!
> Look with your own two eyes, you yourself,
> while you act as the one who is there.[b]
> (By) the scribe of the Necropolis Amen-nakhte,
> the son of Ipuy.

[a] Thin and limp?
[b] Perhaps comparable to the expression, 'the servant there', a humble reference to self.

107. Menna's Letter

This literary composition takes the form of a letter from the draughtsman Menna to his son, Pa-iry, lamenting the latter's wayward life. It is best known for its allusions to two Middle Egyptian classical texts, the *Tale of the Shipwrecked Sailor* and the *Tale of the Eloquent Peasant*, both of which are otherwise unattested in copies from this period; Menna's letter is, in fact, the only evidence that these were remembered after the end of the Middle Kingdom. Certainly neither story was used as a school text in the village, suggesting that Menna studied them on his own, for pleasure. As the letter translated here attests, he was not only well-read, but also a accomplished author in his own right.

It happens that we know a considerable amount about Menna and his son. As a draughtsman, Menna was not one of the local officials and did not receive higher pay than the other workmen, but was able to use his artistic talents to make substantial sums on the side. His name occurs frequently in economic transactions and in legal disputes that arose when his partners failed to live up to their part of the bargain. His son's real name was Mery-Sekhmet, Pa-iry being a nickname. The boy is well documented as a wild young man about town, frequently getting into trouble.

Menna's composition differs from other examples of the abusive letter in several respects. First, it is more serious—Pa-iry is said to be lost almost without hope of deliverance and Menna's tone is despairing rather than chiding. There does not seem to be any attempt at raillery. Second, the piling up of quotations is unusual. Menna quotes not only the two Middle Kingdom classics, but also unspecified 'proverbs and the discourses', although the quotation from the *Eloquent Peasant*, at any rate, is not apt (Pa-iry is identified with the worthy peasant, although the rest of the text paints him as a scoundrel). And finally, it is surprising to find a man composing a highly literary piece, a showpiece, the theme of which was the failings of his own son.

The draughtsman Menna
speaks to his son, his assistant,
the scribe Pa-iry:
The storm was foretold to you before it had come,
my sailor, wretched in mooring.
I set words of all sorts
before you; but, look, you did not listen.
I pointed out every path
where the crocodile was in the undergrowth,
saying, if you go without sandals,
would not every thorn bring you back?
I looked after you in everything
that other people seek out;
I did not allow you to say 'if only!' in the night,
while you lay tossing and turning.
You are on the wanderings of the swallow
with her fledglings.
You have reached the Delta in the great migration.
You have mingled with the Asiatics,
having eaten bread with your blood.[a]

Your sense is no longer with you,
Rover! Sea-wanderer!
Would that I might report about you that I had saved (you);
'You have come and entered your village;
you brought water for your stone.'[b]
I have said in my heart, he has forgotten the words
that I spoke to him before.
I shall speak to you again!
'Remove yourself (from) the enclosure of the crocodiles',
[say] the proverbs and the discourses,
'in speech, in name, in action.' The boat before you does likewise.
If it capsizes ⟨in⟩ a great storm,
they will speak to you with the roaring of lions,
while you are alone.
[. . .]
'If the son obeys the father
(it is) a great instruction for eternity,' they say.
But, look, you have not heard any instruction
that I spoke to you before.
You turned away and sailed without heeding me;
you demolished the planks,
you strode freely to plunder the watery depths,
and (now) you are in the water of your sailing.[c]
Who will say to the little boat,
'Go (over) the rough seas'?[d]
Look, you sink in the abyss of the deep—
I do not know how to save you!
Look, I have brought a thorn of one cubit,
instructing the drowning one.[e]
But it is impossible to recount.
You are in the situation of the one who says,
'You kill me, my asses are taken away,
and complaint is seized from my mouth.'[f]
You truss the one who seizes your goods.[g]
You are helpless before me;
other helplessness is magnified
when it acts without me.
Look, may you turn to consideration of my words;
you will find my counsels to be effective.
Attend to heeding my instruction,

to carrying out my every counsel.
I allowed you to forget them all together—
you became like a *weneb*-plant.[h]
The one like me is not very great
although he equips you with a house;
but, indeed, a man like you is found
to allow the ignorant [. . .] to act,
and you have become like one on horses,[i]
although [your] heart is with me.
You shall guard this letter; it will be an instruction.

[a] A symbolic act to establish blood-brotherhood. See Jaroslav Černý, 'Reference to Blood Brotherhood among Semites in an Egyptian Text of the Ramesside Period', *JNES* 14 (1955), 161–3.

[b] These lines may refer to the ritual of 'pouring water' for a deceased person, in this case a relative since it is said to take place inside the village. Menna wishes that he could report that Pa-iry was at home, carrying out his family duties. On 'pouring water' at Deir el-Medina, see K. Donker van Heel in *Village Voices*, 19–30.

[c] Perhaps, 'a bed of your own making'?

[d] Because a little boat is not suited to rough waters.

[e] Very obscure. Menna may mean that his efforts to instruct Pa-iry have only brought him pain, a thorn in his flesh.

[f] i.e. one who has been robbed of everything, even the right to complain. The quote is from the *Tale of the Eloquent Peasant*.

[g] Very obscure; I have no explanation.

[h] An unidentified flower or plant.

[i] One who gallops around, out of control?

<h2 style="text-align:center">STORIES</h2>

108. *The Blinding of Truth*

The *Tale of the Blinding of Truth*, like the magnificently preserved tale of Horus and Seth, is recorded on a papyrus belonging to the Qen-her-khepesh-ef family archive. The two tales have some striking similarities, including fraternal conflict and a series of legal disputes before the Ennead, but the *Blinding of Truth* is explicitly an allegory of Truth and Falsehood, right and wrong.

The first part of the tale, some of which is lost, describes how Falsehood used an outrageous lie to prosecute his elder brother Truth for theft. The Ennead sentenced Truth to be blinded and made him doorkeeper of Falsehood's house; but Falsehood, still unsatisfied and enraged by his brother's virtue, ordered Truth's own slaves to throw him to the lions. In

true folk-tale style, they yielded to his entreaties to spare his life and merely
reported to Falsehood that Truth was dead. The hero was discovered lying
under a hillock by the servants of a wealthy lady who brought him to her
house. Struck by his beauty, she slept with him that night and conceived a
boy. The extract takes up here. Needless to say, the son of Truth triumphs
over Falsehood in the end.

> Now many days after this,
> she gave birth to a son
> whose like did not exist in the entire land.
> [He was] tall [. . .];
> he resembled a divine child.
> He was sent to school
> and learned to write very well.
> He mastered all the military arts,
> and he surpassed his older companions
> who were at school
> with him.
> Then his companions said to him:
> 'Whose son are you?
> You have no father!'
> And they tormented him (*lit.* you)
> and mocked him (*lit.* you):
> 'Hey, you have no father!'
> Then the boy said to his mother,
> 'What is the name of my father,
> that I may tell it to my companions?
> Indeed, they quarrel with me
> —"Where is your father?" they say to me—
> and they mock me.'
> Then his mother said to him,
> 'Do you see this blind man
> sitting beside the door?
> He is your father.'
> So she said to him.
> Then he said to her,
> 'You deserve to have your family gathered
> and a crocodile summoned.'
> And the boy brought his father,
> sat him down in a chair
> and placed a footstool under his feet;

he set food before him
and let him eat
and let him drink.
Then the boy said to his father,
'Who blinded you?
I will avenge you!'
He said to him,
'My younger brother is the one who blinded me.'
And he told him
everything that had happened to him.

The tale goes on to describe the boy's revenge on his uncle Falsehood. By tempting his uncle to steal a beautiful ox, the boy obtains an excuse to take him to court before the Ennead. At first he gives an outrageously exaggerated description of the wonders of his ox, parallel to the lie that Falsehood had told earlier. When the latter protests, the son quickly reveals his real purpose; to avenge his father. Falsehood then condemns himself, in effect, by swearing that Truth is dead, a claim that is easily refuted, and the penalties invoked in Falsehood's oath are inflicted upon him.

109. *Khonsu-em-heb and the Ghost*

The following short tale, the beginning and end of which are missing, is set in the villagers' own world of the Theban necropolis and the temple of Amen across the river. It concerns a High Priest's encounters with the unhappy ghost (an *akh-* spirit; see No. 76) of a Middle Kingdom official whose tomb had decayed. The High Priest promised to provide a new burial and revive his offerings, and despite the ghost's initial scepticism, he appears to have been true to his word.

The most complete text of the tale was inscribed on a series of large pots. Posener was able to reassemble the surviving fragments of two of the series, and noted that the lower edge of one pot was marked 'second' while the group for 'third' was written on the base of the other. Evidently the pots were 'paginated', and there was originally a 'first' and presumably at least a 'fourth' pot, both now lost. The assembled fragments of the 'third' pot measure 0.85×0.85 m. so that the complete vessel may have been a metre in height as well as in diameter. This seems an extraordinarily clumsy medium for a long work of fiction, but remarkably, fragments from a second copy of the same text also came from large pots. The duplicate text was marked 'second' and 'third' at the very same points as the other copy, suggesting that both copyists were working from the same original on papyrus, transferring each column of text to its own pot.

One of the two copies of the text is verse-pointed and the other is not. The translation below is presented in prose throughout.

[. . . according to] his plan [. . .] according to the plan that had been made [. . . He ferried] over and he reached his house, and ordered [. . . saying, 'I will bring] every good thing [when I go] to the West.' He went up to [his] roof [and he spoke to the] gods of heaven and the gods of earth—south, north, west, and east—and the gods of the necropolis, saying to them, 'Send to me this august spirit!' And he (the spirit) came and said to him, 'I am your [. . . companion whom you met (?)] at night next to his tomb.'

THEN the High Priest of Amen Khonsu-em-heb [said to him, 'Please tell me your name, the name of] ⟨your⟩ father and the name of your mother, so that I may offer to them and do for them everything suitable [to those of their character.'

Then the] august spirit said to him, 'My name is Niut-bu-semekh; my father's name is ꜥAnkh-men, and my mother's name is It-em-shaset.'

THEN the High Priest of Amen-Re, king of gods, Khonsu-em-heb said to him, 'Tell me what you desire so that I may have it done for you, and I will (also) let a [new] burial be prepared for you and let a coffin of gold and *zizyphus*-wood be made for you, and you shall [see its beauty (?)]; I shall let there be done for you everything suitable to one of [your character.'

Then the august spirit] said to him, 'There is no warmth for [the one who] is naked to the winds in winter, who hungers, without food [. . .] It is not my desire to flow like the inundation, without [. . .], without seeing [. . .], without reaching it. Say [. . .]'

Now AFTER (he) finished speaking [. . . Then the High Priest of Amen-Re, king of gods,] Khonsu-em-heb sat and wept beside him, with a face [full of tears, and he addressed the] spirit, saying ['How miserable are these spirits], without eating, without drinking, without age, without youth, without the sight of the sun's rays, or the smell of the north wind. Darkness is in [their] eyes every day, and they shall not rise in the morning to depart!'

Then the spirit said to him, 'When I was alive on earth, I was Overseer of the Treasury of King Mentuhotep, and I was lieutenant of the army, I being foremost among men and (just) behind the gods. I went to rest in Year 14—in the summer months—of King Mentuhotep, l.p.h., and he gave me my four canopic jars and my sarcophagus of alabaster. He ordered for me all that was suitable to one of my character, and he laid me to rest in my tomb, its shaft being 10 cubits (deep). Look, the ground beneath it is [decayed] and fallen away; the wind makes a fluttering and it seizes the tongue.[a] Now as for the speech you made to me, "I will have a new burial made for you," it is the fourth time for me that they (the promises) will be acted on. Now, what can I do with these things that are said to me (yet) again, so that all of these words will come to pass?'

Then the High Priest of Amen, King of Gods, Khonsu-em-heb said to him, 'Please give me a good commission worthy of carrying out for you,[b] and I will have it done for you; or I will (simply) let five men and five women slaves be dedicated to you to pour libations for you,[b] and I will give a sack of emmer daily to be offered for you, and it will be the Overseer of (Ritual?) Things who will pour libations for you.'

Then the spirit Niut-bu-semekh said to him, 'What is the point of the things you will do? Does not a tree grow in sunlight? And does it not produce branches? Stone does not grow as it ages; it crumbles to [. . .]'[c]

. . . (*gap of uncertain length*) . . .

[. . .] Mentuhotep, l.p.h. [Then the High Priest of] Amen-Re, king of gods, Khonsu-em-heb [summoned] three men, each [. . .] and he ferried across and he went up [and instructed them to search] beside the holy temple of King Neb-hepet-Re [l.p.h. Son of Re Monthuhotep] l.p.h.[d] And they [found . . .] in it, at a distance of [. . .] 25 cubits from the royal causeway of Deir el-Bahri.

Then they went down to the riverbank and they [ferried across to tell the High Priest] of Amen-Re, King of Gods, Khonsu-em-heb, and they found him [at] his duties in the temple of Amen[-Re King of Gods]. And he said to them, 'Ha! You have come back after finding the excellent place for making the name [of this spirit Niut-bu-semekh], as he is called, endure for all eternity!'

Then the three men said with one voice, 'We have found the excellent place for [making the name of this august spirit endure!'] And they sat before him and made holiday, while his heart became joyful because of what they had said [. . .]

The sun arose from the horizon. Then he summoned the deputy of the estate of Amen, Monthu-Kau [. . .] about his project. He came in the evening to spend the night in Thebes, and he [. . .]

(*The rest of the tale is lost.*)

[a] An obscure passage.

[b] Here, and several times further on, the text has 'me' where 'you' is clearly meant.

[c] Perhaps the spirit means that the libations will be no good to him if his tomb is not repaired.

[d] The funerary temple of Mentuhotep at Deir el-Bahri, south of the later funerary temple of Hatshepsut.

110. Love Songs

All the known love songs from Pharaonic Egypt come from Deir el-Medina except the cycle of verses on Papyrus Harris 500 (which is said to have been found in the Ramesseum). This is not so very surprising because this intimate genre was presumably produced and transmitted within settlement sites, most of which are lost. On the other hand, the distribution of texts within the workmen's village is unexpected; two groups of love songs are preserved on a papyrus and the rest occur on ostraca. The so-called Cairo Love Songs, translated here, were in fact written on a very large pot, 36.5 cm. high and 43 cm. in diameter, over an effaced copy of the *Instruction of a Man for his Son*. The same type of surface was used for the tale of *Khonsu-em-heb and the Ghost* (No. 109). Such bulky copies could hardly be kept for long periods and indeed we know that the pot was broken and scattered during the site's occupation—some fragments were found in the Great Pit, the community's dump, and others above ground. Similarly, the love songs on ostraca were presumably also for casual and temporary enjoyment since verses on fragments of stone are not conveniently stored. It is striking that there is no duplication of even a single text, so that there does not seem to have been a canon of classics. On the other hand, one example bears a month-and-day date typical of student exercises; this means at least one tutor felt the genre significant enough for instruction.

In contrast to the examples on ostraca, the songs on Papyrus Chester Beatty I in the library of the Qen-her-khepesh-ef family were kept for several generations. The collection is headed 'The beginning of the sweet sayings found in a book container, copied by the scribe of the Necropolis Nakhte-Sobek'. However, Nakhte-Sobek, a carpenter who used the title scribe by virtue of his ability to write, had erased a portion of the existing text to insert his own name, and was therefore an owner but not the copyist of the manuscript. He in turn gave the text to a member of the Qen-her-khepesh-ef-family, probably his friend, the workman Amen-nakhte. This gives some indication of the readership of the Love Songs.

The following extract is from the slightly less well known verses on the Cairo pot described above. The translation draws heavily on the work of M. V. Fox (see Notes).

First cycle
(*girl*)
[. . .] your love by day and night,
in the hours when I sleep
and when I wake at dawn;
[when the sun rises and] when it sinks (?).
I shall say, whenever [. . .]
Your grace animates the hearts;
your charm [. . .];
your voice rejuvenates [my] limbs [. . .]
like fat mixed with honey.
[No one else is] in balance with his heart,
except me alone.

Your love has joined to [me . . .
like a seal-ring (?)] to the finger [of a maiden (?). . . ;
like ointment (?)] to the limbs of princes;
like garments to the limbs of the gods;
like incense to the nose of [. . .]
It enters into [. . .]
It is like a mandragora in the hand of a man;
It is like the dates he mixes with beer;
It is like [beer] with bread.
We will [. . .]
We will (still) be together when the peaceful days of old age have
    come.
I will be with you every day,
offering [food to you like a maidservant] before her lord.

O my god! O my lotus!
[. . .] the north wind [. . .]
It is sweet to go in order to reach [. . .]
breath [. . .] flower [. . .]
I desire to go down
to wash myself before you.
I shall let you see my beauty in a tunic
of the finest royal linen,
soaked with cinnamon oil,
[pushing through] the reeds.
I will come down to the water with you;

and I will come out to you
carrying a red fish,
excellent on my fingers.
I will place it before you,
gazing [on your beauty].
My warrior! My brother!
Come and behold me!

(*boy*)
The love of my sister is on yonder shore.
The river surrounds my limbs;
the flood is mighty in the season [of . . .],
and the crocodile waits in the shoals.
I have gone down to the river
to wade through the waters,
my heart reckless in the channel.
I have found the crocodile to be like a mouse,
and the surface of the water like land to my feet.
It is love of her that makes me strong!
She shall cast a water spell for me.
I see my heart's love standing right before my face!

My sister has come!
My heart thrills, my arms stretch out to embrace her.
My heart is carefree in its place,
like a red fish in its fish-pond.
Oh night, you are mine for ever,
since (my) mistress has come to me.

I embrace her,
her arms are stretched out,
and I am like one who is in Punt.[a]
What is it like?
The rushes have come forth
at the proper time [to shield us?]
Her fragrance is the *iber*-balm.

I kiss her,
her lips are parted,
I am exhilarated without beer.

Oh, how the gap has been bridged!
Menket[b] is adorned here,
leading (me) together with [her]
[. . .] her bed.
Come here that I may speak to you!
'Place fine linen between her limbs,
spread the bed for her with royal linen,
attend to the embroidered white textiles.'
As for the *nekha* (*unknown word*) of her limbs [. . .],
her limbs are found to be
like something drenched in cinnamon oil.

Second cycle
Would that I were her Nubian slavegirl,
who is her companion in secret!
She would bring her (a bowl of) mandragoras [. . .]
and it would be in her hand while she was smelling it.
In other words,
she would grant me the complexion of her whole body!

Would that I were the washerman of (my) sister's clothes
for a single month!
I would be renewed by taking [the clothes . . .]
that were near her body,
and it would be I who washed out the ointment
that was in her kerchief.
I would wipe my limbs with her cast-off clothing (?)
and she [. . .]
[I would be in] joy and rapture;
[it would make] my body young.

Would that I were her little seal-ring,
which is the companion of her finger.
I would see her love every day.
[. . .] I [. . .]
[And it would be I] who stole her heart.

Would that I had a morning of seeing (her),
like one who spends her lifetime (doing this).[c]
Beautiful is the land of Isy;[d]
Brilliant is its craft!
Joyful is her mirror

Into which she gazes
[. . .]

Would that my sister were mine every day,
Like the greenery of a wreath.ᶜ
[. . .] the rushes are sunny,
the safflower blooms,
the *merbeb*-plants are fresh,
the blue plants and the mandragoras
have come forth
[. . . the flow]ers from Hatti ripen (?),
the fennel bloo[ms . . .]
[. . .]
the greenery and the willows,
when she is with me every day
like the greenery of a wreath.
All the flowers will flourish in the ground
[when she is mine] entirely.

Would that she might come
[so that I could] see [her!]
I would make festival to the god
who stops her from staying away.
May he give me my mistress daily!
She will not be absent from [me for ever].
If I spend a moment without seeing her,
I turn in my stomach [. . .]
Then I shall hasten to answer
[. . .]

[Would that . . .] his soul.
I shall honour him
in the deep of night,
I shall present offerings
[. . .]
May my heart go down to [its] place!
[. . .]

She [will ban]ish every evil from [my] limbs
[. . .] who seeks (my) sister,
so that I cannot approach her body.
May she exorcize [my illness?].

^a A land south of Egypt on the Red Sea which was the source of exotic luxuries.
^b Goddess of beer.
^c i.e. the mirror, which faces its owner every day.
^d A place from which copper and metalwork were imported.
^e The green branches of a wreath, which are intertwined.

Praise of Cities

One of the striking features of the New Kingdom was the growth of cities, reflected in a new genre of poetry celebrating the great cosmopolitan centres. Thebes with its splendid temples at Karnak and Luxor, its government offices and royal palaces, and the resulting concentration of wealth, was celebrated in several compositions, perhaps in conscious rivalry to similar praises of Memphis and Pi-Ramesse. The emphasis in the poems is on the abundance and luxury of the city, the splendour of its architecture, and the excitement generated by crowds and festivals.

iii. Longing for Thebes

This short poem focuses on the author's feelings for his home town rather than on the individual attractions of the city, though three local landmarks are mentioned.

> Behold, I do not want to depart from Thebes.
> Save me from what I abhor!
> Every time I leave on a journey,
> I travel north
> with the city beside me,
> with the Temple of Amen on my path (may I reach it!),
> Medamud before me,
> and Tenet Khonsu together with me
> in the boat of my mission.^a
> Bring me to your city, Amen!
> Because I love it;
> it is your city that I love,
> more than bread and beer, Amen,
> more than clothes and oil.
> (I) love the soil of your town
> more than the ointment of another land.

ᵃ Medamud was the cult centre of Monthu, 7 km. east of Karnak; Tenet Khonsu is unidentified.

112. Amen-nakhte's Praise of Thebes

Here we have another composition by the scribe Amen-nakhte (see No. 102). Like the author of the preceding piece, he imagines the feelings of those who are absent from Thebes, but his reflections are less personal and encompass also the envious inhabitants of other towns. Amen-nakhte is also more specific about the city's attractions. If the starred words (*), which are obscure, have the meaning given them here, he seems to be describing the viewing of processions; he then adds that the bread is better and the water sweeter than anywhere else. Amen-nakhte evidently considered himself to be a citizen of Thebes even though he lived several miles from the city proper.

> What do they say to themselves
> in their hearts every day,
> those who are far from Thebes?
> They spend the day
> dreaming (?) of its name, (saying)
> 'If only its light were ours!'
> Its windows are for
> the clothesless*,
> its boat-seats* are for the notables.
> The bread which is in it is more tasty
> than cakes made of goose fat.
> Its [water] is sweeter than honey;
> one drinks of it to drunkenness.
> Behold, this is how one lives in Thebes!
> The heaven has doubled (fresh) wind for it.

> The scribe of the Necropolis Amen-nakhte, son of Ipuy.

Hymns

113. Hymn on the Coronation of Ramesses IV

As Catherine Keller has demonstrated, Ramesses IV was deeply venerated by the workmen of Deir el-Medina, probably because in the second year of his reign the gang was expanded to 120 members. This meant that the sons of workmen were recruited to the gang and the community flourished. The workmen expressed their devotion by placing simple stelae honouring

Ramesses IV in the very tomb of Ramesses VI, his rival and the king who abruptly cut the gang back down to its former size. At least seven workmen also incorporated the name of this king in that of their children, such as, for example, the name Heka-Maʿat-Re-sekheper-djamu, 'Heka-Maʿat-Re nourishes the next generation'—a phrase which appears also in the hymn translated here. This hymn is yet another composition by the scribe Amen-nakhte, the author of Nos. 102, 106, and 112 above. There are no verse-points, but the repetitive structure of the clauses sets up an obvious pattern.

Oh happy day! Heaven and earth are in joy, (since) you are the
   great lord of Egypt!
Those who had fled are come back to their cities;
Those who were [hidden] have emerged;
Those who were hungry, they are sated and content;
Those who were thirsty are drunken;
Those who were naked, they are clad in fine linen;
Those who were dirty are radiant;
Those who were in prison, they have been released;
⟨Those⟩ who were hard pressed are joyful;
The troublemakers in this land, they have become peaceful;
High Niles have come forth from their caverns, to refresh the
   hearts of the people.
The widows, their houses are open; they allow travellers to enter.
The wet-nurses rejoice, singing their lullabies, since they are fitted
   with male children, babies of good delivery (?).
He nurtures the young generation! He nurtures the young
   generation!
Oh ruler, l.p.h., you will exist for ever and ever!
The boats, they rejoice on the water;
They have no ropes, (but) they are moored by the wind and the
   oars. They have done with storms, because of my Dual King,
   Heka-maʿat-Re Setep-en-Amen, l.p.h.—he has resumed the
   white crown!—Son of Re Ramesses—he has received the kingship of his father!
The whole of the Two Lands say to him,
'Beautiful is Horus on the throne of his father Amen-Re, the one
   who sent him, the protector of the ruler, l.p.h., who brings
   every land!'
Made by the scribe of the Necropolis Amen-nakhte in year 4, first
   month of inundation season, day 14.

114. Hymn of Transfiguration by Pa-nefer

The following spell is addressed to a dead person for the purpose of promoting his transfiguration into an *akh*, an effective spirit. Such spells were recited by lector priests as part of the funerary cult; they characteristically address the deceased directly, in the second person, and focus on the freedom of movement he will enjoy in the afterlife and on the blessings he will receive from the gods of the hereafter. This example is included here, rather than in Chapter 3 ('Religion') because it is signed by an individual whose name is unfortunately broken but appears to be Pa-nefer.

> Awake! May your heart be happy with delights,
> every evil being far from you!
> May you be alert as a living one,
> rejuvenated every day,
> healthy in millions of occasions of good sleep,
> while the gods protect you,
> protection being around you every day.
> No disorder approaches you,
> and the worm is punished[a]
> as something presented ⟨to⟩ you by *Iepet weret*.[b]
> Make protection!
> You are life, stability, and dominion.
> May the day be illuminated for the night;
> may the land be illuminated for you in health;
> may your feet tread every beautiful way;
> may you address the common people.
> Made by the scribe Pa-nefer (?).

[a] Presumably the snake Apophis, the enemy of Re in the underworld.
[b] The goddess of Luxor.

115. Praise of Amen by the Scribe Amen-mose

This little hymn is written by, or dedicated to, a certain Amen-mose who calls himself 'scribe' although, since no professional scribe Amen-mose is known, he is using the title here merely by virtue of his ability to read and write.

> [Rul]er of rulers,
> king of kings,
> the greatest of the great,

whose name is hidden[a] from men and gods;
you are [. . .] breath for the noses of the common people
[. . .] the entire land [see]s (?) the joy [. . .]
by (or for) the scribe Amen-mose [. . .] neferu.

[a] The word 'hidden', *amen*, is also the name of the god.

116. Appeal to Amen by Pa-gefy

This is probably a succinct variation on the appeal to Amen to support
the poor man in the law court against his wealthy and powerful opponents.
The author, Pa-gefy, says that he is the son of Kha-em-nun and Naunakhte,
but the famous will of Naunakhte and associated documents do not
name him among her children so he may have died before his parents.
He is unlikely to have been more than a stonecutter, like his father and
brothers.

Come [. . .] I am alone while they have their supporters, their helpers
and their lieutenants. Amen is mighty, the helper for the man
without a voice.

   Made by the scribe Pa-[g]efy son of Kha-em-nun. His mother is
Naunakhte.

117. Hymn to the Sun by Hor-Min

The main interest of this little hymn is that it was written by Hor-Min son
of Hori, who wrote the instruction text quoted above. Hor-Min was the
student of Amen-nakhte, the most prolific author known from the village.

Receive a (long) life, double blessedness,
enter into the praise of [. . .]!
My eyes follow the sun-disk,
who illuminates every path for me,
[. . .] for joy belongs to the one who sees the sun-disk.
My arms are in a position of adoration, my mouth is full of joy
[. . .] Atum,
That which is hidden is known to him,
lord of the deep,
whose body has the sight [. . .]
[. . .] necropolis, West of Thebes.
Hor-Min son of Hori, born to Is.

History

The workmen of Deir el-Medina were surrounded by monuments commemorating the kings and officials of old and, closer to home, by the tombs and memorials of their own ancestors; furthermore, like almost everyone else in West Thebes, their job was to secure the eternal existence of individual mortals. But how much did they know or care about the past? We must remember that the workmen's experience of the antiquity was different from ours in several fundamental ways. In the first place, the Egyptians did not have a linear dating system which automatically provided an orientation for historical events; to know when Amenhotep II lived, a workman would have had to consult a list of kings and the lengths of their reigns and add up the number of intervening years. Nor was it easy to tell the age of a monument by its appearance, since styles changed slowly and the aridity protected against decay. Secondly, the workmen experienced the ancient kings actively through their cults in the necropolis. Interest in these pharaohs is therefore often religious rather than historical.

Nevertheless, there is some evidence for historical awareness at Deir el-Medina, especially among the more learned members. For instance, works of fiction, including those used as student exercises, often had a historical setting which carried with it some information. Further evidence of an interest in the past is furnished by the two texts presented below.

118. King List

The distinctive handwriting of the following king list identifies it as the work of Qen-her-khepesh-ef, the scribe who founded the extensive library described above (No. 98). His list opens with the name of Ramesses II, the reigning king, followed by the kings of the New Kingdom in their proper order—of course with the exception of Queen Hatshepsut and the Amarna kings. As mentioned above, the kings were the objects of cults, but the fact that Qen-her-khepesh-ef placed them in chronological order demonstrates at least a knowledge of and probably also an interest in them as historical figures. The cartouches of Ahmose and Horemheb written side by side on the verso of the ostracon may be particularly significant from this point of view; Ahmose was regarded as the father of the New Kingdom—he is also the earliest king on the *recto*—and Horemheb is perhaps paired with him as the founder of a new Dynasty after the execrated Amarna kings.

recto

King Weser-ma'at-Re Setep-en-Re	(Ramesses II)
Neb-[pehty]-Re	(Ahmose)
Djeser-ka-Re	(Amenophis I)
A'o-kheper-ka-Re	(Thutmosis I)
A'o-kheper-en-Re	(Thutmosis II)
Men-kheper-[Re]	(Thutmosis III)
A'o-kheperu-Re	(Amenophis II)
Men-kheperu-Re	(Thutmosis IV)
Neb-Ma'at-Re	(Amenophis III)
Djeser-kheperu-Re Setep-en-Re	(Horemheb)
Men-pehty-Re [. . .]	(Ramesses I)
Men-Ma'at-Re [. . .]	(Seti I)

verso

Fourth month of summer day 2[1]. 20 [. . .]10 *bit*-cakes.
Fourth month of summer day 22. 1,000 units of firewood for the right side.

Djeser-kheperu-Re Setep-en-⟨Re⟩	(Horemheb)
(Neb)-pehty-Re	(Ahmose)

119. Historical Fiction

This fragment appears to belong to a type of story which draws its heros from the great kings of old. A more complete example of the genre is *The Capture of Joppa*, in which Djehuty, a official of Thutmosis III, directs a clever stratagem for taking that strategic city, reminiscent of the Trojan horse; the Egyptians, pretending to send provisions into the city, conceal a soldier in each of the enormous baskets going in. At night, these spring from their hiding places and open the gates to the pharaoh's army. Too little is preserved of this comparable story from Deir el-Medina to reconstruct the plot. In the legible portion of the text, translated here, Thutmosis III evidently finds himself on the brink of disaster on a battle-field. An individual called Pa-ser encourages him—something that would be very unusual in an official text, where the king needs no urging from mortals—and he rallies. Three manifestations of the war-god Monthu are sent to him in a wind, and together they rout the enemy. Here the text breaks off again.

'[. . .] before my face.
[He] will find [me?] like a bird pinioned
in the hand of a fowler who has learned his secret.'

NOW AFTER A LONG TIME,
Pa-ser the (son) of Ta-aʿotia (*fem.*) answered,
'Allow me to say,
take heart, king Men-kheper-Re, l.p.h.!
Behold, Amen-Re, King of Gods, your good father,
has come to you to do for you all that you desire.'
I found courage, my heart rejoicing.
All that I did became like Monthu.
Their horses became like Seth, great of strength,
like Baʾal in his hour,
when he shoots to the right
and captures to the left;
while I was acting with my hand to the south of Amen-Re, King
   of Gods.[a]
[. . .] may you let one of the hostile winds come to me,
in which there are three Monthu's,
hidden [. . .]
[. . .] gold:
with Monthu lord of Hermonthis (at) my right [hand],
Monthu lord of Armant at my [left hand;
and Monthu] lord of Thebes wiping them out
before king Men-kheper-Re, l.p.h.
I found that Amen had made [. . .]
great lions [. . .]
He fled headlong together with their chariotry (?) [. . .]
Men-kheper-Re l.p.h slew the [. . .] of the donkey of the chief of
   Syria [. . .]

   [a] 'To the south' perhaps relates to the way the army was drawn up.

5

Law

THE SOURCES

Most of the surviving legal records from Deir el-Medina were drawn up for individuals and most are on ostraca. They do not seem to have carried any particur legal weight in themselves but were kept primarily as reminders for future reference; at any rate, no such document is ever produced in the course of a later proceeding, though litigants are evidently drawing on their family archives when they cite names, dates and events from many years in the past and even several generations before their own. The function of these legal records is reflected in their contents. They are relatively laconic, concentrating on the plaintiff's statement of the case, the court's verdict, and the names of judges and witnesses; moreover, they generally concern private disputes over economic transactions or property, or property arrangements such as wills and testaments. Crimes against individuals such as murder, assault, and rape are hardly documented in our sources, not because they did not occur, but because no one had an interest in keeping a record of the event and its aftermath.

Official records *were* kept of everything to do with crimes against the state such as tomb robbery or embezzlement. These documents were stored in the mortuary temples or across the river in the city of Thebes, however, and not in the village; the local officials did not have the authority to deal with such cases, and as soon as they came to the attention of the vizier's office, the suspects were whisked off for interogation elsewhere. At most, the journal of the Necropolis and other local sources record the very earliest stages of an investigation, namely, the detection of the crime, the report to higher authorities, and the arrest of suspects, and very occasionally there is an incidental allusion to the fate of individual criminals. The official records of the interrogations and their outcomes are mostly lost, with the significant exception of the Great Tomb Robbery papyri which came, via the dealers, from the archives of the temple of Medinet Habu.

Principles of Judgement

120. Justice

Our texts contain nothing that could be called jurisprudence. The following rather pompous introduction to a record of a civil suit is one of the few explicit statements that the court was to be guided by the principles of Ma'at, a concept which embraces our notion of justice as well as correctness as opposed to mistakenness, and order as opposed to confusion.

Year 38, first month of inundation, day 3, in the reign of the dual king Weser-ma'at-Re Setep-en [Re, son of Re] Ramesses Mery-Amen (Ramesses II), given life for ever and eternity while Pre endures in heaven.

   Let the court of the Necropolis act in conformity with the laws of Ma'at! [. . .]

      the chief workman Ka-ha
      the scribe Ra-mose
      the scribe [. . .]

   This day of judging between Hori son of Mer-waset and the [chisel] bearer [. . .] (*remainder very fragmentary*)

121. The Litigant's Prayer

One genre of text that does comment on justice—or the lack thereof—is the appeal to the god Amn to help the poor litigant who is at the mercy of a corrupt legal system. The petitioner in these texts calls himself a *nemeh*, a lone man, one not bound to an institution and therefore without powerful connections; but these sophisticated literary compositions were collected by individuals who were neither poor nor powerless, and may be compared to Christian psalms which take the form of laments by the downtrodden and oppressed but are also sung by congregations including very few members of this description. It is therefore difficult to say that they reflect a perception of the court system as favoring the rich and powerful.

Amen-Re, the one who intercedes for the lone man when he is in distress, may he cause the court to be of one voice when they answer concerning the lone man! (So that) the lone man becomes justified and the one who carries gifts is grieved.

122. Laws and Precedent

Whether the Egyptians had 'laws' in the sense of explicit rules binding on the courts is a matter of continuing debate. The word *hep*, which is often translated 'law', could also be translated 'custom' in most cases and still make good sense. Only one legal text from the New Kingdom cites a *hep* by that name as a basis for the court's decision, and that is the case presented here. The same text is one of the very few to refer to a legal precedent (No. 144 is another example of this practice).

The text in question records an appeal to the oracle to decide a dispute over inheritance in the presence of the officials, who would presumably implement the god's decision. The speaker, who is identified on the verso of the papyrus as Huy, testifies that he provided for the burial of his mother, Ta-gemyt, by himself, without the help of his brothers and sisters. He argues that this entitles him to his mother's full estate, and in support of his claim he cites a *hep* of pharaoh saying, 'Let the property be given to the one who buries.' This does not shine much light on the nature of *hep*; it may be a special exception to the general rule that children inherit, decreed by the pharaoh, or it could be a general principle or custom of the country. Huy then refers to an earlier case in which the oracle gave the real property of a woman to the child who buried her, that of Ta-nehesy's son Sa-Wadjyt. Quite miraculously, this case history has also been preserved; it is now known as O Petrie 16 (*HO* 21, 1), and it dates to the very early Twentieth Dynasty, that is, only shortly before the date of the text translated here. Sa-Wadjyt's case would thus have belonged to recent memory.

List of the things [. ...] which he gave to the lady Ta-[gem]yt, his mother:
    1 burial place
after he had given her coffin to Pa-[tjau-em]-di-Amen, makes 40 *deben*.
    Again, what he gave to her:
    1 coffin for her burial
after he had provided a burial-place for Huy-nefer, his father.
    But look, the children of the lady Ta-gemyt contest this today in order to claim her property, although they did not bury their father, and although her children did not bury her herself. That which they

claim today is her property, although they did not bury together with my father when he buried his father and mother.

'Give the property to the one who buries,' so says the *hep* of Pharaoh. My good lord, l.p.h.! Look, I am in the presence of the magistrates—let the right thing be done!

Now, look, the place of Ta-nehesy was given to Sa-Wadjyt after (he) buried her, and he gave her his coffin. He was given her share in the presence of the magistrates, for it was King Amenophis who gave it to him in the court.

The Authorities and the Court

Three legal bodies had jurisdiction over legal matters in Deir el-Medina: the local court, the oracle of the deified Pharaoh Amenophis I, and the office of the vizier. Ultimately, all three represented the state and they naturally interracted closely with one another, with scribes from the vizier's office sitting on the court and local officials carrying out the orders of the oracle. Their areas of jurisdiction also overlapped with some exceptions; e.g. criminal cases were not tried in the village and questions concerning real property were reserved for the oracle or the office of the vizier. The mechanics of the local bodies are well documented, but, as noted above, the records of the vizier's office have not survived and we know much less about how legal questions were dealt with there.

The details of procedure in the local court, or *kenbet*, will be illustrated by the selections below, so only a brief introduction to the subject is necessary. The magistrates of the court (members of the court were collectively called *seru*, 'magistrates', whatever their rank in daily life) varied from sitting to sitting but almost always included one or more of the captains of the gang and often also outside officials such as scribes of the vizier or chief policemen. Simple workmen also sat on the court but supply staff, such as water-carriers, were never included among the judges. There is very little information about the relationship between the various members of the court, that is, whether their judgements all carried equal weight and whether they reached their verdict by majority decision or had to be unanimous. On the few occasions when a text identifies which of the judges questioned the litigants, it is the highest ranking member; this may indicate that he was a sort of president. On the question of how the judges arrived at their joint decision, one can only point to the prayer to Amen (No. 121 above) which expresses the hope that the court will be unanimous in its verdict for the powerless litigant, but this does not necessarily mean that unanimity was required.

The evidence presented in court is entirely oral; we never hear of litigants producing documents and the ostraca themselves do not appear to have had any evidentiary value. The court is sometimes said to question the litigants, and in a handful of cases, it also asks for witnesses to corroborate a particular point. It is in the nature of our documents, most of which were drawn up for successful plaintiffs, that they rarely report the testimony of the defendant, but they do sometimes record his denial of the charges under oath. Although an oath carried substantial weight in the village, it was not necessarily considered conclusive and in at least one case the court continued its enquiries even after the defendant had sworn (No. 144). Particularly in cases of interest to the state, such as those involving state property, the authorities might carry out investigations on the spot—at the site of a disputed tomb, for instance, or in the home of a suspect. What we never see at Deir el-Medina is examination of parties or witnesses under torture, a practice that may have been reserved to the higher authorities outside the village.

In general, the key characteristic of the court seems to have been its flexibility; there were no fixed rules of procedure that we know of. Neither does the court appear to have been bound by written laws. Presumably it was guided by custom and tradition, but there seems to have been room for equity as well; the many cases in which deadlines for payments by the defendant were extended may reflect equity-based judgements, as also the court's failure to carry out penalties when, strictly speaking, these were due.

123. Women on the Court

The court of the following text is unique in having two women among its members and probably also unique in including no officials. The subject matter of the dispute is largely lost, but it may be that the 'judges' were in effect merely witnesses to an oath. Whether this means women could in principle join the court or whether the term kenbet, 'court' itself is being used loosely is not clear.

Year 28, third month of winter, day 22. Court of this day:
   the workman Nakhte-Min
   the workman [Pen-ta]-weret
   the workman Nefer-hotep
   the lady [. . .]
   the lady Merut-Mut
The [work]man Weser-hat said, 'As Amen endures, as the [ruler]
endures, [. . .]'

124. The Use of Witnesses

Although written records do not seem to have been used as evidence, the
testimony of witnesses did carry legal weight in court. Hence the importance of carrying out transactions in the presence of reliable witnesses. In
this little text, a doorkeeper swears to be satisfied with the price of 50 *deben*
for his ox in the presence of Nefer-hotep, whom we know from other
sources to have been the watchman on duty that day. The court itself could
also serve as a notary to transactions, as for instance in the case of the
testament of Naunakhte (No. 14), which was reported in the court.

Year 25, third month of inundation day 13. Oath of the lord, l.p.h.,
sworn by the doorkeeper Kha-em-waset: 'As Amen endures, as the
ruler, l.p.h., endures, (the price of) this ox is 50 copper *deben*. I will
not contest it in the future.'
   Before the workman Nefer-hotep.

ENFORCEMENT OF THE VERDICT

125. Penalty for Non-Compliance

The standard oath in contracts and before the court when one party
promises to compensate another before a certain date names a penalty of
double payment and a beating for non-performance. The following text
provides a typical example. The courts, or perhaps the litigants themselves,
were slow to impose this penalty, however. There are no recorded instances
in which the double penalty was exacted, and blows were administered only
after repeated failures to pay, as in the next case below (No. 126).

Year 9, third month of winter, day 7. What the washerman Bak-en-
werl said: 'As Amen endures, as the ruler, l.p.h., endures, if I do not
(hand over) these 4 skeins of yarn to the workman Ptah-shed on the

third month of winter, day 10, I will get 100 blows and they will be reckoned against me double.'

126. Reluctant Enforcement

One of the most striking features of legal disputes at Deir el-Medina is that they could go on almost interminably; the same dispute could come before the court repeatedly over a period of up to eighteen years. This suggests the court's inablity or unwillingness to enforce its verdicts, or, alternatively, that the plaintiff himself was reluctant actually to demand punishment for his opponent. The longest-running cases were those in which the offender was of relatively high status like the chief policeman Monthu-mose; a water-carrier was more likely to pay the price of his failure to comply with the verdict. In the case translated here, the water-carrier Pen-niut had ignored four verdicts against him. He was finally taken before a special court of officials from inside and outside the village who carried out his punishment, presumably the standard '100 blows' invoked in the oath to pay.

Year 22, second month of winter, day 5. Court of this day:
   the 4 administrators of the interior
   the 4 administrators of the riverbank
The workman Kha-em-nun reported to them, saying, 'As for me, the water-carrier Pen-niut took my donkey together with her foal. They died in his possession. Now, I reported him in court four times; he was ordered to pay me for the donkey and the foal on all four, but he has not given me anything.'
   His testimony was heard. He said, 'This workman is right; I was indeed ordered to pay him.' Punishment was administered to him. He repeated the oath of the lord, l.p.h., once again, saying 'Pen-niut will make [. . .]'

verso
What he brought to me in year 22, second month of winter, day 26: $\frac{1}{4}$ sack of barley.

127. The Bailiff

Where it looked as though the losing party might refuse to comply with the court's instructions to compensate the plaintiff, the officials could send a messenger to his home to confiscate some appropriate items of property. This was not necessarily the end of the matter, however, since in at least two cases, the recalcitrant litigant resisted the messenger. It is not clear that the magistrates of Thebes who sent out the two messengers mentioned in the following extract from a letter were members of a court, but there is no doubt about the letter-writer's contempt for the agents of the authorities.

[. . . of the] protected [Necropolis], in l.p.h., (in the praise) of Amun-Re, King of Gods. I tell Sobek, Amen, Mut, and Khonsu to let you be healthy, to let you live, to let you be young, to let you have a long life and a great old age for ever and eternity.

To the effect that: The magistrates of Thebes sent two messengers, and they took hold of the donkey that you gave me. But I was stronger than them; I took it (back), and I am sending it to you via the scribe Ser-Amen.

Now look, look—I have a good donkey! Look, the best! And you shall accept it—indeed, its face is large—and do not seek a quarrel. But you should act for your own peace of mind, and do it well, doing the right thing. Look, it was in year 6, third month of summer, day 25 that I sent your donkey to you. Now, it was together with the other things that I was buying that I sent you the sack of grain.

Farewell.

THE ORACLE

Legal oracles at Deir el-Medina were delivered by the deified Amenophis I, the pharaoh who founded the workmen's community. On special occasions, his image was placed on a litter and carried in procession on the shoulders of eight priests. In principle, he could be asked about any matter at such times and many short questions addressed to the oracle survive, but only the legal consultations have been preserved at length. The god answered by moving, or rather, by making his bearers carry him in various directions—the statue itself did not make gestures or sounds. He moved backwards to express 'no' and forwards for a 'yes'; and, if various answers on ostraca were put on the ground in front of him, he moved towards the one he wished to choose. Probably he could also shake violently to express agitation. How it all 'really' worked has not been satisfactorily explained, but it is unlikely that the oracle was manipulated by the priests, who were simply workmen serving as lay officiants; the whole procedure also took place in public in the open air where such manipulations would have been detected. Quite possibly the bearers anticipated the god's answer and believed that he was directing them in one direction or another.

The oracle was asked to decide a variety of legal disputes, including some straightforward disagreements about economic transactions such as whether one villager had paid another as agreed. More often, it was asked to identify a thief, either because the petitioner did not know who had robbed him, or because he did not have enough evidence to come before the secular authorities. It was questions involving real property, however, that were the court's special domain. Almost every question about ownership of houses and tombs was submitted to the god rather than to the court, possibly because so much property in the village was state owned and thus did not fall under the jurisdiction of the local court. The two bodies worked closely together on these as in all matters; in many cases, the oracle almost seems to be used as a fact-finder by the civil authorities (Fig. 17).

128. The Oracle in Action

The following text provides some useful information about the use of a stela to publish a claim to a hut, but it is included here primarily to illustrate the oracle procedure. In this case, the petioner addressed the god directly with yes-or-no questions. The answer to the first question is an emphatic 'no', which the god expressed by moving backwards—or rather, by making his bearers carry him backwards. The question is then put to him again, but is now phrased so that the answer is 'yes'; the god moves forward in a gesture of concurrence. At the very end of the text, the god is said to 'say' something to one of the parties. This can hardly mean the statue was made to utter the words but is presumably shorthand for an answer elicited through yes-or-no questions like those that went before.

Year 27, first month of summer, day 19. This day, the workman Kha-em-waset reported to King Amenophis, l.p.h., s[aying, 'Come] to me, my lord! Judge between me and the workman Nefer-hotep. Shall [one] take the hut of Baki, my anscestor, that is in the Great Field (Valley of the Kings) on account of the share of Sekhmet-nofret, Oh, my Great Light?' And the god moved backwards emphatically. Then one said to him, 'Shall one give it to Kha-em-waset?' And the god moved forwards emphatically. Before:

the chief workman Khonsu
the chief workman [In]-her-khau
all the bearers
He (the god) [said to I]n-niut-ef, 'Do not enter the hut!'
    Calling to Amenophis, l.p.h., saying, 'Oh, my [Great] Light! [. . .]
Hori [. . .] a stela. He erected it in the hut upon [. . .] exactly.' And
the god said to him, 'Do not enter [. . .] remove your stela [from
there].'

129. Enforcement: The Oracle

Litigants who were convinced of their own innocence were no more willing
to accept the oracle's verdict than that of the court; and if the bystanders
also doubted the justice of the god's decision, they might not back it up
with pressure on the loser to submit. These appear to be the circumstances
in the following case. A tentative reconstruction of the background to the
dispute is that the policeman Amen-kha had served as a middleman in a
donkey transaction between the plaintiff, Hor-min, and the water-carrier.
The policeman failed to deliver the donkey to the plaintiff, his defence
being that the water-carrier had not given him the animal. Hor-Min took
the case before the oracle, but Amen-kha twice ignored the god's order to
pay for a donkey. After a third oracle, he swore before the entire gang to
replace the animal, but then, when the case appeared to be settled, the
water-carrier Pa-wekhed was brought forward as a witness for the already
victorious plaintiff and testified that the donkey had indeed been given to
Amen-kha, while two further witnesses were asked to confirm this fact.
Apparently, the bystanders were not convinced of Amen-kha's guilt even
after three oracles, and wanted some extra testimony to convince them.

[. . .] This [day]. King Amenophis, l.p.h., ordered the policeman
Amen-kha to pay for the donkey of the draughtsman Hor-Min.
    Year 4, first month of winter, day 9. This day. The god ordered
the policeman Amen-kha [to pay] 9 *deben*.
    First month of winter, day 10. He reported him again and he (the
god) ordered him to pay yet again, for the third time. He made him
take an oath of the lord, l.p.h., saying, 'If I renege and dispute again,
I (*lit.* 'he') will get 100 blows of a stick, and the donkey will be
counted against me (*lit.* 'him') double.' Before
    the priests of the god
    the chief workman Nakhte-em-Mut
    the chief workman In-her-kha
    the scribe Hori-sheri

the scribe of the Necropolis Hori
[. . .]
the doorkeeper An-hotep
the doorkeeper Pen-pa-mer
the officer Pen-ta-Weret
the officer Djehuty-nakhte
the gang in its entirety.
Bringing the water-carrier Pa-wekhed before the god (and) the gang
in its entirety. He took an oath of the lord for the god, l.p.h., saying,
'I handed over the donkey to the policeman Amen-kha in the
presence of the doorkeeper An-hotep and the child of the Necropolis
Neb-Amen [. . .]' They were brought. They said, 'Right [. . .] we (*lit.*
'they') saw that it was really handed over.'

PROPERTY

130. Official Property

All of the houses in the village, along with many of the structures outside
the walls, were owned by the state and allocated to individual workmen
only for their use while they were employed in the Necropolis. (For a
description of a Deir el-Medina house, see the Introduction, pp. 11–13.)
Along with his house, a workman was assigned a hut near the Valley of the
Kings, a tomb and a chapel. Naturally, a son who joined the gang would
hope to be assigned his father's dwelling, in which he himself had grown
up, but it did not always work out that way. In the broken opening lines of
the following text, the workman Amen-niut-nakhte, perhaps a new recruit,
seems to have appealed to the oracle to give him the property of his father,
A'o-nakhte. He was disappointed, however, because A'o-nakhte's 'set' of
four structures went to another workman, Mose, while Amen-niut-nakhte
received those of a certain Tener-Monthu. The actual transfer of the
property took place as a separate event in the presence of two officials, who
made Amen-niut-nakhte swear his acquiesence in the arrangement.

[. . . Amenophis], l.p.h. And I [. . .] to share in the property of his
(*sic*) father [. . . in the presence of]
    the chief workman Hor-mose
    the chief workman Nakhte-em-mut
    [. . . and those] carrying the god:
        the *wab*-priest Nefer-renpet
        the *wab*-priest Nefer-her

the *wab*-priest Ta
the *wab*-priest Neb-nefer
and the entire gang all together.

He was given the house of Tener-Monthu, and also his chapel, his hut (in) the Valley, (and) his tomb. The house of Aʿo-nakhte, his chapel, his tomb, and his hut in the Valley were given to the workman Mose.

The workman Amen-niut-nakhte took an oath of the lord, l.p.h., saying, 'I will not argue about any structure of Aʿo-nakhte, their (?) father: they are for the one who lives in his house.' So he said, speaking in the presence of the chief workman Nakhte-em-Mut (at) the Enclosure of the Necropolis.

(Written by) the scribe Amen-hotep of the Necropolis.

131. Private Property

Not all of the structures around the village belonged to the state; some were privately owned and could be bought and sold. In particular, huts built by the workmen themselves in their free time became their own property. (See also Chapter 1, 'Family and Friends', No. 17.) Such structures rarely feature in the preserved records of economic exchange, but do appear in documents concerning inheritance, especially inheritance by women. The following testament lists five small buildings and a pyramidion intended for a woman called Ta-Weret-hotep; they evidently represent half a legacy, the other half of which will go to a woman named Mut. Although the locations of the huts and storehouses cannot be identified precisely, they seem to be scattered among the temples and chapels to the north of the village and in the cemetery to the west, that is, outside the walled village but nearby.

Its half belongs to Mut.

What is for Ta-Weret-hotep:
The storehouse of Osiris, it belongs to Ta-Weret-hotep
The storehouse that is beside the temple of Ptah, it belongs to Ta-Weret-hotep
The hut that is beside the temple of (Amen-Re), *ditto*, *ditto*
The storehouse that is beside the tomb of Seba, it belongs to Ta-Weret-hotep
As for the little shrine (?) that is beside [. . .], *ditto* Ta-Weret-hotep

As for the pyramid that is on the tomb of Amen-em-ope, it belongs to Ta-Weret-hotep

Being 1 share of 2. 1 is for Mut, 1 [is for Ta-Weret-hotep (?)]

132. Land Sale

The following short text documents the sale of a plot of land. Even for a small building plot, the price (5 *deben*) seems very low indeed.

(*one line or more lost at the beginning*)
[. . .] the plot of the workman Hori son of Huy-nefer. Its price, in the presence of the chief workman Kha and the deputy Any-nakhte: 5 *deben*.

133. Land outside the Village

In this extract from a quarrel over a donkey, one of the parties suggests that she will pay for the animal with fields in Armant, some 10 km. south of the village. This is valuable evidence that her counterpart—possibly the workman Nefer-senut named in the verso—had the opportunity to acquire agricultural land, although he did not accept. There is some further evidence from Deir el-Medina that some workmen did engage in farming, in the form of both textual references and agricultural implements found at the site.

'[. . .] the donkey. I will buy it and I will give you [its] price [from f]ields in Armant.' I wrote to her, 'I will not accept [. . .] fields. Now give (me) the donkey *itself*!'

134. A Ruined Chapel Belongs to Him Who Rebuilds It

The following dispute over the ownership of a chapel (*hnw*) was touched off by yet another outrageous ploy of the young scoundrel Mery-Sekhmet (see No. 22). Kenna, the plaintiff, had rebuilt a collapsed and presumably abandoned chapel and thus made it his own. According to his testimony, Mery-Sekhmet then announced that a god had authorized him to share the dwelling. Kenna quite reasonably decided to check this with the god Amenophis himself, and the oracle confirmed his suspicion that Mery-Sekhmet's story was a fabrication.

Kenna based his claim on the fact that he had rebuilt the chapel, and rejected Mery-Sekmet's encroachment on the grounds that he had not

helped with the work. This suggests that a ruined building belonged to
whomever built it up again, even though, as in this case, the previous owner
was known.

The text is also interesting for its clear account of a legal oracle. Here, the
scribe of the Necropolis put the actual question to the god; the god is said
to have 'spoken' his verdict, but we may understand this to mean that he
chose one of two pre-phrased answers. The spot at which the oracle was
delivered is identified; it was the site of the tomb of the chief workman
Kaha, Theban Tomb 360, near the south-west corner of the village.

recto

Year 4, fourth month of inundation, last day. On this day, the
workman Kenna son of Wadjyt reported to King Amenophis, l.p.h.,
the god, l.p.h. of the village, saying: Come to me, my good lord! I am
the one who rebuilt the chapel of the workman Pa-khal when it was
collapsed. Now, look, the workman Mery-Sekhmet son of Menna
does not allow me to dwell in it, saying, 'It is the god who told me
to share it with you.' So he says, although he had not rebuilt it with
me. [. . .]

verso

[. . .] share.' So he said, speaking to the god. When the scribe of
the Necropolis [Hori]-sheri repeated (it) to him, he said, 'Give
the chapel back to Kenna, its owner! It is his through an order of
Pharaoh, l.p.h., and no man shall share it.' So said the god, speaking,
(in) his presence, and in the presence of

    the chief workman Nakhte-em-Mut
    the chief workman In-her-khau
    the scribe Hori
    the bearers of the god
    the entire gang

at the entrance of the tomb of the chief workman Kaha.

He (Mery-Sekhmet) took an oath of the lord, l.p.h., saying, 'As
Amun endures, as the Ruler endures, he whose manifestation is
worse than death, (namely) Pharaoh, l.p.h., my lord, if I revert and
dispute about it (again), I (*lit.* 'he') will get 100 blows, being deprived
of a share.'

135. An Easement

In the crowded valley of Deir el-Medina where tombs, chapels, and dwell-
ings stood cheek by jowl, the only access to one villager's building might be

across the property of another. The following dispute submitted to the oracle appears to concern such a right of way—what today would be called an easement. (The word translated 'right of way' here, *meten*, is unparalleled and its meaning must be inferred from the context.) A certain Kener had owned a right of entrance and exit in connection with his storehouse, and when Kener's property was divided (perhaps on his death), this easement was passed to Hay.

Ten months later, Pen-ta-Weret, the owner of the land that was affected by the easement, contested Hay's right before the oracle, but without success. Hay then took advantage of the opportunity to ask the god to confirm the right of a certain Hut-iy to remove wooden fixtures from the storehouse.

(Note that the accession of Ramesses III fell on first month of summer day 26, so that the first month of summer day 16 falls after the third month of summer of the same year, counterintuitive though that is.)

Year 14, third month of summer, day 24. Arrangement for dividing the storehouse of Kener so as to give the passage to the workman Hay, by

the chief workman Nakhte-em-Mut
the scribe Wenen-nefer
Khonsu
the draughtsman Hori

Said by the chief workman Nakhte-em-Mut, 'Look, this right (?) [belonged to] Kener formerly, and he gave it to the workman Hay son of Huy [. . .]'

Year 14, first month of summer, day 19. The workman Pen-ta-Weret called out to Amenophis on this day, saying, 'My good lord! I will not give to Hay the right (?) of entering and leaving this plot of land.' So he said. Then the god moved backwards. Then he repeated (it) to him, saying 'Shall one give him the right (?) of entering and leaving?' And the god agreed very greatly. Then the workman Hay called out to him, saying 'My Light! As for the property of this place, consisting of boards, of beams, and of a door, do [you] not agree that the lady Hut-iy takes them?' And the god agreed very greatly, saying, 'She shall take her things.' In the presence of witnesses:

the chief workman Hay
the scribe Wenen-nefer
the police inspector Khonsu
Ipuy
the *wab*-priest Nefer-hotep

the *wab*-priest Iy-er-niut-ef
the *wab*-priest Any-nakhte
the *wab*-priest Amen-nakhte
the *wab*-priest Kener
the *wab*-priest Nefer-her
the gang in its entirety

He took an oath of the lord, l.p.h. in the presence of (?) Amen,
saying [. . .]

136. Equity

Fragmentary though it is, the following text has two interesting features.
First, it seems to record a rare case in which the officials arranged a
compromise between two litigants. The workman Wen-nefer—the 'I' of
the text—claimed a right to his father's hut, which was, however, occupied
by another workman who also had an interest in the structure. The two
took their dispute before the chief workman Khonsu and a deputy who
evidently decided that Wen-nefer should have the hut, but that he should
pay the other workman for the improvements he had made during his
occupancy. A list of the items given in payment follows. This sort of
equitable arrangement is otherwise unknown, and may indicate that the
two officials were acting as arbitrators rather than judges; it is at any rate
striking that Khonsu and his colleague are not referred to as a 'court'.

The second unusual feature of this document is its format; instead of
being written in ink, the text has been cut into the ostracon and filled with
blue frit. This almost monumental treatment suggests a special use for this
document. It is possible that it was to be set into the wall of the disputed
hut to publicize Wen-nefer's claim to the building, like the stela which the
oracle ordered another workman to remove from a hut in No. 128 above.

[Reporting by] the workman Wen-nefer (and) the work-
[man . . . saying, Let?] there be given to me the hut (of) my father
[. . .] in the presence of:
    the chief workman Khonsu
    the deputy [. . .]
[. . .] And they said to me, 'Give him grain [. . . for the construction]
that he made in it.' List of the silver [given to him: . . .]
    box: 2 *deben*, 3 *oipe* of it belonging to me
    [. . . from his?] wood
    And I made for him a staff [. . . from?] his wood
    and I made for him a [. . . from?] his wood
    and [. . .] *hen*-box, X *deben* [. . .]

Our best evidence for the law of contracts is from the texts recording donkey sales and rentals, which have been included in Chapter 2, Nos. 56–62.

137. Dunning the Dead

Death did not cancel debts in Deir el-Medina; in this text, the deceased workman Sa-Mut is held liable for twenty sacks of grain, which are collected from his widow by an officer of the court. The verso apparently lists the various creditors who are to be paid off; or, less likely, the friends of the family who chipped in to help make up the required sum.

recto
Year 9, third month of summer, day 18. This day, coming by the scribe [. . .] to approach the court, saying: 'Let the grain be exacted against the workman Sa-mut, who is dead. The messenger [Pen]-pa-mer was sent to collect from his wife, Hut-ia, and exacted 12 sacks of emmer and 8 sacks of barley.

verso
Specification thereof, list of [. . .] expenses [. . .]

made by the draughtsman Nefer-hotep	1 *deben*
Ipuy	2 sacks
[. . .]	
Iy-er-niut-ef	1 sack
[. . .]	
List of [. . .]	
[. . .]	$\frac{1}{2}$ sack
Hay	2 sacks
[. . .] Ken-her-hepesh-ef	2 sacks
Nakhy	1 sack
Huy	2 sacks

TORTS

138. The Oracle Names the Thief

It was not often that an ordinary chisel-bearer accused a member of a powerful family of misconduct, and when this did happen a certain amount

of diplomacy was in order. In the following case the guilty party was not an
official but the daughter of the scribe of the Necropolis Amen-nakhte,
which, if anything, made the problem even more delicate. A charge against
Amen-nakhte would presumably have been brought before the vizier, but
his daughter would be tried in the village where Amen-nakhte himself
would ordinarily preside over the court. This is probably one reason why
the chisel-bearer Ka-ha chose to ask the god to identify the thief of his two
garments rather than take her to court himself.

Another reason why a villager might approach the oracle with questions
of this sort is that he did not have enough hard evidence to win a case before
the court. We do not know what level of proof was required by the secular
judges but presumably an unsupported accusation would not satisfy them.
The problem of evidence could be sidestepped by letting the god name the
culprit; however, the god's verdict necessarily reflected the suspicions of
some members of the community and no action would be taken against
Amen-nakhte's daughter unless a substantial number of people were at least
not surprised by the identification. In other words, an oracle of this kind,
in the open air, articulated the suspicions of the community, whether or not
there was good evidence against the accused.

Year 5, third month of inundation, day 28. The chisel-bearer Ka-ha
called to King Amenophis, l.p.h., saying, 'My good lord, come
today, because my two garments have been stolen!' And he brought
the scorpion-charmer Amen-mose, saying, 'Read out the houses of
the settlement!' They were read out. Now when the house of the
scribe Amen-nakhte was reached, he (the god) agreed, saying, 'They
are with his daughter.'

In the presence of witnesses:
the scribe [. . .]
A'o-pa-tjau
Nefer-hotep
Iy-er-niut-ef
Hay
the guardian Khay
And the gang was standing [. . .] Then the scribe Amen-nakhte stood
in the presence of the god, saying, 'As for the garments you mentioned, did the daugher of the scribe Amen-nakhte steal them?' And
the god agreed.

139. The Perplexed Victim

The petitioner in the preceding case may have used the oracle to single
out a suspect whom he dared not accuse himself, but others who came

before the god were genuinely at a loss to know who had taken their property. A number of small ostraca bearing short questions for the god attest to some simpler form of oracular consultation than that used by Kaha (see No. 78), and many of these relate to theft. In some cases (*a–f*), the question is open-ended, in others (*g–h*), the petitioner clearly suspects someone in particular.

(*a*) Has a man of the gang stolen them?
(*b*) Someone stole it.
(*c*) Did the men of the army steal it?
(*d*) Is it a person who did it?
(*e*) Is it a stranger?
(*f*) Is it someone of the inner Necropolis?
(*g*) Is it he who stole this mat?
(*h*) Is it Nakhte?
(*i*) Is it another thief who stole it?

140. Compensation

Few texts document the penalty for theft from a private person, but Černý was able to demonstrate that this took the form of a threefold restitution of the stolen items. One of the two New Kingdom texts cited by Černý came from the Deir el-Medina; it lists the objects to be exacted from the workman Ruti and their *tjaut*, 'penalty', a word derived from the verb *tjau*, 'to steal'.

What will be exacted from Ruti to be given to the chief workman Hay:

20 *hin* of fat	its penalty: 40 *hin*	makes $\frac{3}{8}$ sack
1 loincloth	its penalty: 2	makes 3 loincloths
1 stick	its penalty: 2	makes 3
1 shabti-box	its penalty: 2	makes 3

141. Incarceration as Punishment?

The following fragmentary and obscure statement by the workman Amen-em-one suggests another penalty for theft; confinement in the Enclosure of the Necropolis. The suspects in the Great Tomb Robberies hearings were locked up in the granary of the temple of Maʿat, and possibly the granary of the Necropolis served the same function. On the other hand, being 'made to sit at the Enclosure' may have some different meaning altogether. We are not told what was stolen by the culprit in this case and thus cannot tell whether it was state property or privately owned.

What the workman Amen-em-one said: Now when this theft was
effected through the agency of Khnum-mose, he was taken and
made to sit at the Enclosure. And [he spent] 40 days there, sitting. I
made [. . .] in the form of pigments and strips of cloth. Now when
one caused [. . .] chief of police [. . .].

(Narrative continued on verso, but too broken for translation.)

142. Slander

There is only one prosecution for slander in our material and it is peculiar
in several respects. The background to the case is that the chief workman
Hay overheard three workmen and a woman saying that he, Hay, had
cursed Seti II, the reigning king. He acccused the scandalmongers
before the local court, and under questioning, they first disagreed among
themselves over how to answer and then confessed that they had never
heard Hay make any such seditious statement. Presumably they did not
deny spreading the rumour, however, because the court not only made
them swear never to charge Hay with treason in the future, but also gave
them each a severe beating.

There are at least three unusual features of this trial. First, chief workmen
did not usually appear before the local court whether as plaintiff or
defendant. Possibly cases involving officials automatically went to the
vizier; possibly, too, chief workmen could apply direct pressure to workmen
who offended them. Second, it is striking that there are no outside officials
on the court, although there would usually be at least a chief policeman
or a scribe of the vizier among the judges when an important case was
being heard. And finally, the ostracon was probably found in the Valley
of the Kings, suggesting that the court was sitting in or near this remote
gorge.

All of these features would be explained if Hay was not prosecuting the
workmen for slander so much as silencing them before their words reached
the Theban officials. Simply punishing the alleged slanderers would not
have cleared him of blame, while taking them before an ordinary court
would have drawn the attention of the vizier's agents in the Necropolis.
Therefore, Hay approached a specially assembled court at some distance
from the village on a day when the scribes of the vizier were absent, and his
fellow chief-workman Pa-neb got the accused to withdraw their accusation.
We may assume that this was not standard procedure in a case of slander;
the local court was rather exceeding its jurisdiction in the hope of avoiding
an official inquiry.

Year 5, third month of summer, day 2. [The] court of this [day]. The
chief workman Hay approached the court together with Pen-Amen,

Ptah-shed, Wen-nefer, Ta-weseret, in the presence of the magistrates
of the court:
  the chief workman Pa-neb
  Neb-semen
  Amen-nakhte
  Nakhte-em-Mut
  Huy
  Pa-shed
  Ra-hotep
  Neb-nefer son of Pen-nub
  Neb-nefer son of Wadje-mose
  Huy son of In-her-khau
  Mery-Re
  Ipu
  the complete gang
The chief workman Hay said, 'As for me, I was lying in my hut when
Pen-Amen came out together with his people. They mentioned
an accusation concerning the greatness of Pharaoh involving Hay,
(namely, that) he uttered a curse against Seti.'

The court said to them, 'Tell us what you heard!' But they went
back on their testimony to argue (among themselves). The chief
workman Pa-neb said to them, 'Tell us what you heard!' And they
said, 'We did not hear anything.'

The court said to them—to Pen-Amen, Ptah-shed, Wen-nefer,
and Ta-weseret—'Say "as Amen endures, as the ruler endures, there
is no accusation concerning (him) involving Pharaoh, l.p.h. If we
(*lit.* "you") conceal it today to come out with it in the future, may
our (*lit.* "his") noses and ears be cut off [. . .] evil."' And they were
given 100 severe blows of the stick.

CRIMES

Neither the local court nor the oracle had jurisdiction over criminal
matters; these were tried by outside authorities including the office
of the vizier. Less is known about criminal than civil matters because,
as mentioned above, the records were not kept in the village, but a
few extraordinary texts do shine a fascinating light on particular
details of a criminal inquiry.

143. Assault

A. There are remarkably few references to violence at Deir el-Medina, and no case of assault or murder is known to have come before the village court. This is almost certainly due, at least in part, to the nature of our sources; records of cases concerning property or economic transactions, or even theft, were kept by the winning party for future reference, but neither the victim nor the defendant wanted a permanent record of a trial for assault. In addition, violent crimes may have been beyond the jurisdiction of the local authorities. However, there are a handful of incidental references to assault which at any rate suggest that it was a crime punished by penal labour. The following extract from the journal of the Necropolis mentions stone-cutting in the Theban necropolis, the Place of Truth, as a punishment; the stonecutters of the gang did this work every day, of course, so that we must assume Aʿo-nakhte was either of a higher rank not accustomed to heavy labour, or a tomb-builder made to work overtime. This penalty was certainly not imposed by the local court but by some higher agency.

Year 6, third month of summer, day 16. Setting Aʿo-nakhte to hammering (stone) in the Place of Truth (for?) striking the head of Djaydjay, Pa-idehu, and Montu-pa-Hapy. Pouring water for the dual kings on this day.

B. Another reference to penal labour as a punishment for assault is contained in the following extract from a letter. The policeman in question was evidently sentenced and punished in some other town, not Deir el-Medina, and indeed he is not known to have been associated with the Necropolis; but the letter is addressed to a member of the gang and may therefore be included among our material.

[. . .]

Furthermore: I heard your message about the affair of the policeman Nakhte-Seti. The policeman Nakhte-Seti is in the compulsory labour since he hit with the stick and was like every enemy of Pre. If Amen allows me to live long enough to come South, I will bring him and I will stand with you and I will see the fate that he has brought upon himself, and it will be done.

144. 'The theft of copper is the abomination of this village'

The following two records of criminal cases, both brought before the local court by the same plaintiff on probably the same day, provide almost as much information about criminal procedure as the rest of the material from Deir el-Medina put together.

The importance of this first text lies in the court's active inquiry into the merits of the case through questioning and investigations on the spot, something we do not see in civil cases, as well as in the explicit statement that cases of a certain gravity were taken out of village hands to be dealt with by the higher authorities.

The original charge against the accused, a woman called Herya, was that she had stolen a copper chisel from the workman Neb-nefer. He had done his own detective work by asking everyone in the village to swear that he knew nothing of the theft; and the effectiveness of this method is demonstrated when one of the women had an attack of conscience (a 'manifestation of god', see above No. 73) and confessed that she had seen Herya take the chisel.

Before the court, Herya was questioned and asked whether she was able to declare her innocence under oath. Although this suggests that the oath was regarded as an ordeal which would test her innocence, the result was not regarded as conclusive and the court proceeded to examine her. 'Examination' is an ominous word in the context of a criminal case and may suggest torture; at any rate, the interrogation was effective and shortly thereafter, accompanied by a servant of the court, she went home and brought back the stolen chisel. Unfortunately for Herya, the chisel was found to have been buried with other copper objects belonging to one of the local cults; she was now definitely guilty of a crime and beyond the jurisdiction of the local court. Her case was accordingly set aside for the vizier.

The text then changes tone and addresses the vizier directly. The author stresses the fact that Herya stole copper, and notes that in the past a woman who stole even a tiny amount of the metal was 'taken to the riverbank' by the scribe of the vizier, presumably for interrogation and punishment. (See No. 148). Theft of private property was otherwise a tort; this is the only indication that the nature of the stolen object might raise the offence to a crime.

Year 6, third month of summer, day 10. This day, the workman Neb-nefer son of Nakhy approached the law court and reported the lady Herya. The workman Neb-nefer said: 'As for me, I buried a chisel of mine in my house after the war, and it was stolen. I made everyone in the village swear to his innocence regarding my chisel. Now, after many days, the lady Nub-em-nehem came to say to me, "A manifestation of god has come about! I saw Herya taking your chisel." So she said.'

Then the court said to Herya, 'Are you indeed the one who stole this chisel of Neb-nefer, or not?' Herya said: 'No! I am not the one who stole it.' The court said to her: 'Are you able to take a great oath of the lord, l.p.h., regarding this chisel, saying "I am not the one who stole it"?' Then Herya said, 'As Amun endures, as the ruler, l.p.h., endures, the one whose manifestation is worse than death, (namely) Pharaoh, l.p.h., if I am found to be the one who stole this chisel . . .'

Now, an hour later, the court examined her. The servant Pa-shed was sent out with her and she brought the chisel; it was buried in her possession together with a copper-*weshbu* (image?) of Amen of the Good Encounter—she had buried them in her house after she had stolen the copper-*an* (*unidentified*) of the *weshbu* of Amen, although she had taken a great oath of the lord, l.p.h., saying, 'I am not the one who stole this chisel.'

Then the court said, 'The lady Herya is a great false one worthy of death; the workman Neb-nefer is right.' Her case was set aside until the vizier should come.

Court of this day:
the chief workman Pa-neb
the chief workman Hay
the scribe Pa-shed
the scribe Pa-ser
the scribe Pen-ta-Weret
the chief policeman Monthu-mose
the guardian Ipuy
the entire gang

Now, the theft of copper from here is the abomination of this village. And in the matter of the widow—to inform my lord of the custom of the place: the lady Ta-nedjem-hemsi took one small cup of $\frac{1}{2}$ *deben* here in the village before, in the time of the vizier Nefer-hotep, although she was the wife of Pa-shed, the son of Heh. The vizier sent the scribe Hat-iay, and he had her taken to the riverbank. May my lord let this woman who stole the chisel and also the *weshbu* be punished, so that no other woman in her position will do the like again! See, I have informed my lord. Now, the vizier is the one who knows: let him carry out any plan he wishes.

May they (*sic*) take notice.

145. Theft of State Property Brought before the Court

Unlike the preceeding case, the following was known to concern theft of state property from the beginning. The same plaintiff, Neb-nefer, accused a fellow workman of stealing three copper chisels before what appears to be the very same court as before. It is something of a mystery why such a charge should come before the village court in the first instance rather than the Theban authorities; the answer may be that since the representatives of the vizier happened to be among the judges (the scribes Pa-ser and Pen-ta-Weret) they chose to carry out their initial investigation in this setting.

One of the most interesting features of the hearing is the role of Neb-nefer as a sort of private prosecutor. He not only brought the accused, Huy son of Huy-nefer, to the attention of the authorities, but was asked to supply witnesses against him. Neb-nefer himself was made to swear that if his allegation proved to be groundless, he would suffer some terrible penalty (which cannot be identified because three of the key words are otherwise unknown). This can only be a safeguard against false accusations, a precaution which would not seem to be in the state's interest since it might discourage reports to the authorities.

The proceedings are run by the scribe Pen-ta-Weret of the vizier's office, who questions Neb-nefer and the two witnesses. Their testimony is more detailed than that recorded in most of our cases, but in the end the main instruments for discovering the truth appear to be the oaths administered to the various parties. No verdict is given at the end of the hearing. This probably means that the case would be forwarded to the higher authorities for further investigation, as in the preceeding text.

recto

[. . .]

This day: the workman Neb-nefer son of Nakhy approached [the court] and he reported the workman Huy son of Huy-nefer, saying, 'The workman Huy son of Huy-nefer stole the three chisels of Pharaoh, l.p.h.; I found them in his hut in the Valley (of the Kings).' So he said.

Then the scribe Pen-ta-Weret said to him, 'As for these chisels of Pharaoh, l.p.h., which you said Huy stole from the place of Pharaoh, l.p.h., do you have witnesses against him or not?'

Neb-nefer said, 'I have witnesses; he stole the chisels of Pharaoh, l.p.h., in the presence of the workman Huy son of Kha and the chisel-bearer Khamu.'

Then the workman Huy son of Kha and the chisel-bearer Khamu were brought before the court. They swore an oath of the lord, l.p.h.; 'As Amen endures, as the ruler, l.p.h., endures, the one whose manifestation is worse than death, Pharaoh, l.p.h., we shall speak the truth (of) Pharaoh, l.p.h.; we shall not speak falsehood; if we speak falsehood, we will be beaten with 100 blows and the chisels will be exacted from our (*lit.* 'their') houses, being given to Pharaoh, l.p.h.'

So they said. They said, 'It is true that we saw two chisels in the hut
of Huy son of Huy-nefer in the Valley after the war, but we do not
know [if they belonged to Pharaoh.'] So they said about the two
chisels [. . .]

verso
[The scribe] Pen-ta-Weret [said] to te workman Neb-nefer, '[As for
these chisels] which you said Huy son of Huy-nefer stole, (do) they
belong to Pharaoh, l.p.h., or do they belong to himself?'

Neb-nefer son of Nakhy said, 'They belong to Pharaoh, l.p.h.'
Oath of the lord, l.p.h., that he swore, (namely) Neb-nefer: 'As
Amen endures, as the ruler, l.p.h. endures, the one whose manifestation is worse than death, Pharaoh, l.p.h., behold, these chisels stolen
by Huy son of Huy-nefer belong to Pharaoh, l.p.h. If one learns in
the future that they do not belong to Pharaoh, l.p.h., they will put
(me) in hard labour (?) on account of it and I will be removed (?)
from my house which will be given to Pharaoh, l.p.h. Now look,
he has also had another 28 copper *deben* made into a cauldron for
himself. Now, 2 female donkeys were also sent to him in exchange
for them.' So he said.

Oath of the lord, l.p.h., spoken by Huy son of Huy-nefer: 'As
Amen endures, as the ruler endures, he whose manifestation is worse
than death, Pharaoh, l.p.h., if there is an investigation and it is found
that these chisels do not belong to me [just as] they belonged to
Huy-nefer my father, I (*lit.* 'he') will be cast [. . .]'

[Court of] this [day]:
Chief workman Pa-neb
Chief [workman] Hay
[Scribe Pa]-ser
Scribe Pen-ta-Weret
Chief policeman [Monthu-mose]
Guardian [Ipuy]
The entire gang

146. Reporting Crime

Legal historians must use P Salt 124, the papyrus from which the following
extract is taken, with caution. It is a catalogue of the villainous deeds of
the chief workman Pa-neb addressed to the vizier by a man who felt
Pa-neb's job should by right have been his own, so that it is almost

impossible not to suspect bias. Moreover, although it is addressed to the vizier, it was never sent to him; the papyrus was bought on the market and not discovered in the course of excavation, but there is reason to believe that it was found at Deir el-Medina and never left the village for East Thebes. And finally, the charges against Pa-neb are intended to prove that he is 'unworthy of this office (of chief workman)', as the final lines state. This does not necessarily mean that every individual offence listed was actually illegal.

On the other hand, some of the activities attributed to Pa-neb were most certainly criminal, such as his notorious theft of stone from the royal tomb; this incident and its repercussions are actually cited as a precedent in a later case (No. 147). The other little case history included in the extract below concerns a threat to kill his predecessor in office, Nefer-hotep, in the days when Pa-neb was still a mere workman; and his assault on nine other villagers on the same day. According to the text, Nefer-hotep reported Pa-neb to the vizier who ordered him to be punished with a beating. If this account is reliable, it furnishes our only information about how assault might be prosecuted and punished. Pa-neb allegedly had his revenge; the text states that he complained to Mesy, thought to be the shadowy Pharaoh Amenmose, and brought about the vizier's own dismissal. This cannot be confirmed.

[Said by the workman] Amen-nakhte: 'I am the child of the chief workman Neb-nefer. My father died, and Nefer-hotep, my brother, [was appointed] to his place. Then the enemy killed Nefer-hotep [and, although I was] his brother, Pa-neb gave 5 of my father's slaves to Pre-em-hab, who was vizier, [and was appointed to the place of m]y father, although the place was not his. . . .

Charge concerning his setting the men to cut stone on the top of the work of King Seti-Merneptah, l.p.h. They took (it) to his tomb every day, and he erected four columns in his tomb with this stone; he stripped the place of Pharaoh, l.p.h. While the stonecutters were standing and working on top of the work of Pharaoh, the people passing by in the desert saw them and heard their voices. And he took the chisels of Pharaoh, l.p.h., and the pickaxe to work in his tomb.

List of the stonecutters who worked for him: Aᶜo-pehty, Kasa, Kasa son of Ramose, Hor-em-wia, Ken-her-khepesh-ef, Roma, Pa-shed son of Heh, Neb-nakhte, Nakhte-Min, Neb-semen, Hor-em-wia son of Baki, Khonsu, Nakhte-Min, Pa-yom, Wenen-nefer, Aᶜo-nakhte. Total: 16.

Charge concerning his bringing away the large chisel of the work in progress, and he broke it in his tomb.

Charge concerning his running after the chief workman Nefer-hotep, his brother, although it was he who raised him; and he locked his doors before him, and he took a stone and he broke his doors, and people were set to guard Nefer-hotep because he said, 'I will kill him in the night!' And he beat nine men in that night.

And the chief-workman Nefer-hotep reported him to the vizier Amen-mose, and he punished him, and he (Pa-neb) reported the vizier to Mesy and had him dismissed from the office of vizier, saying, 'He carried out my beating.'. . .

Now, (he) is not worthy of this office. Indeed he is behaving like the *wadjet-eye*,[a] (although) he is like a madman (?). He killed these men so that they would not be able to make a report to Pharaoh, l.p.h.! Look, I have let the vizier know his behaviour.

---

[a] J. F. Borghouts suggests that 'behaving like the wadjet-eye!' may mean something like 'playing Providence' (in Leonard H. Lesko (ed.), *Pharaoh's Workers* (Ithaca and London, 1994), 127).

147. The Duty to Report

The author of the preceding text had a personal motive for accusing Pa-neb to the authorities, but it was also his duty to report suspicious goings on in the Necropolis. This duty was imposed on all members of the gang by their 'oath of office' (*sedjfa-teryt*). Ordinary workmen would report to the local officials, and these in turn notified the vizier. The following extract from an official journal records charges made by a workman to two of the captains concerning appropriation of stone from a royal tomb, theft of a temple ox, and adultery. In the course of his report the speaker alludes to the fate of Pa-neb, the villain of extract No. 146 above; it seems that the vizier Hori punished him for taking stones, but, unfortunately, the nature of the punishment is not specified.

Year 29, first month of summer day, 16. What the workman Pen-anket said to the scribe Amen-nakhte and the chief workman Khonsu: You are my superiors and you are the administrators of the Necropolis. Pharaoh, l.p.h., my good lord, made me take an 'oath of office' that I will not hear of a matter, I will not see a theft in these great and deep places and conceal it. Now look, Weser-hat and Pen-ta-Weret removed a boulder from the top of the tomb of the Osiris, King Weser-Ma'at-Re Setep-en-Re (Ramesses II), l.p.h., the great god. And he brought an ox branded with the brand of the Ramesseum; it is standing in his stall. And he slept with three married women: the lady Menat when she was with Kenna; the lady Ta-iu-en-es when she was with Nakhte-Amen; and the lady Ta-Weret-hotep when she was with Pen-ta-Weret. Now, you have seen the standpoint of the vizier Hori regarding the bringing away of stones when it was said to him, 'The chief workman Pa-neb', my father, 'caused men to bring away stones from there, [. . . like (?)] him precisely. And Kenna the son of Ruty did it in the very same manner on top of this tomb of the royal children of King Osiris Weser-Maʿat-Re Setep-en-Re (Ramesses II), l.p.h., the (great) god. Let it be known what you will do to them, or I will make a report to Pharaoh, l.p.h., my lord, l.p.h., and also to the vizier, my superior.

148. The Place of Examination

A number of texts mention that individuals suspected of crime were 'taken to the riverbank', which was the site of the ominously named Place of Examination. The officials of the Place of Examination feature in the trials following the Great Tomb Robberies and the Harem Conspiracy (leading to the assassination of Ramesses III); it seems clear that their job was to interrogate suspects, but very little is actually known about their activities. The first text below records that two villagers, Nakhte-em-Mut and Isis, were taken to the riverbank on the first month of winter, day 15, where they were imprisoned in the place of examination and then released ten days later. The reason for their arrest is lost. Remarkably, the second text refers to the same incident, noting that Nakhte-em-Mut was examined on the 25th, the day of his release. The experience does not seem to have hampered his career, judging from the fact that he later appears as chief workman of the gang.

A. *verso*
[Year 25], first month of winter, day 15. [Tak]en to (*lit.* in) the riverbank [. . .]

recto
Year 25, first month of winter, day 25. On this day, Nakhte-em-Mut son of Khonsu was brought up, together with Isis, the wife of Any-nakhte [after they had been] imprisoned in the place of the examination on account of [. . .] of the Necropolis.

B. Year 25, first month of winter, day 25. [. . .] examining Nakhte-em-Mut.

149. Punishments

The punishment for those found guilty of tomb robbery was death, but we
have little information about the range of punishments available for lesser
offences. In Chapter 6, 'Work on the Royal Tomb', No. 182 (from which
this brief extract is taken) the scribe of the vizier Pa-ser announced to the
gang the outcome of a trial involving himself and the draughtsman Neb-
nefer; Neb-nefer was found to be in the wrong and was sentenced to a
beating and set to breaking stone in the Necropolis until he was pardoned
by the vizier. The text may also say that Neb-nefer was to be branded but
it becomes almost illegible at that point. Neither the grounds of the dispute
nor the court are named. The case did not come before the local court, as
we know from the fact that Pa-ser had to inform the gang of the result;
and the reference to the vizier's pardon suggests that this high official may
himself have presided over the trial.

'The scribe Pa-ser was in court together with the draughtsman Neb-
nefer, and the scribe Pa-ser was found to be in the right, while the
draughtsman Neb-nefer was found to be in the wrong. The court
said: Give him 100 blows with a stick as well as 10 (??) brand marks
(??), and set him to breaking stone in the Place of Truth until the
vizier pardons him.'

THE GREAT TOMB ROBBERIES

The records of the Great Tomb Robberies investigations of the late
Twentieth Dynasty make some of the most thrilling reading from
Ancient Egypt. At this time, gangs of Thebans were systematically
looting the tombs of the Theban necropolis, and the authorities
launched one series of investigations and trials after another in a
futile effort to stop the pillaging, keeping meticulous records of
every step of the proceedings. The testimony of the suspects, who
were examined under torture, is particularly fascinating because it
includes virtually the only statements by lower-class Thebans about
their own activities in their own words. Some, indeed, threw caution
to the winds and boasted of their exploits, almost taunting the judges
for their impotence; one ended his spellbinding account of a thieving
expedition with the remark that everyone in Thebes was involved
in the thefts. The community of Deir el-Medina was split by these
events. Some families joined the thieves, others helped the investigat-

ing officials; both sides, of course, took advantage of their unique familiarity with the Theban necropolis.

150. The Initial Report

The following extract is from Papyrus Abbott, which documents the earliest recorded investigations, those of the 16th year of Ramesses IX. The first part of the papyrus describes how a commission of inspection was dispatched to the necropolis following a report by the mayor of Thebes Pa-Ser that certain royal tombs had been violated. Ten royal tombs were inspected, including that of Amenhotep I, the patron saint of the workmen; all but one were found intact. On the other hand, all the private tombs in the area had been robbed and their owners dragged from their coffins and cast on the desert. The commission reported back to the vizier and gave him a list of suspects, who were seized and interrogated that same evening and confessed their crimes. The next day, the vizier and other judges visited the Valley of the Queens (the 'Place of Beauty') to examine the tombs of the royal mothers, wives, and children. They took with them a suspect supposed to have robbed the tomb of a queen Isis, wife of Ramesses III, but this suspect turned out to know nothing of the tomb in question, and not only it but all the other tombs of the royal relatives were found intact—a result that was seen as a complete vindication of the Necropolis staff and a defeat for the mayor Pa-ser.

Our extract picks up here and is relatively self-explanatory. The Necropolis staff embarked on a noisy celebration of the commission's findings which brought them to the very home of the mayor of Thebes. He reproached them for turning into the affair into a personal contest between themselves and him, and reminded them that investigation had revealed one violated royal tomb. Most importantly, he announced that two scribes of the Necropolis had made serious accusations to him which he would be forwarding to the Pharaoh. His colleague and rival, the mayor of West Thebes, attempted a pre-emptive strike by informing the vizier about the charges before they could reach Pharaoh. Both men stress that it was their inescapable duty to alert their superiors about the matter, which we may understand as a reference to the oath of office. The mayor of West Thebes insisted, however, that the scribes ought to have made their charges to the vizier, their immediate superior, and at the end of the extract below, he recommended that the vizier take the situation back into his own hands. In fact, in the succeeding passage of the papyrus, the Great Court of Thebes is assembled primarily to condemn the mayor of Thebes for having made false accusations about the tombs found intact in the previous investigation.

The magistrates examined the seals of the great tombs in the Place of Beauty, where the royal children, the queens, the royal mothers, and the beneficent ancestors and ancestresses of Pharaoh, l.p.h., rest. They were found to be intact. The great magistrates caused the administrators, the captains, and the workmen of the Necropolis, and the chief policemen, policemen and all the supply staff of the Necropolis to go around West Thebes in great celebrations as far as Thebes.

Year 16, THIRD MONTH OF INUNDATION, DAY 19. This day, in the evening, beside the temple of Ptah, lord of Thebes, there came the royal butler and scribe of Pharaoh, l.p.h., Nesu-Amen and the mayor of Thebes Pa-ser. They found the chief workman Weser-khepesh, the scribe Amen-nakhte, and the workman Amen-hotep of the Necropolis. This mayor of Thebes spoke to the people of the Necropolis in the presence of the butler of Pharaoh, saying, 'As for this celebration you make today—it is not a celebration, it is your song of triumph that you are making.' So he said to them. He took an oath of the lord, l.p.h., before this butler of Pharaoh, saying, 'The scribe Hori-sheri son of Amen-nakhte of the inner, protected Necropolis and the scribe Pay-bes of the Necropolis have made to me five very great capital charges against you. Now I will write about them to Pharaoh, l.p.h., my lord, l.p.h., to cause people of Pharaoh, l.p.h., to be sent out to arrest you all.' So he said.

Year 16, THIRD MONTH OF INUNDATION, DAY 20. Copy of the letter that the mayor of West Thebes and chief of police of the Necropolis Pa-wer-aʿo presented to the vizier respecting the words spoken by the mayor of Thebes Pa-ser to the men of the Necropolis in the presence of the butler of Pharaoh, l.p.h, and the scribe of the overseer of the Treasury, Pay-nedjem.

What the mayor of West Thebes, Pa-wer-aʿo said:

To the effect that: I came upon the butler and scribe of Pharaoh Nesu-Amun while the mayor of Thebes, Pa-ser, was with him standing and quarrelling with the men of the Necropolis beside the temple of Ptah, lord of Thebes. And the mayor of Thebes said to the men of the Necropolis, 'You exult over me at the very door of my house. What is this? I am the mayor who reports to the ruler, l.p.h. If you are exulting because you found that this (tomb) in which you carried out your inspection is intact, still King Sekhem-Re-shed-Tauy, son of Re, Sobek-em-sa-ef, l.p.h. (Sebekamzaf II of the Seventeenth Dynasty), has been violated, together with Nub-Kha-es, his queen; a great ruler who executed ten weighty comissions for Amen-Re King of Gods, this great god. His monuments stand in his midst to this day.'

Now, the workman Weser-khepesh, who is in the charge of the chief workman of the Necropolis Nakhte-em-Mut, said, 'As for all the kings together with their queens, royal mothers and royal children who rest in the great and noble Necropolis, and also those who rest in this Place of Beauty, they are intact; they are guarded and protected for ever. The good counsel of Pharaoh, l.p.h., their child, guards them and examines them rigorously.'

This mayor of Thebes said to him, 'Your deeds contradict your words!'

Now, it is no small charge that this mayor of Thebes made. This mayor of Thebes spoke to him again a second time, saying, 'The scribe Hori-sheri son of Amen-nakhte of the inner, protected Necropolis came as far as this great side of Thebes to the place where I was in order to make three very great charges to me. My scribe and the two scribes of the district of Thebes wrote them down. And the scribe of the Necropolis Pay-bes made another two charges to me, total five, and they were written down also, since they do not belong to the sort of thing about which one can keep silent—they are major crimes leading to mutilation and impalement and every punishment. Now, I will write about them to Pharaoh, l.p.h., my lord, l.p.h., to have Pharaoh's men sent to arrest you.' So said this mayor of Thebes to them. He took ten oaths of the lord, l.p.h., saying, 'I will do this!'

I heard these words spoken by the mayor of Thebes to the men of the great and noble Necropolis of millions of years of Pharaoh, l.p.h., on the West of Thebes (and) I have reported them to my lord. Now, it is a crime for one in my position to hear (such) matters and conceal them. Now, I am unable to fathom these very great charges that the mayor of Thebes said, 'These scribes of the inner Necropolis made them to me standing in the midst of their men'; indeed, I cannot fathom them. I am making a report to my lord so that my lord may get to the bottom of these charges of which the mayor of Thebes said, 'The scribes of the Necropolis made them to me and I will write about them to Pharaoh, l.p.h.' So he said. It was a crime on the part of these two scribes of the Necropolis to go to the mayor of Thebes in order to report to him, since their predecessors had not reported to him but to the vizier when he was in the southern district, and if he happened to be in the northern district, the police of the Necropolis, the servants of his majesty, l.p.h., went downstream to where the vizer was bearing their documents. I bear witness for myself in year 16, third month of inundation, day 20 concerning these charges which I heard from this mayor of Thebes; and I am putting them in writing before my lord in order to get to the bottom of them immediately.

151. Workmen Arrested and Interrogated

In the preceding extract, the gang of the Necropolis celebrated the results of an investigation which showed the tomb of Queen Isis, among others in the Valley of the Queens, to be intact; within 14 months, the same tomb had been smashed to bits by a gang of 8 workmen from Deir el-Medina. Two papyri record the recovery of the loot from the individuals to whom they had passed it on, and in addition the journal of the Necropolis periodically relates the latest developments. The first of the extracts below describes a more sobering inspection of the tomb of Isis than that of Papyrus Abott; the second is a broken fragment of testimony of one of the thieves, explaining how his companions had given him directions for breaking into the queen's burial place.

A. Year 17, third month of winter, day 21. The gang of the Necropolis was idle. Going up to the Place of Beauty by the butler (Nesu-Amen?), the city-governor and vizier Kha-em-waset, and the gang of the Necropolis together with their captains to inspect the king's mother, king's wife Isis, l.p.h. They opened her tomb and they found that the granite stone (sarcophagus?) had been smashed in the *menet* (*unknown word*) by the eight thieves. They had caused wanton devastation everywhere inside, having smashed the western door [. . .]

B. [. . . ta]king the testimony of the thief Nakhte-Min son of Pen-ta-Weret of the Necropolis. [. . .] thieves. And the thief Amen-wa and the thief Pen-ta-Weret [. . . said to us, 'Go] to this tomb and break through the corner stones of the tomb,' so they said to us, [. . . You will go] up and hack away opposite the [. . . corn]er stone of the tomb.' So they said to us. We went up to the tomb [and we] reached the proper place, and [we] opened the doors, and we entered. [List of what we took:]
    4 bronze [. . .]-vessels
    [. . .]

2 bronze *sema*-vessels
2 bronze *mehbek*-vessels
[. . .].

152. Rough Company

Tomb robbery was hazardous business; the robbers were exposed not only to the danger of detection and trial, but also to the ruthlessness of their companions in crime. The following extract from the testimony of a thief mentions quite incidentally that a member of the Deir el-Medina community had been murdered so that he might not betray his fellows. The extract goes on to describe the robbery of the tomb of Ramesses VI in the Valley of the Kings, which is known to have taken place not many years after the burial took place (see No. 195). Cyril Aldred has pointed out that the remains in the tomb itself attest to the impatience of the thieves to get at the royal treasure: the sarcophagus was tipped onto its side before the precious oils used in the burial had congealed, so that these flowed down towards the floor leaving streaks on the sarcophagus that are still visible today. One of the most surprising aspects of the tomb robberies is how little awe was inspired by the Pharaohs as soon as they were dead. The tomb of Tutankhamen was partially looted by the very priests responsible for the burial.

The list of items stolen from the tomb of Ramesses VI does not include the gold one associates with a royal burial, perhaps because the thieves were interrupted before they got beyond the first chamber. Even so, the 100 *deben* of copper which fell to the share of each was equivalent to roughly 10 months' grain ration for a Deir el-Medina workman.

Now after some days, we joined up with the foreigner Pa-is, the coppersmith Pen-ta-hut-nakhte, Hori, and the foreigner Nes-Amen; total, five men. We went up as a group. The foreigner Nes-Amen took us up and showed [us] the tomb of King Neb-Ma'at-Ra Mery-Amun, l.p.h., the great god (Ramesses VI). We said to him, 'Where is the child of the Necropolis who was with you?' And he said to us, 'The child [of the Necropolis] was killed, along with the young servant who was with us, so that he would not give us away.' So he said to us. I spent four days breaking into it, all five of us being [present]. We opened the tomb and we entered it. We found a sack lying on sixty [. . .] chests (?). We opened it and found

bronze [. . .]
a bronze cauldron
3 bronze washbowls

a bronze washbowl and ewer (for) pouring water over the hands
2 bronze *kebu*-jars
2 bronze *punt*-jars
a bronze pillar-type *kebu*-jar
a *ker*[. . .]
3 bronze *irer*-vessels
6 inlaid beds
8 copper lamps
We weighed the copper of the cast vessels and we found there to be
[500] copper *deben*, 100 *deben* falling to the share of each [man].
We opened two *gawut*-boxes filled with clothes, and we found:
35 kilts, shawls, kerchiefs, and clothes of fine thin cloth
[7 garments] of fine thin cloth falling to the share of each man.
We found a sack of clothes lying there. We opened it and we found
25 shawls of smooth cloth in it, 5 shawls of smooth cloth falling [to
the share of each man . . .]

Work on the Royal Tomb

INTRODUCTION

The *raison d'être* of the community of workmen was the construction of the royal tombs in the Valley of the Kings. These tombs are rich in imagery, illustrating and magically promoting the passage of the deceased king through the Beyond. The king hoped to travel with the god Re in his sun-bark as he journeyed through the Netherworld during the twelve hours of the night towards the Gates of the Horizon where the sun, and the king, would be reborn. The perils and adventures of this nocturnal journey are recorded in great detail in the Books of the Netherworld, which form the basis of the decoration in the royal tombs, the various corridors and chambers corresponding to specific hours of the night. From the reign of Seti I on, the walls of the entire tomb, from the entrance down to and including the burial chamber, were covered with figures cut in low relief and painted with the full Egyptian palette—if indeed the king reigned long enough for this ambitious programme to be completed.

In the construction of the tomb, the workmen all had their own special tasks. The stonecutters or quarrymen hollowed out the tomb with chisels, smoothed the walls, and plastered them in preparation for decoration. The figures were then drawn in outline on the walls by the draughtsmen and carved in low relief by the chisel-bearers. Finally, it was the draughtsmen's turn again to paint the reliefs. Scaffolding enabled them to reach the upper walls and ceilings, and this was presumably built for them by the carpenters. After a given point, all of the specialists were working at once, the artists decorating prepared surfaces near to the entrance while, deeper down, the stonecutters were opening up new chambers. The two sides of the gang, left and right, were each responsible for the corresponding half of the tomb, and Cathleen Keller and Maya Müller have shown that the decoration on opposite walls of the same chamber, though so similar as to be almost indistinguishable, is in fact the work of two separate teams of workmen.

The passages in this chapter are taken especially from official records. Like every branch of the Egyptian administration, the Necropolis kept detailed registers and accounts of all of its operations. A continuous day-journal recorded such events as deliveries of the supplies to the Necropolis, visits by outside authorities, and incidents connected with the progress of the work. The character of

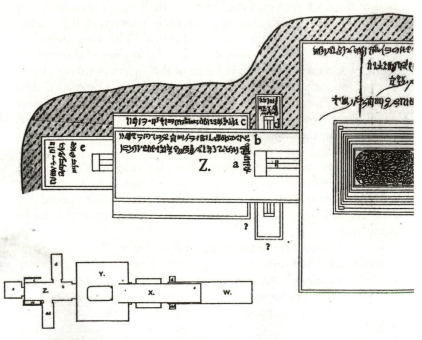

PORTION OF MR. CARTER'S PLAN ILLUSTRATING THE PAPYRUS.

Fig. 23. Plan of the tomb of Ramesses IV from a papyrus in Turin. See Text 153. (Reproduced with the kind permission of the Egypt Exploration Society from Howard Carter and Alan H. Gardiner, 'The Tomb of Ramesses IV and the Turin Plan of a Royal Tomb', *JEA* 4 (1917), 130–158, pl. xxix.)

the entries changes over the centuries, depending on what the scribe of the time thought to be worth noting. Day to day events were initially recorded on ostraca from which a final account covering the entire year would eventually be drawn up on papyrus for the archives. About these archives of the Necropolis not much is known; they were apparently kept in the temple of Medinet Habu during most of the Twentieth Dynasty. Before that time, official documents may have been kept in the Ramesseum or other funerary temples, from which little has been recovered, though we do of course have memoranda and complete texts from the village itself.

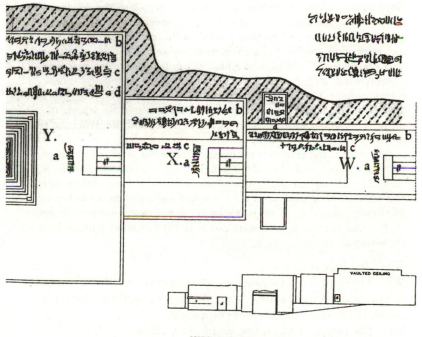

PORTION OF MR. CARTER'S SECTION ILLUSTRATING THE PAPYRUS.

Fig. 23. *Continued.*

153. Plan of the Tomb of Ramesses IV

Several plans or partial plans of royal tombs have survived, of which this is the most complete. It may well be a record of the tomb when it was finished rather than a design drawn up in advance.

The lower portion of the plan has been lost, as has the right end of the papyrus, including the first three corridors of the tomb; but the main body of the design is perfectly preserved. Attractive details include the irregularly shaped brownish surface around the tomb, hatched with diagonal lines of black and red droplet shapes, which clearly represents the mountain-side into which the tomb was cut. The corridors are shown blocked by double doors fastened with bolts; these are painted yellow, presumably to indicate that they were made of gilded wood. The sarcophagus is red mottled with black, corresponding to the rose granite sarcophagus found in place in the tomb; and the scene on the lid of the sarcophagus of the plan, of Isis and Nepthys on either side of the king, is also faithful to the original. The yellow rectangles around the sarcophagus were something of a mystery to Carter and Gardiner when they published this plan in 1917, but Carter's discovery of the tomb of Tutankhamen five years later revealed that the king's body rested in shrines of gilded wood. Legends to the plan give the measurements and the state of completion of the various chambers and corridors designated by names related to their function. Thus the corridors are called 'god's passages', the god being the sun-god Re whose journey through the underworld is recreated in the tomb; and the 'House of Gold in which one rests' was the burial chamber with its large gilt shrines. 'The resting place of the gods' was of course the chamber in which statues of the gods were placed, and where depictions of those statues still adorn the walls. As the legends explain, the figures on the walls and ceilings of the tomb had first been drawn in outline on the smoothed surface, then cut in low relief, and finally painted in. There is at least one inaccuracy, however; the figures of the innermost passage, Z, were not in fact cut in relief, perhaps because the workman ran out of time.

Wa2. Its door is fastened.
Wb. The fourth god's passage, of 25 cubits; width, of 6 cubits; height, of 9 cubits, 4 palms; being drawn with outlines, cut with the chisel, filled with colours, and completed.
Wc. The ramp, of 20 cubits; width, of 5 cubits, 1 palm.
Wd. This chamber, of 2 cubits; width, of 1 cubit, 2 palms; depth, of 1 cubit, 2 palms.

Xa. Its door is fastened.
Xb. The Hall of Waiting, of 9 cubits; width, of 8 cubits; height, of 8 cubits; being drawn with outlines, cut with the chisel, filled with colour, and completed.

Xc. End of the ramp, of 3 cubits. (*This legend should be in the burial chamber.*)

Ya. [Its] door is fastened.

Yb. House of Gold in which one rests, of 16 cubits; width, of 16 cubits; height, of 10 cubits; being drawn with outlines, cut with the chisel, filled with colour, and completed; being equipped with furniture of his majesty, l.p.h., on every side of it, and with the ennead who are in the Netherworld.

Yc. Total, from the first god's passage to the House of Gold, 136 cubits, 2 palms.

Yd. From the House of Gold to the Innermost Treasury, 24 cubits, 3 palms. Total: 160 cubits, 5 palms.

Za. [Its] door is fastened.

Zb. The god's passage which is the shabti-place, of 14 cubits, 3 palms; width, of 5 cubits; height, of 6 cubits, 3 palms, 2 digits; being drawn with outlines, cut with the chisel, filled with colour, and completed. The south of it as well.

Zc. The resting place of the gods, of 4 cubits, 4 palms; height, of 1 cubit, 5 palms; depth, of 1 cubit, 3 palms, 2 digits.

Zd. Left treasury, of 10 cubits; width, of 3 cubits; height, of 3 cubits, 3 palms.

Ze. Innermost Treasury, of 10 cubits; width, of 3 cubits; height, of 4 cubits.

(*Upside-down legend giving further details of the Treasury and the spaces opening from it*):

The god's passage which is on the inner side of the House of Gold [. . .]

The place, the southern one, on the right, which [. . .]

The treasury which is on the left in the *sedet-buti* (*unknown term*) [. . .]

The second god's passage which is at the rear of the House of Gold [. . .]

ACCESSION OF A NEW KING AND
THE CHOICE OF A TOMB SITE

154. The Death of Seti II and Accession of Siptah

In the following extract from the Necropolis journal, the death of the Pharaoh Seti II is announced to the gang. Seti died relatively young—his mummy shows him to have been about 25 years old—and his tomb was unfinished. The accelerated preparations for his burial, followed immediately by the beginning of work on the tomb of his successor, were expected to make heavy demands on the crew, and were therefore accompanied by extra payments, which may explain the rejoicing reported on the first month of winter, day 22. Note that work on the new Pharaoh's tomb, heralded by the issue of chisels to the workmen, began almost at once, some three months after the beginning of the reign.

(Year 1), first month of winter, day 19: remained (in the village). Day that the chief-policeman Nakhte-Min came, saying, 'The falcon has flown to heaven, namely Seti; another has arisen in his place.' The gang was idle.
Day 19: [. . .]
Day 20: remained (in the village)
Day 21
Day 22: remained (in the village). They rejoiced and the gang came to the Valley (of the Kings) in the first month of winter, day 22, in order to work. . . .
Year 1, fourth month of winter, day 21. Day of giving the chisels to the gang.
Year [1, fourth] month of winter, day 21. Day of ordering the work for Sekha-en-Re Setep-en-Re, l.p.h., the Lord of Appearances Ramesses Siptah, l.p.h.

155. Announcement of the Accession of Ramesses VI

Some fifty years later, at the beginning of the reign of Ramesses VI, this pattern of announcing a new reign, issuing wages, and setting to work immediately, was repeated.

Year 1, second month of winter, [day X]. The city-governor, [vizier Nefer-renpet] came to the Enclosure of the Necropolis; and he read out to them a letter, saying, 'Neb-Ma'at-Re Amen-Khepesh-ef Ramesses Mery-Amen, the god, the ruler of Heliopolis, l.p.h. (Ramesses VI), has arisen as great ruler of the whole land.' And they rejoiced very greatly. And he said, 'Let the gang go up (to work).' The three captains went (?) to him to receive the dues of the Necropolis.

156. Choosing the Tomb Site for Ramesses IV

Very important decisions, such as the location of the new tomb and its design and decoration, were of course made by the vizier and other high officials. Choosing a suitable site for a tomb required not only familiarity with the natural features of the Valley, but also information about the locations of existing royal tombs. The officials did sometimes make mistakes; Tomb 11, begun by Sethnakhte, had progressed for several passages when it ran into the earlier tomb of Amenmesses, the course of which had been miscalculated or forgotten although that king had only been dead for fourteen years. Sethnakhte abandoned the project at this point and simply appropriated the tomb of his predecessor Tawoseret, but the half-finished Tomb 11 was later taken over by Ramesses III. His architects simply circumvented the obstacle by giving the tomb a sharp turn to the right and then resuming its course straight into the cliff.

The following extract from the official journal records a visit to the Valley of the Kings by the vizier and two royal butlers, to choose a site for the tomb of Ramesses IV. Royal butlers were members of the king's personal staff; they were often of foreign extraction and owed their position and allegiance only to him. At this time, when the royal capital was at Pi-Ramesse in the Delta and the king was beginning to loose his hold over the powerful southern officials, the royal butlers were often sent to Thebes to work with the vizier and High Priest of Amen and to keep an eye on them. Oddly, although work on the royal tomb ordinarily began as soon as possible after the king's accession, here the choice of tomb site is dated fifteen months into the new reign; it has been suggested that was related to problems with the grain ration and protests by the gang at about this time. (Cf. Nos. 187–9 below.)

(Year 2, second month of inundation, day 17)
The city-governor, vizier Nefer-renpet arrived at Thebes, and also the royal butler Hori and the royal butler Amen-kha son of Tekhy.
Day 18. They went up to the [Great] Valley to seek out a place to cut the tomb of Weser-Ma'at-Re Setep-en-Amen (Ramesses IV).

THE WORK IN PROGRESS

157. Lighting the Work

The further the tomb was driven into the cliff, the more the artists relied on artificial light to carry out their work. This was supplied by wicks, tightly

Fig. 24. A figure representing eternity holds a bowl with three candles of the sort used by the workmen to light their work in the royal tomb. From the tomb of Nefer-abu (Tomb 5). (Reproduced with kind permission of the IFAO in Cairo from J. Vandier, *Tombes de Deir el-Médineh: La Tombe de Nefer-Abou*. MIFAO 69 (Cairo, 1935), pl. XXI.)

twisted lengths of cloth greased with fat or oil. The workmen made the wicks themselves, and since the oils used were valuable commodities, strict accounts were kept of every stage of the process. In the following texts, grease and rags are distributed for the making of wicks; the second also records an issue of lights from the storehouse as well as the quantity consumed on a given day.

The finished wicks were probably set in shallow bowls, to judge by depictions in several Deir el-Medina tombs. Salt was traditionally added to lamps to prevent them from smoking and despite the absence of salt from the accounts, we may suppose it was used by the workmen, since the tombs show no trace of ancient smoke.

Černý noted that roughly equal numbers of wicks were consumed in the morning and in the afternoon, suggesting that the men worked for two equal periods with a lunch break in between. In the second text below, the regular use of 32 candles per day perhaps indicates a policy of never exceeding this quantity.

A. Fourth month of winter, day 2. Day of greasing the wicks that were drawn from the storehouse.

Grease, 8 *hin*-measures. 200 wicks were greased (from?) the 100 *deben* of rags brought by the scribe [. . .]. They were distributed among the gang.

B. (*Across top*) The jar of sesame-oil [for] greasing 400 wicks.

Year 6, third month of inundation, day 26. Day of giving sesame-oil for lighting to the gang when they came to work.

Third month of inundation, day 27. Brought (from) the storehouse, 95 greased wicks.

Consumption of them on this day: 16 plus 16 wicks, makes 32.

Third month of inundation, day 28. Consumption of wicks on this day: [16 plus 16] wicks, makes 32.

32 plus 32 makes 64. Remainder: 35 (*sic*).

Fourth month of inundation, day 3. Brought (from) the storehouse: 118 wicks.

Consumption on this day: 32 wicks.

Fourth month of inundation, day 4. Consumption of wicks on this day. 16 wicks plus 16. Total, 22 (*sic*).

Fourth month of inundation, day [. . .]. Consumption of wicks on this day, 32 [. . .]

Fourth month of inundation, day 7. Consumption of wicks on this day, 16 plus [1]6 wicks. Total, 22 (*sic*).

(*The text continues in the same fashion to fourth month of inundation, day 28.*)

CHISELS FOR THE STONECUTTERS

The Theban mountains into which the tomb was cut were of relatively soft limestone, but this was crossed by bands of flint and the workmen's soft copper chisels quickly became blunt. Coppersmiths were specially assigned to the Necropolis to reforge them. Copper was a valuable commodity and, like grain, a form of currency, so strict records were kept of the chisels issued to the workmen and the authorities kept a stone counterweight with which they could later verify that the full weight of the chisel had been returned.

158. Chisels are Issued to the Gang

[YEAR 1], FOURTH MONTH OF WINTER, DAY 21. Day of [issuing] the chisels to the gang.

Chisels, 68. Itemization:

34 on the right side
34 on the left side
Total, 64 (*sic*)

159. Blunted Chisels Are Collected to Be Reforged

Year 6, THIRD MONTH OF SUMMER, DAY 23. Handing over the blunted portion of the chisels of Pharaoh by the ⟨three⟩ captains, the two deputies, and the two police inspectors. They (*lit.* you) went to the Enclosure of the Necropolis to (?) the doorkeeper Kha-em-waset, the policeman Amen-mose, the policeman Nakhte-Sobek, and Had-nakhte, the scribe of the treasury of Medinet Habu. They found 307 *deben* of copper.

Fig. 25. Sketch of a stonecutter at work with a mallet and chisel. The brawny arms, round head, thick neck and unshaven face are in marked contrast to the elegant features depicted in formal Egyptian art. The stonecutter appears to be working on his knees and is panting from the stress of his labour. (Drawn by Marion Cox after EGA 4324-1943 *recto* in the Fitzwillian Museum, Cambridge.)

GYPSUM FOR PLASTERING THE WALLS

Gypsum, also known as plaster of Paris, was used to repair flaws in the freshly-cut tomb walls; the whole area would then be white-washed with a fine gypsum-solution to give a smooth surface for decoration.

A naturally occuring composite of calcium sulphate and water, gypsum could be found in various parts of Egypt just below the desert surface. To make plaster, it had to be burnt, powdered, and mixed with water. At temperatures over 100°C, gypsum loses about $\frac{3}{4}$ of its moisture; when the resulting substance is recombined with water it sets and eventually becomes very hard. This can then be cut as though it were stone.

160. Preparing the Raw Gypsum

The gypsum used in the royal tomb was prepared as the work progressed. Sometimes this was the work of a special gypsum-maker assigned to the supply staff; at other times of workmen released from their normal duties for this task. This entry from the Necropolis journal records the average yield of the gypsum-maker of the right side of the gang over a four month period.

Year 17 First month of inundation: work of the gypsum-maker, right side, (received) by the scribe Wen-nefer:

Preparinging gypsum, amounting to	$\frac{1}{8}$ sack of gypsum daily
Makes, left-side, (per) 10 (days)	$1\frac{1}{4}$ sacks
Makes (per) month	$3\frac{3}{4}$ sacks
Makes (per) 4 months, makes	15 sacks gypsum
Left side	15 sacks gypsum
Total, right and left, 30 sacks	

161. The Plasterers' Progress

The following graffito recording the progress of the plasterers in the third corridor of the tomb of Ramesses IX shines through the whitewash which was applied subsequently.

Fourth month of inundation, day 22. Laying gypsum in the god's passage.

162. Running out of Gypsum

Without a steady supply of gypsum the work of decoration would grind to a halt. The following is a letter to a man who has interrupted his labours for lack of gypsum. Since he appears to have been working on his own, however, it is possible that he was employed on a private commission rather than the royal tomb.

As for your statement, 'It has been a full month since gypsum was brought to me' and this is (the reason for) your coming down (from) the work; look, I am sending to you. Do not quarrel with me, and Ptah will allow you to get (gypsum). There will be no waiting to get it at all! Now look, I will assign the men to[day].

PAINTING THE TOMB

163. Pigments Issued to a Painter

A. The basic colours of the Egyptian palette, blue, green, red, yellow, black, and white, are reflected in this list of pigments issued to an artist of the Necropolis. He would grind them himself and mix them with gum, which served as the binding material necessary for applying the colours to the surface. Blue pigment could be azurite or blue frit, an artificial compound containing copper; yellows and reds were obtained from ochres and sulphides of arsenic. Various minerals were used for green pigment, especially malachite. Black and white pigments are missing from the list; black would ordinarily be made from soot or lampblack, while whiting or gypsum would be used for white. Perhaps the draughtsman was expected to procure such readily available items for himself.

What was given to the draughtsman Ra-hotep:

gum (?)	10 *deben*
[. . .]	
blue-pigment	20 *deben*
green-pigment	30 *deben*
red ochre	4 *deben*
green-frit	20 *deben*
orpiment (the yellow sulphide of arsenic)	2 *deben*
realgar (the red sulphide of arsenic)	1 *deben*
yellow ochre	5 *hin*

B. The following record of paint deliveries is unusually detailed in that it specifies not only what part of the tomb was being painted, i.e. the ceiling of the door-reveal of the tomb of Ramesses IV, but also the draughtsmen responsible for the scenes in question. Egyptian artists did not sign their work and only very rarely can we identify the creator of a painting or sculpture but the individual draughtsmen of Deir el-Medina are so well known from texts, signed drawings on ostraca, and their own tombs that some of them have been matched up with particular areas of the royal tombs.

Year 4, second month of summer, day 25. This day, beginning to paint the reveal of the tomb on its ceiling on year 4, second month of summer, day 25.
  ochre, 10 *hin*
What was given to the draughtsmen:
  good blue pigment, 18 *deben*
  good malachite, 9 *deben*
Third month of summer, day 16. Once again, (given) to them:
  blue pigment for painting, 36 *deben*
  ochre, 10 *hin* . . .
Fourth month of summer, day 17. This day, once again, given to the draughtsman Amen-hotep and the draughtsman Hori-[sheri]:
  very good blue pigment, 10 + X *deben*
The draughtsman Amen-hotep:
  good blue pigment, 5
  malachite, 4 *deben*
Once again, (given) to him
  blue pigment for painting, 23
Through (?) the scribe Amen-hotep:
  5 *deben*

164. A Painter Asks for Help with His Work

As described in the introduction to this chapter, the left and right sides of the gang worked in parallel, but independently, preparing the corresponding halves of the tomb. The draughtsman who wrote the following letter to his father was working alone on the drawings of the left side since his brother and colleague was ill, and found himself falling further and further behind the other half of the gang. One may suppose that the sculptors were being kept waiting while Hor-Min struggled to prepare the outlines of the figures they would complete. His efforts to get an assistant have been hampered by red tape; the local officials resented his attempts to go over their heads to the High Priest of Amen, but did nothing to help. Now he asks his father to persuade the captains to grant him a colleague.

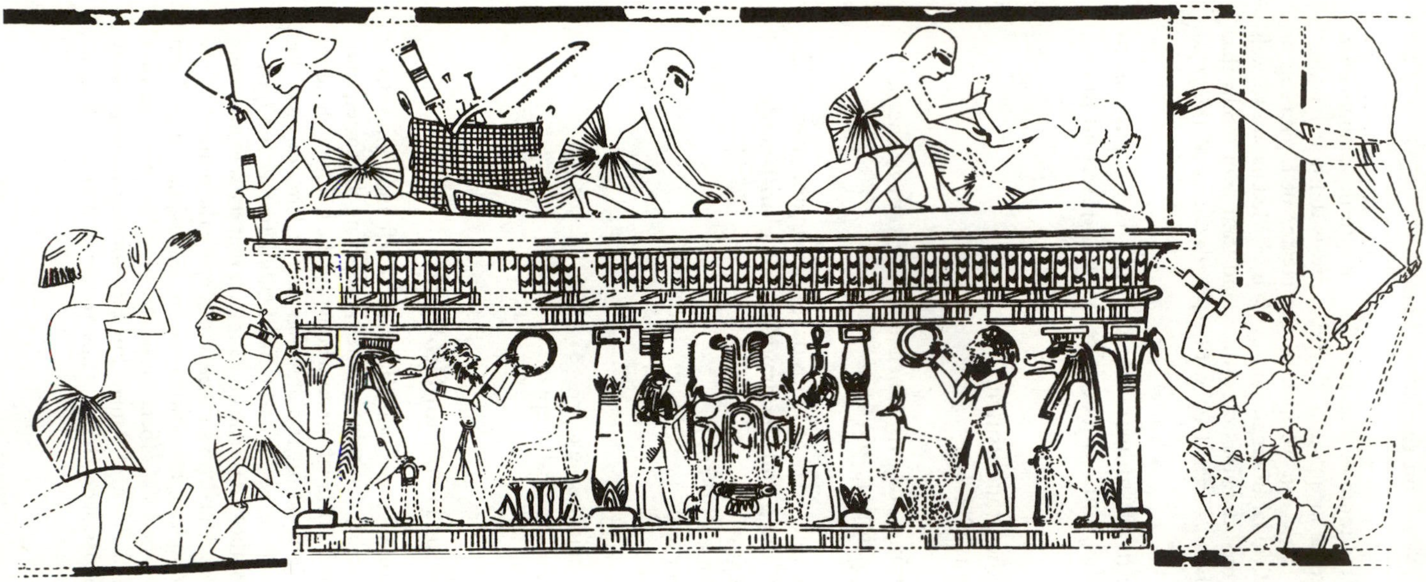

Fig. 26. Detail from a scene in the tomb of the workman Ipuy depicting craftsmen building a shrine for the deified pharaoh Amenophis I (TT 217). The workman on the left, who is calling up to a colleague above him, has dropped his mallet on the foot of another colleague. The latter looks back, startled, and hops on his uninjured foot. In the upper right, a workman tries to rouse a sleeping comrade. (Reproduced with the kind permission of the Metropolitan Museum of Art, New York, from Norman deGaris Davies, *Two Ramesside Tombs at Thebes* (New York, 1927), pl. 37.)

Interestingly, he is willing to bear the expense himself, and offers to share his rations with the newcomer.

Hor-Min's father, the scribe Hori, was an influential member of the gang whose duties were primarily administrative, although he does not seem to have been one of the captains; he may have supervised the supply staff. Hori had two other sons, either of whom could be the draughtsman whose illness prompted Hor-Min's letter.

The draughtsman Hor-Min to his father, the scribe Hori [. . .] in life, prosperity and health, in the praise of Amen-Re, King of Gods.

To the effect that: I say to Amen-Re, King of Gods, Mut, Khonsu, and the ennead of Karnak, Grant that you be healthy! Grant that you live! Give to you strength, health and happiness!

Further: when my letter reaches you, you should send for the man who will go to receive the grain (for?) the donkey. Look, the god's-father of the temple of Hathor wrote me saying, 'Come to receive it.'

And you should write to reason with the captains so they will promote the servant of yours, so that he will give me a hand with the painting. I am alone, since my brother is ill; those of the right side have carved a chamber more than the left-side. Now, he will consume my rations with me.

Now, witness a commission of Pharaoh, l.p.h., like this one when men are doubled for it![a] Now when I told it ⟨to⟩ the High Priest, the captains said to me, 'We will bring him up (to the work site). It is not the responsibility of the High Priest.' So they said. Write [. . .] As for everything my mouth said, I will double it, and more.

[a] i.e. how quickly the work would progress if there were more staff to carry it out!

165. The Pigments Are Exhausted

Our copy of the following letter to the vizier is certainly not the original; it is one of four letters transcribed onto a single ostracon, probably by a student learning the basics of official epistolography. The many corruptions in the text, with some words garbled beyond recognition and others left out altogether, show that the copyist did not entirely understand what he was writing, and the handwriting is juvenile. There is always some doubt about whether such 'model letters' are copies of genuine documents which were actually sent or whether they were composed for classroom use; the latter possibility would of course lessen their value for the historian. In the following example, both the writer and his correspondent, the vizier Hay, are well known from the reign of Ramesses II; the subject matter, pigments

for work on the tomb, is also quite routine. It is therefore not impossible
that this is a copy of an official letter of the Nineteenth Dynasty.

The workman in the Place of Truth In-her-khau greets his lord, the
fan-bearer on the right hand ⟨of the king⟩, the overseer of the gang
in the Place of Truth, the city-governor, the vizier who does justice,
Hay, in life, prosperity and health. It is a communication to inform
my ⟨lord⟩.
    Another communication for my ⟨lord⟩, to the effect that: we are
working ⟨in⟩ the places of which my lord said, 'Let the decoration be
made very well!' But the pigments in it are [exhausted?]. May my
lord act so that I may carry out his good plans. May Pharaoh, l.p.h.,
be written and informed; and may a dispatch be sent to the major-
domo of Thebes, to the High Priest of Amen, ⟨to⟩ the second priest
(of Amen), to the mayor of Thebes, and the administrators who
administer in the treasury of Pharaoh, l.p.h., to supply us with all
that we require.
    To inform my lord:
    yellow ochre
    gum
    orpiment
    realger
    red ochre
    blue frit
    green frit
    fresh fat for burning
    old clothes for wicks
And ⟨we⟩ will execute ⟨every⟩ commission that my ⟨lord⟩ has
ordered.

MONITORING PROGRESS

166. Measuring the Stonecutters' Progress

The higher authorities inspected the work in the tomb periodically to
monitor the gang's progress, as recorded in the following journal from the
first year of the reign of an unnamed king. The records begin, logically
enough, with the 'first god's passage', that is, the open descent towards
the door of the royal tomb. The next segment, the first part of the tomb

underground, is called by various names including the 'other god's passage' and the 'other first god's passage'. Each of these passages is said to be 30 cubits long. The work progressed rapidly; depending on how the scribe is reckoning, which is not entirely clear, the gang seems to have cut either 47 or 60 cubits, that is, 24.5 or 31.5 m. in three months.

Year 1, second month of inundation, day 12. Day of registering the work by the city-governor, the vizier Hori.

The pushing beyond, 13 cubits. What was done in it after the vizier registered the work, pushing beyond, [. . .] cubits.

Third month of inundation, day 2. Day (of) adding to the god's passage to make 30 cubits.

Third month of inundation, day 28. Day (of) opening the other god's passage. Work done in it: 17 cubits.

First month of winter, day 11. Day (of) separating the left side from the right side. The pushing beyond, 13 cubits; in addition to the earlier 17 cubits from the other first god's passage. Total: 30.

As for the registering the work [. . .] from first month of winter, day 8 up to the [first (?) month] of winter, day 17: work in the god's passage, 5 cubits.

167. Progress Reports

The following letter to the vizier from the scribe Nefer-hotep, an ordinary workman, is the very model of the Egyptian official letter combining fawning servility with complaints, here in the guise of a progress report. Note that the author names three main sources of supply to the workmen; the Granary, which provided the grain ration; the Treasury, responsible for other foodstuffs, firewood, and clothes; and the storehouse, where lamps and tools were kept.

The elaborate salutation, characteristic of letters to officials of very high rank, invokes gods of West Thebes, such as the first king of the Eighteenth Dynasty, Amenophis I, and his mother, Queen (Ahmose-) Nefertari; the latter is said to be 'of Menset', the name of her mortuary temple. A manifestation of Amen that was worshipped in her temple is named as well. (On the format of Egyptian letters in general, see the introductory remarks to Chapter 1.)

(To) the fanbearer on the right hand of the king, city governor, the vizier Ta. The scribe Nefer-hotep greets his lord, in life, prosperity and health. It is a letter to inform my lord.

Another communication for my lord, to the effect that, Every day I say to Amen-Re, King of Gods; Mut; Khonsu; Pre-Herackhti; to Amen of Menset (the temple of Nefertari); to Nefertari, may she live!, of Menset; to Amen of the Thrones of the Two Lands; to Amen of the Beautiful Encounter; to Ptah of Ramesses Mery-Amen, l.p.h.; to Ptah of the Place of Beauty (the Valley of the Queens) (to) the south of the village; to Hathor, Mistress of the West, (to) its north; to Amenophis, l.p.h., who dwells in the midst of the West Side: 'Make healthy Pharaoh, l.p.h., my good lord! Let him achieve millions of jubilees as great ruler of the whole land for ever, while you are in his favour every day!'

Another communication for my lord, to the effect that, I am working in the tombs of the royal children which my lord ordered to be constructed. I am working very well and very efficiently, with good work and with efficient work. May my lord not be concerned about it! Indeed, I am working very excellently; I do not tire at all.

Another communication for my lord, to the effect that, we are exceedingly weak; everything for us that is ⟨in⟩ the Treasury, that is in the Granary, and that is ⟨in⟩ the storehouse has been stopped, being exhausted. A load of *den*-unit of stone is not light![a] Moreover, 6 *oipe* of grain have been taken from us, to be given to us as 6 *oipe* of dirt. May my lord act to make for us a means of sustenance. Indeed, moreover, we are dying; we do not live at all. It (the means of sustenance) is not being given to us in any form whatsoever.

    [a] i.e. carrying stones, as we do, is not easy.

168. A Vizier's Answer

The following letter from the vizier Hay was written many years before the one translated above, but it is an answer to a very similar report. The vizier when addressing his subordinates eschewed elaborate compliments and circumlocutions, and went straight to the point. The foreman Neb-nefer had asked about the gang's rations; the vizier seems to say that everything had been arranged by the administrators of the Necropolis and the captains of the gang should simply apply directly to the Treasury to collect the rations. On the other hand, he implicitly acknowledges that all is not as it should be when he promises to inform the pharaoh (respectfully called 'One') of the gang's circumstances. He also arranges for further communication with the gang through his scribe Pa-ser.

The fanbearer on the right hand of the king, the royal scribe, the city governor, the vizier Hay speaks to the chief workman Neb-nefer to the following effect:

This letter has been brought to you to say, Please may you be extremely diligent in executing very well every commission of the great place of Pharaoh, l.p.h, in which you are. Do not allow yourselves to be reproached.

Further: It is *you* who should inquire about the dues of the gang that are in the Treasury of Pharaoh, l.p.h.. Do not allow any of it to be delayed, because I have written to the administrators of the Necropolis about your (*lit.* our) dues that are in the Treasury of Pharaoh, l.p.h., saying, Let it be brought to them.

Now, I will go north to the place where One is, and I will make Pharaoh, l.p.h., aware of your situation. See, I will have the scribe Pa-ser come with a commission to Thebes. When he comes to you at the Enclosure [of the Necropolis], you will come to him there, and you will send him to us with information about your condition.

169. An Attendance List

For certain periods, most notably the reigns of Seti II and Amenmesse, the journal of the Necropolis included full particulars of who was absent from work on any given day and for what reason. A particularly complete text from year 40 of Ramesses II has been studied by Janssen, who observed that at that time the gang as a whole worked an average of only one day in four. The king's tomb would have been long finished by this point in his reign, and although the gang would have been assigned to other projects they were evidently not pushed very hard. On days when there was work, the main reason for absences was 'illness', usually unspecified. The doctor, a workman with medical skills, might also be excused from work to look after a particularly sick colleague or other member of the community (see Chapter 2, No. 25). Workmen are also said to have been absent in connection with the funeral of a relative, or because their wives or daughters had given birth, or to make preparations for a religious festival.

The following selection is a part of the journal of the Necropolis drawn up on an ostracon; it was from such notes that a final record, such as that described above, would have been compiled. The only reason given for absences in this text is illness. Six members of the gang were too ill to work on the first day of the journal; most seemed to recover quite quickly, but for Mery-Sekhmet and Baki the illness lingered, and though they made it to the Valley of the Kings once or twice, they were too weak to do any work. Note that no absences are given for days 8–11 and 19–20. These were weekends, the first a long weekend, and the whole gang was free from work.

Fourth month of inundation, day 7. The scribe Qen-her-khepes-ef, ill; Mery-Sekhmet, ill; Baki, ill; Kasa son of Ra-mose, ill; Mose, ill; Hori-nefer, ill.

Day 8. Mery-Sekhmet, ill; Baki, ill; Mose came to work; Ka-sa son of Ra-mose, ill; Hori-nefer, ill.

Day 11. Mery-Sekhmet came to the Valley (of the Kings) but did not go to work; Baki, ill; Hori-nefer came to work; Ka-sa, came to work.

Day 12. Baki, ill; Mery-Sekhmet came, but he was not able to work.

Day 13. Baki, ill; Mery-Sekhmet came, but he was not able to work.

Fourth month of inundation, day 14. Baki, ill; Mery-Sekhmet, in the village.

Fourth month of inundation, day 15. Baki, ill; Mery-Sekhmet, ⟨in⟩ the village.

Day 16. Mery-Sekhmet, ditto; Baki came to the Valley, but he did not work.

Day 17. Mery-Sekhmet, ditto; Baki came to the Valley, but he did not work.

Day 18. Mery-Sekhmet, ditto; Baki came to work.

Day 21. Mery-Sekhmet, ⟨in⟩ the village.

Day 22. Ditto, ditto.

Day 23. Ditto, ditto.

Day 24. Mery-Sekhmet came to work.

FINAL PREPARATIONS FOR THE BURIAL

Tradition allotted seventy days between a king's death and his burial, allowing time for the process of mummification. If the pharaoh had reigned for many years, his tomb and its furnishings would have been finished long before his death, but even so, many arrangements had to wait until the last minute, such as the assembly of the coffins and shrines around the king's body and the installation of the grave goods. Two papyri evidently record the final preparations for the burial of Ramesses IV in the first year of his successor. The first passage below (No. 170) records the transport of some very heavy object or objects, for which a total of 450 men were enlisted, including the full complement of workmen of the Necropolis. The dragging of the object may have begun at the Ramesseum or perhaps passed this structure, which is mentioned along with the funerary temple of Ahmose-Nefertari in the passage preceding that translated below. Although the text does not state explicitly that they were moving funerary goods, this is a reasonable assumption in the light of No. 172, which is dated twelve days later and describes last-minute work on the funerary equipment, already installed in the tomb.

170. Transporting the Funeral Equipment for Ramesses IV

Year 1, first month of summer, day 25. Last day, total of [. . .] the Necropolis [. . .]. Work at dragging (??) this day.
Men who were dragging, and [. . .]

Police	60 men
Older children	60 men
Marines of Pharaoh	20 men
Place of Truth	40 men
Crew members of the sailors and fishermen	150 men
[. . .] of the Residence	
Workmen of the Necropolis	120 men
Men who were dragging	450 men

171. Preparing to Install the Funerary Equipment

The following Necropolis account, which speaks of 'tombs' in the plural, probably concerns the Valley of the Queens. The main section records the delivery of gear such as may have been used for the installation of heavy funerary furniture. Some of the grave goods were already in place, including coffins and a shabti-box. In addition, we read in the opening lines that 'monuments' had been brought to the tombs on the day before; the word is determined by a mummiform figure, suggesting that it may refer to statues of the gods as mentioned in No. 173, below. Saying 'Ha!' by the workmen was presumably an expression of joy.

Year 1, second month of summer, day 24. This day, saying 'Ha!' on account of the monuments in the entrance of the Valley and of putting them in the opening of the tombs.
Day 25. Bringing gear ⟨for⟩ the men of the Necropolis:
  9 pinewood beams
  7 well-made cords

75 wooden blocks of wood
3 ropes of palm fibre
9 thick bundles (?) of reed
6 posts of acacia-wood
1 wooden 'arm'
1 wooden 'seat' of sycamore wood
22 wooden *seniu* (*meaning unknown*)
14 empty *menet*-jars
30 wicks daily (?)
What rested in them (i.e. the tombs):
    5 coffins treated with varnish, their bands worked with gold; the
       second (also); (and) another, (total) 3 (coffins worked with
       gold?), 2 varnished with sesame-oil (??)
a shabti-box loaded with shabtis (and) treated (with) varnish.

172. Installing the Funerary Equipment

The following excerpt from the journal of the Necropolis describes the
introduction of shrines in the tomb of Ramesses IV under the supervision
of the vizier, the high priest of Amen, and other top officials. The shrines,
which fit one inside the other, were of various materials. The outermost
shrine was of granite and already *in situ*; the next was of *mry*-wood, which
Janssen suggests is a red wood, possibly imported. Inside this was placed a
shrine of alabaster, and this in turn contained silver equipment of an
unspecified kind. It would seem that the alabaster shrine was not designed
as part of this funerary equipment; there was some question about whether
it would fit, and alterations had to be made to the decoration at the last
minute.

    A comparison can be drawn between this assemblage and the canopic
chest of alabaster from the tomb of Tutankhamen, which was enclosed in
a shrine of guilded wood. This chest may also have been altered for use in
the young king's burial, as the containers for his organs certainly were, the
names having been changed from Ankh-kheperu-Re. In Tutankhamen's
case the alabaster shrine held miniature gold coffins containing the internal
organs removed in the embalming process; these presumably correspond to
the 'equipment of silver' found in the alabaster shrine of our text.

YEAR 1, SECOND MONTH OF SUMMER, DAY 7. WORKING IN THE THREE
BOOTHS.
Consumption of wicks, 92; night, 22
Coming by the officials:
    the vizier Nefer-renpet

the High Priest of Amen Ramesses-nakhte
the royal butler Seti-her-imeny-ef
the royal butler Pre-nakhte
[the overseer of the] treasury, Monthu-tawy
the royal butler Tem-nakhte
the royal butler Sobek-hotep
the overseer of bowmen Pa-iry

in order to install the equipment in the large piece of equipment of granite. The *mry*-wood shrine was installed, and its wooden pole put on it. And the pole of *kedey*-wood was put in them up to the [. . .] of the granite shrine [. . .] And they let the alabaster shrine be dragged (down) in order to install it in the shrine of *mry*-wood; and it fit perfectly within it; while on the inside, it fit the silver equipment. And the craftsmen of the Place of Truth were set to hammering on it while the royal butler Kha stood over them.

(*13 lines recording grave goods*)

The royal butler Amen-kha sent for the 4 overseers of the alabaster-cutters together with two men. They escorted (?) them down the passage, and the scribe Amen-nakhte let them into the tomb, and they spent the night hammering on the exterior of the alabaster shrine, as well as its interior, until daybreak. They finished, and it was painted with figures.

173. Final Preparations for the Burial of Merneptah

Here we have a record of the installation of funerary equipment in the tomb of Merneptah, including statues of the gods and the king's coffins. This took place in year 7 over a period of almost a year; first, the statues of the gods are said to have been dragged to the royal tomb, then some nine months later the vizier supervised the installation of the sarcophagus and coffins. Two months after this the northern vizier and overseer of the Treasury came to see the work; they brought with them a sculptor who spent two days in the tomb doing some final work on one of the coffins. Merneptah reigned for almost two more years after this; during that time the tomb may have been sealed, ready for the day it would be needed.

Note the distribution of extra payments to the gang at the end of the extract. These were special payments called 'rewards' which the workmen received in addition to their regular wages of grain, fish, and vegetables. They included foods such as fruit, meat, and breads; and manufactured goods including clothes, oil, and other supplies. High-ranking officials came to the village to deliver the 'rewards', especially when extra work was required from the gang, as at the beginning of a reign when the new tomb was begun.

Year 7, [third month of inundation, day 2]3. On this day the gods of the Dual King [Ba-en-Re] Mery-Amen were conveyed to their place by the city governor, vizier Pa-nehesy.

Year 7, fourth month of summer, day 13. On this day, the vizier Pa-nehesy came [to the village (?)], but he did not find the gang there. He came to the Necropolis, and he said, 'Go up to the Valley [to lower the sarcophagus of?] alabaster to the coffin of cedar-wood.' He said, 'Let the officials come with me.'

Year 7, fourth month of summer, day 14. On this day, the butler Ramesses-em-per-Re and the scribe Pen-pa-mer came together with the vizier Pa-nehesy to the Valley to let the coffins of Pharaoh, l.p.h., descend to their place.

   . . . (*the gang receives rewards*)

Year 8, second month of inundation, day 13. This day, the scribe Inpu-em-hab, the scribe Pa-ser, the chief of police Nakhte-Min, and the chief of police Hori arrived, saying, 'The overseer of carpenters Roma is arriving at the Enclosure of the Necropolis.' The captains were brought to him, and he said to them, 'Pharaoh, l.p.h., has sent the vizier Pen-Sekhmet, the overseer of the Treasury Mery-Ptah, and the scribe of the sculptor's workshop Huy.'

They (the high officials) came to the mouth of the Valley bearing the document of Pharaoh, l.p.h., on the second month of inundation, day 14, but the vizier Pen-Sekhmet did not come with them. They told the captains that the Pharaoh, l.p.h., had ordered rewards for them because of the commission they had executed.

He (the vizier?) came on the second month of inundation, day 16, together with the scribe of the sculptors workshop Huy, and Huy spent two days staying there and working on the coffin. And the overseer of craftsmen came to the Valley on the second month of inundation, day 18 and registered the work on the coffin [. . .] and he came to the Enclosure of the Necropolis to reward the gang on the second month of inundation, day 20. He rewarded the gang, giving them (as) rewards:

9,000 loaves

20 *menet*-jars of sesame oil

9,000 [. . .] fish
20 sacks of salt
600 blocks of natron
400 blocks of salt
6 sacks of malt
[. . .]
3 sacks of beans
[. . .] of *kdy*-beer
[. . .]

THE BURIAL

174. The Burial of Ramesses III

The actual burial of the Pharaoh Ramesses III, who had reigned for 32 years, is reported surprisingly tersely in this journal of the Necropolis from the first year of his successor, Ramesses IV.

First month of inundation, day 4. Weser-hat (on duty). 1 *des*-jar [of beer], 8 bundles of vegetables. This day, the burial equipment reached the Great Valley. . . .
First month of inundation day 24. Min-kha (on duty). What came via the builder Baku:
    3 jars. The burial of the coffin took place.

175. Ramesses V Is Buried and his Tomb is Sealed

The following text records the burial of Ramesses V in the second year of Ramesses VI, who was probably his uncle though of roughly the same age. Such a long delay before the interment is very unusual, and is probably connected in some way to the fact that Ramesses VI took over the tomb intended for his nephew; the first four corridors of KV 9 are inscribed for Ramesses V, but from there on the decoration is in the name of Ramesses VI. However, Ramesses VI did provide a burial for Ramesses V, and the latter's body was found along with those of other New Kingdom kings in the tomb of Amenhotep II to which they were later moved for safety; he died young, less than 30 years old, and possibly of smallpox. It is thought by some that uncle and nephew shared the adapted sepulchre, and by others that Ramesses VI had a simple tomb cut for the earlier king, which, if it was undecorated, is no longer identifiable.

Year 2, second month of inundation, day 1. This day, Sekheper-en-Re arrived at the west of Thebes, in funeral. The doors of his tomb were carpented in the second month of inundation, day 2.

CIVIL WAR AND FOREIGN
INVADERS INTERRUPT THE WORK

176. Libyan Nomads Reach Thebes

In the Nineteenth and Twentieth Dynasties, large population movements across the Near East brought waves of immigrants hoping to settle in the fertile Nile valley, while food shortages in Libya and the western desert led to pressure on Egypt's western borders as well. The Egyptian annals record one magnificent victory after another over the foreigners, but by the reign of Ramesses IX foreign marauders were a threat even as far south as Thebes. From then on, the journal of the Necropolis recurrently notes that the gang was prevented from working because of the danger posed by Libyans and Meshwesh. The following extract from years 10 and 11 of Ramesses IX records the movements of the raiders and the suspension of work on the tomb for some period. The 'desert dwellers' are first reported to have reached Semen, a town some 25 km south of Thebes; this is the point where the trade route from the Kharga oasis reached the Nile valley. Ten days later they were in West Thebes itself, and they are now more precisely identified as Meshwesh. However, the delivery of vegetables on the epagomenal days shows that the village was not cut off by the nomads; the concern was rather that they might swoop down at any moment.

The desert dwellers descended from the town of Semen.
Year 10, fourth month of summer, day 26. Inactivity of the gang of the Necropolis because of the desert dwellers [. . .]
Year 10, fourth month of summer, day 27. Inactivity of the gang of the Necropolis because of the desert dwellers [. . .]
Year 10, fourth month of summer, day 28. Inactivity of the gang of the Necropolis because of the desert dwellers [. . .]
The Servant of Truth Baki came, and he took hold of Pal together with those who [who belonged] to the temple of Men-[. . .]-Re; and he took Pal's captain together with [. . .]
Year 10, fourth month of summer, day [29]. Inactivity of the gang of the Necropolis because of the desert dwellers [. . .]
Year 10, fourth month of summer, [day 30]. Day the gardeners of the Necropolis, right side, brought [. . .] vegetables, 50 (?) bundles; 21

qeb-jars; 110 + X *tjabu*-vessels [. . .] Pen-ta-Weret, vegetables, 80 bundles; onions [. . .]

[Fifth epagomenal day, the birth] of Osiris. The desert dwellers descended to the West [of Thebes . . .] the great river [. . .]

Day 2. Inactivity of the gang because of the Meshwesh.

177. Mobilizing Defences

The following letter from the vizier perhaps suggests a more substantial threat than small-scale raids. It is addressed to people in Per-hebyt, a town in the Delta, and so very far from Thebes; but the chief policeman sent by the vizier may be the Ser-Monthu attached to the Necropolis. This is perhaps sufficient excuse for including here the text which most vividly evokes the panic caused by the invaders.

The vizier of the land [says to . . .]: When the chief policeman Ser-[Monthu reaches you, you will] come quickly with him, and with all the people of the officials and police who are with you in Per-hebyt, the village. Do not keep back anyone of those whose names I will read out, which I have in writing; but you will come only when you know the route of the Meswesh very, very well. Do not be slack at all. Take note of these things you will do!

178. Civil War

The following text dates to the reign of Ramesses V or of Ramesses VI, and is therefore much earlier than the two extracts given above. The threat here is said to be from 'people who are enemies'. There is some doubt whether the scribe used this vague term because he was not yet familiar with the names of the bedouin peoples, or whether the antagonists in this case were in fact Egyptians. Černý has argued that the hostilities described here were episodes in a civil war between the supporters of Ramesses V and Ramesses VI. The latter does seem to have been on poor terms with his predecessors, inasmuch as he erased the cartouches of Ramesses IV and usurped the tomb of Ramesses V. The disturbances are also more serious than those recorded later; a policeman announces to the gang that the town of Per-nebyt, an otherwise unknown location, has been plundered and its people burned. Some days later the gang itself appears to have been in danger.

Despite these crisis conditions, life, and even work, went on. The birth of a baby is reported in the middle of the policemen's announcement; while construction on the royal tomb appears to have continued in the face of the enemy.

Year 1, first month of winter, day 13. Inactive because of the enemy. Coming by the two chief policemen to say: The people who are enemies have come and reached Per-nebyt.

Giving birth in the night by Men-nefer-em-hab. They plundered everything in it, and burned its people, so they say. Now the high priest of Amen said to us, Bring the police of Per-nebyt together with those who are in the South and those of the Necropolis, and let them stand there guarding the Necropolis.

[. . .] 160. The pushing beyond: 5 cubits; width, 6 cubits; height, 2 cubits, making 30 cubic cubits (*sic*). The 2 watches (?) amounting to 360 cubic cubits. The [. . .]

Year 1, first month of winter, day 10 + X. The chief policeman Monthu-mose [came and] said to the captains of the Necropolis (on) this day: [. . .] Do not go up (to the Valley of the Kings) until you see what will happen. I will hurry to look for you, and to hear what will be said. It is I who will come to tell you to go up.

Year 1, first month of winter, day 27. The gang was inactive because of the enemy on this day.

The Workmen

The officers of the gang usually managed to pass on their positions to one of their sons, and it is likely that, as a rule, the workmen's posts also stayed in the family. However, there was no guarantee that all of the young men would find employment in the gang, and the competition for places was fierce.

The Necropolis also employed several dozen supply staff to provide the gang with water, fuel, and other staples. Their position was much less enviable than that of the workmen; they were assigned quotas which they seem to have been unable to meet and they were given no days off. There is no information about their salaries but these were certainly much less than those enjoyed by members of the gang. The supply staff did not live in the village.

179. List of New Appointments

The following ostracon, dated to year 2 of an unnamed king who is perhaps Merneptah, presents two interesting texts. The first is a report on the excavation of the royal tomb, which is still in its early stages, having progressed only as far as the second corridor and to half its intended height. This is as one might expect so early in the reign. The text on the verso is a very full list of personnel assigned to the tomb, possibly new recruits over and above those already employed, since neither the captains of the gang nor the stonecutters appear to be included. The list mentions artisans and plasterers, for whom there would be steadily more work as the stone-cutters progressed; supply staff, to bring water, fish, and firewood for the others; and a handful of administrative staff such as guardians and police officers.

recto

Record of work done in the Great Place of Pharaoh in year 2, second month of inundation, last day:

> God's passage which is upon the sun's path: length, of 20 cubits, 3 palms; width, of 6 cubits; height, 10 cubits.
>
> Second god's passage, behind it, work done in it: its length, of 15 cubits; width, of 5 cubits; height, of 5 cubits [. . .]

verso

Those who will be brought to the settlement of the Necropolis as craftsmen:

> 2 draughtsmen
> 2 chisel-bearers
> 2 plasterers
> 2 craftsmen of the *kha*-tool
> 2 coppersmiths to make the tools of the gang of Pharaoh
> 2 sandal-makers
> 10 supply staff
> [. . .]
> 1 bearer
> 2 officers
> 2 guardians
> 2 *war-Hor* (unknown)

And this Great Place of Pharaoh will be furnished (?) with them.

180. Career Worries

Concern about the careers of five local boys prompted one villager to submit the following question to the oracle. (On oracle questions, see Chapter 3, No. 78.)

Will the vizier take the five boys?

181. Buying a Promotion

It comes as no surprise that with so much at stake fathers might bribe the local officials to secure a place for their sons on the gang of the Necropolis. In the following text, a father keeps a careful record of the bribe goods he has paid out, and stresses the legitimacy of the transaction with a statement that the items were all his own property. Note that the scribe Hori-sheri receives more than either of the foremen, perhaps because it was he who corresponded with the office of the vizier.

List of [the things] I gave to the administrators [of the gang] so that they would promote the boy, all of which belonged to me personally—none of them [belonged to anyone else.]
The scribe Hori-sheri:

wooden chair	makes 11 (*deben*)
wooden container	makes 2 (*deben*)

The chief workman Nakhte-em-Mut:

leather sack	makes 15 *deben*

The chief workman In-her-khau:

wooden chair with a low seat	makes 30 *deben*

The scribe Hori-sheri:

large folding-stool with a footstool	makes 30 *deben*

182. Mass Job Cuts

The position of a Necropolis workman was, in general, very secure, so it must have come as a severe blow to the community when, in the reign of Ramesses VI, almost half of the gang was demoted at once. Ten years earlier, Ramesses IV had greatly increased the number of workmen to 120, and it was evidently felt that such a level could not be maintained; sixty could stay, and the rest would have to go. The following text records not only the announcement of this decision to the gang, but also the events before and after, from which it seems that the most important members of the community were chiefly concerned with saving themselves. First, they assembled the workmen, perhaps to prepare them for the coming events. Then the scribe Pa-ser sent the chief workmen to report to the others his victory in a legal battle with the draughtsman Neb-nefer; the latter's offence is not named, but the punishment was very heavy and perhaps included even branding, though the text is broken at this point. This statement may have been meant to intimidate the gang before Pa-ser's main announcement, that of the reduction of the gang. It was up to themselves to pick who were to stay and who were to be demoted to serfs. The local officials and other important figures of course survived this selection, and sent two silver chisels to the vizier in gratitude.

Year 2, third month of summer, day 9. This day, mustering the men of the Necropolis by the scribe of the ⟨Necropolis⟩ Hori, the scribe of the Necropolis Amen-em-ope, the chief workman Nakhte-em-Mut, the chief workman In-her-khau, the scribe Amen-nakhte, and the scribe Hori-sheri, behind the wall.

Year 2, third month of summer, day [. . .] This day, the scribe Paser came to the Enclosure of the Necropolis and sent (for?)

the 2 chief workmen
the scribe of the Necropolis Hori
the 2 chief policemen
the scribe of the Necropolis (*sic*—a repetition)
(and ten named workmen)

saying: 'The scribe Pa-ser was in court together with the draughtsman Neb-nefer, and the scribe Pa-ser was found to be in the right, while the draughtsman Neb-nefer was found to be in the wrong. The court said: Give him 100 blows with a stick as well as 10 (??) brand marks (??), and set him to breaking stone in the Place of Truth until the vizier pardons him.' So they said.

The scribe Pa-ser said, The vizier spoke thus: 'Let these sixty men stay here as the gang, all your choice, and let the rest be brought outside. Order them to become supply staff who will carry for you (*lit.* 'us').'

SUPPLIES AND RATIONS

The workmen's wages were all paid in kind and the gang was generously supplied with food, fuel, and clothing by the State. Deir el-Medina is in fact a well-documented example of the redistribution system in action. The Treasury and the Granary were the main suppliers of goods and provisions to the Necropolis, but various temples also delivered foodstuffs, particularly breads from the offerings and occassionally also whole cattle for beef.

The workmen's basic salary was the monthly grain ration, supplied by the Granary; a workman received 4 sacks (*c.*300 litres) of emmer and $1\frac{1}{2}$ sacks (*c.*115 litres) of barley, while the captains were alloted $5\frac{1}{2}$ sacks of emmer and 2 of barley. Emmer and barley were used to make bread and beer respectively, the two staples of the Egyptian diet. The value of these grain-salaries is difficult to convert into modern terms. The 300 litres of emmer received by the workmen was at any rate more than enough to feed a family of ten and there would be some surplus which could be used to buy other goods.

In addition, the supply staff supplied the gang with fish, firewood, water, and vegetables, working to a quota of a given quantity per week. Other payments, including clothes, oils, and luxury items such as meat, were supplied by the Treasury at wider intervals; when high officials visited the tomb, they sometimes distributed such goods to the workmen as 'favours' from the king.

The accounts for fish deliveries are particularly well preserved, and from them it has been calculated that, in, for example, year 27 of Ramesses III, the workmen received an average of 8.4 kilograms of fish per month; fish and beans would have been the main source of protein for the workmen, since meat was a luxury. In the case of other commodities the surviving records are too incomplete for the average monthly deliveries to be estimated. The workmen may have received one or two cakes per month, a half a dozen vessels of beer, and unknown quantities of dates, vegetables, beans, and so on.

183. A Ration Distribution

The following ostracon records a paradigmatic ration distribution to the right side of the gang in the mid-Twentieth Dynasty. The rations are paid in full and on time, namely in the month before that for which they were due. Note that the physician, a workman who also tended the sick when necessary, received an extra ration of 1 sack of emmer and $\frac{1}{4}$ sack of barley, bringing his total to nearly that of a captain. The young men appear in some distributions and not in others; the $1\frac{1}{2}$ sack plus $\frac{1}{2}$ sack they receive is much lower than that of a workman, but still amply sufficient to support a single person. The maidservants were assigned to the gang for grinding grain and perhaps other household tasks. Since it is not known how many maidservants there were, little can be said about their joint ration of $1\frac{1}{2}$ sacks of barley and the same amount of emmer. (The scribe followed the standard practice of using black ink for measures of barley and red ink (small caps. in the translation) for measures of emmer.)

The ostracon was found in the temple area to the north of the village, and it is likely that the grain was issued nearby.

FIRST MONTH OF SUMMER, on the right.
The ration distribution for THE SECOND MONTH OF SUMMER.

the chief workman	2 sacks	$5\frac{1}{2}$ SACKS
the scribe	2 sacks	$5\frac{1}{2}$ SACKS
17 men, each	$1\frac{1}{2}$ sacks	4 SACKS
makes	$25\frac{1}{2}$ sacks	68 SACKS
2 young men, each	$\frac{1}{2}$ sack	$1\frac{1}{2}$ SACKS
amounts to	1 sack	3 SACKS
the guardian	$1\frac{1}{4}$ sacks	$3\frac{1}{4}$ SACKS
the maidservants	$1\frac{1}{2}$ sacks	$1\frac{1}{2}$ SACKS
the doorkeeper	$\frac{1}{2}$ sack	1 SACK
the doctor	$\frac{1}{4}$ sack	1 SACK
total	$32\frac{1}{2}$ sacks	$84\frac{3}{4}$ SACKS

184. Official Corruption

In year 17 of Ramesses III, the gang was being shortchanged by a greedy official who used an undersized measure to distribute the rations and presumably kept the difference for himself. Here the captains bring the problem to the attention of another scribe of the vizier, Akh-pet, who checks the grain-measure and finds that it holds 38 *hin* instead of the standard 40. The workmen had been receiving 5 per cent less than their due.

Year 17, second month of winter, day 29. [T]his day, the captains of the Necropolis spoke to the scribe Akh-pet, saying, 'the *oipe*-measure with which the rations are given is (too) small.' And he said, 'To whom does the *oipe*-measure belong?' And they said to him, 'It was the scribe Pa-ser who brought it.' So they brought a new [*hin*-measure], and measured it with the *hin*-measure, and it made 38 *hin*.

185. A Personal Favour from the King

As noted above (No. 173) the gang from time to time received 'rewards' of luxury items from the Pharaoh. In addition, individual workmen could be singled out for extra payments. The foreman In-her-khau recorded such an exceptional gift on a stela. The commodities were granted by Ramesses III and delivered to In-her-khau by the royal butler Hori; Hori is shown in the upper half of the stela receiving his instructions from the Pharaoh himself. The reason for the donation is not given, but In-her-khau was clearly proud of this evidence of royal favour.

Given as favours from the King, the Lord of the Two Lands, Ramesses III, by the royal scribe, the royal butler Hori [. . . to] the chief workman in the Place of Truth In[-her-khau].

silver *tjebu*-vases [from As]kalon	2
tunics of fine, thin cloth	. . .
[. . .]	2
kerchiefs of fine, thin cloth	2
sashes of fine, thin cloth	2
semau-cloths of fine, thin cloth	2
[. . .]-cloth	1
sheet of smooth cloth	1
bronze *kebu*-jars	[. . .]
[. . .] vase with flowers	1
iredj-vessel	1
Sweet *ben*-oil[a]	[. . .] jars
[. . .]	1
honey	1 *menet*-jar
fat	1 *menet*-jar
cream	[. . .] *menet*-jar
[. . .]	50
sam-plants	20 handfuls
incense	10 *qede[ret]*-units
olives	2 *menet*-jars
fenugreek	20 sacks
emmer	30 (sacks?)
papyrus	50 (bundles?)
flax	200 bundles
sety-fruit	2 *oipe*
big loaves	[. . .]

[a] Made from moringa nuts.

186. Maidservants for the Gang

The state provided the workmen with not only the material necessities of life, but also certain services such as launderers to wash their clothes and those of their families, water-carriers to alleviate the nuisance of living in the desert, and maidservants to turn the monthly grain ration into flour. In the following letter the general Pay-ankh, effective ruler of Upper Egypt in the last years of the Twentieth Dynasty, speaks about five maidservants whom he had given to the gang; if these had not yet arrived, he tells the workmen to go to the God's Wife of Amen, Herere, to collect them.

Now, *à propos* of the matter of these five servants I gave, they belong to you, all of you, from the captains down to all the workmen. And let not any one among you tyrannize over his fellow! But do not give to Her-Amen-pena-ef a share of them; indeed, I have (already) given to him.

Now, if you have not received them, you shall go to the place where Herere is and receive them from her. And you will not be slack concerning any matter of mine. And you will save my letter so that it may serve for you as testimony.

DEMONSTRATIONS

At several periods in the village's history, especially in the latter part of the Twentieth Dynasty, ration deliveries were irregular and incomplete. There is no indication of the cause of the various crises, although Theban officials state repeatedly that they simply did not have the grain with which to pay the gang. The problem must therefore have been further afield, such as a breakdown of the general system of distribution.

The gangs reacted to extended periods of shortage by staging demonstrations to draw the attention of any powerful official who could help. They left the village *en masse*, and might, for instance, gather at one of the great funerary temples, calling out to officials who happened to pass. The best-known demonstrations are those of year 29 of Ramesses III, which are described in a particularly detailed journal of the Necropolis now known as the Turin Strike Papyrus. As it happens, this coincides with one of the periods for which the preserved records of ration deliveries are most complete, so that we can check the validity of the workmen's complaints. It seems they were indeed on very short rations and justifiably distressed.

187. The Turin Strike Papyrus

The Turin Strike Papyrus is in fact a journal recording not only the demonstrations but also various other incidents and events in the Necropolis in year 29 of Ramesses III, but the accounts of protests by hungry workmen are so striking that they have given the modern name to the whole. The author of the papyrus was the scribe Amen-nakhte who features prominently in the first episode below, as appears from his slip into the first person ('I brought them up'). This same Amen-nakhte is known to have kept a record of the shortfalls in his own rations, and must have been sympathetic to the workmen in their plight even though he was one of the captains and supports the higher authorities on this occasion.

In the first incident below, Amen-nakhte supervised the distribution of 2 sacks of emmer to the workmen as rations for the first month of summer. Even if this means 2 sacks per person it would have been far too little, and the foreman Khonsu advised the gang to leave the village and approach the children of the vizier for help. When they had passed one 'wall', the scribe Amen-nakhte stopped them with threats of legal action. The wall in question was clearly not a barrier, and may have been a symbolic boundary to the necropolis area.

In the second incident eleven days later, the gang did in fact reach the temple of Merneptah and managed to obtain a promise of relief from the Mayor of Thebes.

Year 29, first month of summer, day 2: giving the two sacks of emmer to the gang as rations for the first month of summer by Amen-kha and Weser-hat. The chief workman Khonsu said to the gang, 'Look, I am telling you: take the rations and go down to the riverbank to the Enclosure. Then let the children of the vizier tell it to him.'

Now when the scribe Amen-nakhte had finished giving them rations, they betook themselves to the riverbank in accordance with what he had said to them. Now when they had passed one wall, the scribe Amen-nakhte went and said to them, 'Do not pass on to the riverbank! Indeed, I gave you two sacks of emmer within the hour. If you go, I will prove you to be at fault in any court to which one will go.' And I brought them back up.

Year 29, first month of summer, day 13. The gang passed the walls, saying, 'We are hungry!' Sitting at the back of the temple of King Ba-en-Ra Mery-Amen (Merneptah), l.p.h. And they called out to the Mayor of Thebes as he was passing by. He sent Nefer, the gardener of the overseer of cattle, to them, saying, 'Look, I will give you these 30 *khar* of emmer to be a means of life, which Pharaoh gave you (as) rations.'

188. The Shortfalls in the Rations

One member of the gang kept track of the monthly shortfalls in rations in years 28–30 of Ramesses III, covering the period of the famous strikes. He calculated on the basis of an expected income of $5\frac{1}{2}$ sacks per month, which could represent either the combined ration of a workman, or the ration of

emmer alone for one of the captains. In fact, the writer may well have been
Amen-nakhte, the author of the Strike Papyrus, since he is stated elsewhere
to have kept a record of 'the arrears of the Necropolis'.

Only half of this rather long text is presented here to give an impression
of its contents; the pattern continues into year 30, and there does not seem
to have been any improvement in ration deliveries after the demonstrations
of year 29. The very complicated notation for figures is due to the Egyptians' lack of complex fractions.

Year 28, fourth month of summer, last day. This day, taking away
   half of my rations.
List of my balance:
Fourth month of summer. Entered: $4\frac{2}{4}\frac{1}{8}$ sacks. Balance: $\frac{3}{4}\frac{1}{8}$ sacks.
The 5 epagomenal days. Balance: $\frac{2}{4}\frac{1}{8}\frac{1}{16}\frac{1}{32}$ sacks.
First month of inundation. Entered: $4\frac{2}{4}\frac{1}{8}$ sacks. Balance: $\frac{3}{4}\frac{1}{8}$
   sacks.
Second month of inundation. Entered: $4\frac{2}{4}\frac{1}{8}$ sacks. Balance: $\frac{3}{4}\frac{1}{8}$ sacks.
Third month of inundation. Entered: 5 sacks. Balance: $\frac{1}{4}$ sacks.
Fourth month of inundation. Entered: 5 sacks. Balance: $\frac{2}{4}\frac{1}{32}$ (?) $\frac{1}{64}$ (?)
   sack.
First month of winter. Entered: complete.
Second month of winter. Entered: $1\frac{2}{4}$ sacks. Balance: [4] sacks.
Third month of winter. As balance: $1\frac{2}{4}$ sacks.
Fourth month of winter. Entered: 5 sacks. Balance: [$\frac{2}{4}$] sack.

189. Torchlight Demonstrations

Several texts mention protests at night, at which the gang carried torches or,
more literally, 'a torch' or 'the torch' in the singular. This must have been
a striking scene, but the texts are unfortunately very laconic in their descrip-
tions. Not all the occasions of 'carrying torches' were related to protests or
demonstrations, and one text even mentions 'the place of carrying torches',
as though a special area was associated with the activity; the significance of
the activity in general is still far from clear.

The events recorded in the first text below are also described in the Turin
Strike Papyrus (No. 187 above) of the 29th year of Ramesses III; the second
text is dated four years later in year 2 of Ramesses IV.

A. (*opening lines very broken*)
Second month of winter, day 4 [. . .] the [3] captains [. . .], so he
said, falsely. 'Give 2 *oipe* of water to each man,' so he said. And the
chief policeman Monthu-mose sent them 50 jars of beer.

[Second month of winter, day 17.] They all passed (the walls) again in the evening, carrying torches.

Second month of winter, day 17. The overseer of the army of Medinet Habu [. . .] came to the gang, and he heard [their testimony, saying, 'Tell me] the things I will write about to Pharaoh.' The scribe Hori [. . .] the mayor of Thebes told it to me. The [gang . . .] spent the night.

(*The text continues with reports of further demonstrations.*)

B. (Year 2, third month of summer), day 28. Nefer-her . . . The gang carried torches on account of their rations for the third month of summer and the fourth month of summer.

Day 29 . . . The officials came to hear the testimony of the gang: the mayor of Thebes, the overseer of the Treasury Kha-em-tery, the mayor of the river Ra-mose, and also the document scribe Amen-pa-nefer.

190. An Oracle about Rations

A workman who dispaired of learning the truth about the ration situation from the officials finally turned to his god: the following is a question submitted to the oracle of Amenophis I.

My good lord! Shall we be given rations?

Epilogue

191. The Gang is Scattered

Towards the end of the Twentieth Dynasty, when work in the Valley of the Kings was repeatedly interrupted by the proximity of hostile Libyan and Meshwesh nomads (see above No. 176), the situation of the workmen and their families in their isolated valley became increasingly precarious. It was presumably for this reason that they eventually abandoned the village inhabited by their ancestors for over 400 years and moved down to more more densely populated areas, some settling within the massive walls of Medinet Habu and others going as far as East Thebes. No document refers to the decision to leave or the move itself, and the date can only be estimated to fall in the early years of Ramesses XI. The following letter to the deputy of the Estate of Amen-Re, Hori in East Thebes from the scribe of the Necropolis Djehutymose and the scribe of the army of Medinet Habu, Pen-ta-hut-nakhte (the very title suggests the unsettled conditions of the times), indicates to what extent the gang had already been dispersed by the second half of that king's reign.

We heard that you have returned, that you have reached the city of Thebes and Amen has given you a good reception. May he do every good thing for you! Now, we are living here in the Temple, and you know our present way of life inside and out. Now, the children of the Necropolis have come; they are living in Thebes while I am living here alone with the scribe of the army Pen-ta-hut-nakhte. Please let the people of the Necropolis who are there in Thebes be assembled and send them to me on this side. List of them for you:

Pen-neset-tawy
Nefer-Amen
Hor-mose
Wen-Amen
Pa-nakhte-en-ope son of Pa-neb-aku
Amen-hotep
Ka-djadja

Total: 7 men.

Put them under the authority of Butehamun. Send them very quickly! And do not let them procrastinate. And also Pa-khal and Adjar—total, 9 men.

192. New Duties

Ramesses XI was the last king to commission a tomb in the Valley of the Kings, and this was presumably completed long before the end of his 30-year reign. Lower-ranking members of the gang were then assigned to such tasks as making columns for one of the temple ships, while supply staff were at one point employed in the temple of Hathor. The scribe of the tomb Djehutymose and his son Butehamun, in contrast, became the trusted aides of the generals who effectively ran Upper Egypt. Much of our information about the events of this time come from the correspondence of this father and son, including letters sent to and from Djehutymose in the course of his voyage to Nubia on business of the general Pay-ankh who was campaigining in the region against Pa-nehesy, the rebel viceroy of Nubia. Djehutymose did not enjoy travelling, which generally seems to have made him ill. The following anxious letter from a friend, the prophet of Amenophis I, Amen-hotep, reflects the incongruity of a scribe of the Necropolis caught up in a military expedition to the far south.

When my letter reaches you, do not go out to watch the winnowing.[a] Indeed, you have not been taken as an enemy soldier and you have not been taken as a messenger; you have been taken so that you can be consulted. Stay in the boat, and guard yourself against arrows and spears [. . .] And do not abandon all of us. Indeed, you know that you are the father of all of us—there is no one else here whom we can consult about our lives.

I am standing before Amenophis, l.p.h., daily, being pure, and I tell him to bring you back alive, prosperous and healthy. I am writing to let you know [. . .] Pen-neset-tawy, Pen-ta-wemet, Pa-by, Her-Amen-pena-ef, Sadjaa, Pa-her-ta-hat-nakhte, and all your kinsmen, both male and female, tell Amen-of-the-Thrones-of-the-Two-Lands to bring you back alive, prosperous and healthy.

[a] Presumably the fighting on the battlefield.

193. Visits to the Old Haunts

Although they had moved their households down to more populated areas, the members of the gang, especially the captains, made frequent visits to the royal necropolis and to their abandoned village. Some of these visits were in connection with work, including tours of inspection and the reburial of kings whose tombs had been ransacked; others were personal, to celebrate the funerary cult at the family tomb or to consult archives stored at Deir el-Medina (see No. 99). And sometimes the workmen rambled in the hills and valleys of the Theban necropolis simply for their own pleasure. The scribe Butehamun was particularly fond of recording his visits in graffiti, as in the following examples.

A. Third month of summer, day 23 (?). (Day) the gang of the Necropolis finished the work in this Place of Truth. The scribe Butehamun crossed over to Thebes to see the arrival of the General of the Army who was sailing north.

B. Year 12, first month of summer, day 8 to first month of summer, day 9. This day, the scribe Butehamun and the scribe Ankh-ef-en-Amen of the Necropolis (on) the west of Thebes come to the mountains to see them.

C. The scribe in the Place of Truth Butehamun of the Necropolis after coming to see the mountains in Year 11, fourth month of innundation season, day 24 (?).

THE ROYAL TOMBS STAND OPEN

194. Graffito in the Tomb of Ramesses II

Following the wholesale looting of the royal tombs and the removal of the royal mummies to places of safety (see No. 196), at least some tombs in Valley of the Kings were left standing open and accessible to passers-by. The following graffito inside the tomb of the most famous king of the Nineteenth Dynasty, Ramesses II, records a visit by members of the gang, including Butehamun and two of his eight sons. The title 'Scribe of the Tomb', formerly so significant, is now used by the two younger men as well as by the genuine office holder, Butehamun: by this late date, when no more tombs were built in the Valley of the Kings, the title had presumably lost much of its meaning.

Scribe Iy-er-niut-ef
Scribe Butehamun of [the Necropolis]
Scribe Meni-nefer of the Necropolis
Scribe Pa-khy of the Necropolis

195. In the Tomb of Ramesses VI

The following graffito in the tomb of Ramesses VI is dated to the reign
of Ramesses IX, indicating that this tomb was already standing open
and accessible hardly twenty years after the burial of its royal owner. The
draughtsmen who left the graffito say that they had just finished the
decoration in the tomb of Iy-em-seba, now known as Theban Tomb 65, in
the Theban necropolis—a rare indication that members of the gang were
commissioned to paint the tombs of private officials. Presumably they
visited the Valley of the Kings to admire the work of the draughtsmen of
the preceding generation.

Year 9, second month of winter, day 14 (?) under the majesty of King
Ramesses IX. This day, the scribe Amen-hotep with his son, the
scribe, deputy of the draughtsmen Amen-nakhte of the Necropolis,
came to see the temples of truth[a] [. . . after (?)] they executed the
decoration in the tomb [. . . of the overseer of the scribes of the]
temple Iy-em-seba, of the Estate of Amon. [. . .] They came and they
looked at the mountains.

[a] Perhaps, royal tombs.

196. Reburying the Kings of Old

By 1064 BC at the latest it was patently clear that all the major royal tombs
in the Valley of the Kings had been looted, and the best the authorities
could hope for was the preservation of the royal bodies themselves. At first,
their burials were simply renewed, perhaps in the original tombs, though at
this date or later some groups of mummies were also collected together in
a single tomb (see No. 197). Some of the kings had to be reburied several
times. The officials of the gang assisted in this work as their ancestors had
done in the so much more lavish original burials. The following record
from the reign of Semendes was written on the shroud of Ramesses III, the
great king whose mortuary temple, Medinet Habu, sheltered some of the
workmen after they abandoned their village.

Year 13, second month of summer, day 27. This day, the high priest
of Amun-Re, King of Gods, Pay-nedjem, son of the high priest of

Amen, Pay-ankh, sent the scribe of the temple Shed-su-Khonsu and the scribe of the Place of Truth Butehamun to let the Osiris, King Weser-Ma°at-Re Mery-Amen (Ramesses III) endure and last for ever.

197. The Last Two Captains of the Gang

The last word on the gang of the Necropolis comes, appropriately enough, from the burial of a high priest of Amen and the final burial of three kings of the New Kingdom. After the mummies of the pharaohs in the Valley of the Kings had been reburied in their own tombs, then moved to intermediate places of safety, they were finally collected in a common tomb, the so-called cachette in the bay of Deir el-Bahri. In year 10 of Siamen, Ramesses I, Seti I, and Ramesses II were moved to the cachette from the tomb of Seti I, joining the body of Amenhotep I which was already there. Three days later, the high priest of Amen Pinudjem II was buried in the cachette as well, in the sarcophagus of Thutmosis I (his wife Nes-Khonsu had been interred there 5 years earlier). A graffito at the bottom of the tomb shaft records the burial and names the officials responsible, including the scribe of the Necropolis and two chief workmen. Thus over 120 years after the abandonment of the village, there were still individuals who bore the titles and carrying out the duties of the captains of the gang.

In the end almost 40 mummies of kings, high priests of Amen, and their relatives, were deposited in the Deir el-Bahri cachette. The measure was successful, and the royal mummies were not disturbed again until they were discovered in the 1880s; they now rest in the Egyptian Museum in Cairo. After this move, we do not hear of the gang of the Necropolis again.

Year 10, fourth month of summer, day 20. Day of the burial of the Osiris the high priest of Amen-Re, King of Gods, the great chief of the army, the leader Pinudjem (II) by

> the prophet of Amon, overseer of the Treasury, Djed-khonsu-iu-ef-ankh
> the prophet of Amen, scribe of the army, chief administrator, Nes-pa-ka-shuty
> the herald of Amen [. . .]-en-Amen
> the prophet of Amen, Wen-nefer
> the royal scribe of the Place of Truth, Bak-en-Mut
> the chief workman Pa-di-Amen
> the chief workman Amen-mose
> the prophet of Amen, master of secrets, Pa-di-Amen, son of Ankh-ef-en-Khonsu

Notes

Introduction

GENERAL DESCRIPTION OF THE SITE

The Village: Valbelle, *Ouvriers*, 118–21; Bruyère, *Rapport (1934–1935)*, 1–78. I would like to thank Lynn Meskyll for allowing me read her work-in-progress on the archaeology of Deir el-Medina.

Cemeteries: Valbelle, *Ouvriers*, 287–304; B. Bruyère, 'La Nécropole de Deir el Medineh', *Cd'E* 11 (1936), 329–40.

Chapels: Valbelle, *Ouvriers*, 313–18; A. H. Bomann, *The Private Chapel in Ancient Egypt* (London and New York, 1991).

Huts on the Col: Bruyère, *Rapport (1934–1935)*, 345–53 and pls. xxxv–xxxvii.

Great Pit: Bruyère, *Rapport (1948–1951)*, 17–28 and pls. i–viii.

THE HISTORY OF OCCUPATION

Eighteenth Dynasty in General: Valbelle, *Ouvriers*, 1–26; Charles Bonnet and Dominique Valbelle, 'Le Village de Deir el-Médineh: reprise de l'étude archéologique,' *BIFAO* 75 (1975), 429–46 and pls. LXII–LXXII.

Amarna period: Bruyère, *Rapport (1933–4)*, part 1, 104 and pl. XII; Barry J. Kemp, *JEA* 73 (1987), 43–6; Valbelle, *Ouvriers*, 23 n. 11, 25; Bonnet et Valbelle, *BIFAO* 75 (1975), 432–3; and Černý, *Community*, 51–2.

Ramesside: Valbelle, *Ouvriers*, 159–226.

THE EXCAVATIONS

Émile Baraize, 'Compte rendu des travaux exécutés à Déîr-el-Médinéh,' *ASAE* 13 (1914), 19–42; Rudolf Anthes, 'Die Deutschen Grabungen auf der Westseite von Theben in der Jahren 1911 und 1913,' *MDAIK* 12 (1943), 1–68; Bernard Bruyère, 'Historique des fouilles archéologiques faites dans le Village', *Rapport (1934–1935)*, 237–40 and pl. XXVI; Morris Bierbrier, *The Tomb-Builders of the Pharaohs* (London, 1982), 119–44.

Find Spots of Texts: Valbelle, *Ouvriers*, 27–30; P. W. Pestman, 'Who Were the Owners, in the "Community of Workmen", of the Chester Beatty Papyri', in *Gleanings*, 155–72.

Chapter 1: Family and Friends

LETTERS BETWEEN FRIENDS AND FAMILY

1. **A garbled message:** O DeM 123. Translation in Wente, *Letters*, 164 (no. 263).

2. **Letter about a Useless Co-worker:** O DeM 328; also published in K*RI* III. 535. Translation in Wente, *Letters*, 237 (no. 167).

3. **A and B Letters from a Neglected Friend:** P DeM 4–5; also published in K*RI* VI. 264–6. Translations of both in Wente, *Letters*, 151 (nos. 210 and 211). Deborah Sweeney, 'Friendship and Frustration: A Study in Papyri Deir el-Medina IV to VI', *JEA* 85 (forthcoming).

4. **A Jokey Letter:** O Mich 79; also published in K*RI* VI. 254. Translation in Wente, *Letters*, 152 (no. 212).

5. **A Joke that Went Wrong:** Pap. Bibl. Nat. 198, II = Černý, *LRL* 67–8 (no. 46). Translation in Wente, *Letters*, 173 (no. 289); Wente, *LRL*, 79–81.

LOVE AND MARRIAGE

P. W. Pestman, *Marriage and Matrimonial Property in Ancient Egypt* (Leiden, 1961), 6–13, 51–2; Jac. J. Janssen, 'An Allusion to an Egyptian Wedding Ceremony', *GM* 10 (1974), 25–8; S. Allam, 'An Allusion to an Egyptian Wedding Ceremony?', *GM* 13 (1974), 9–11; S. Allam, 'Quelques aspects du mariage dans l'Égypte ancienne,' *JEA* 67 (1981), 116; C. J. Eyre, 'Crime and Adultery in Ancient Egypt', *JEA*, 70 (1984), 101.

6. **A Love Charm:** O DeM 1057. Translation in Smither, 'A Ramesside Love Charm,' *JEA* 27 (1941), 131–2; J. F. Borghouts, *Ancient Egyptian Magical Texts*. Nisaba, Religious Texts Translation Series, vol. 9 (Leiden, 1978), 1.

7. **A Son-in-Law Swears to his Intentions:** *HO* 64, 2 = O Bodleian Library 253; also published in K*RI* V. 485. Translation and commentary in Allam, *HOP* 40–2 (no. 18). See also James E. Hoch, *Semitic Words in Egyptian Texts of the New Kingdom and Third Intermediate Period* (Princeton, 1994), 196–8.

8. **A Case of Domestic Violence:** *HO* 53, 2^r = O Nash 5^r; also published in K*RI* V. 471–2. Translation and commentary in Allam, *HOP* 221–2 (no. 221).

9. **A Domestic Quarrel:** *HO* 72, 1 = O Ashmolean Museum, Oxford No. 1945.39; also published in K*RI* V. 587–8. Allam, *HOP* 24–6 (no. 4).

10. **Paternity Leave:** O Cairo 25517^v 4–7; also published in K*RI* IV. 387–9.

11. **Women Withdraw for Menstruation:** O OIM 13512. T. Wilfong, 'Menstrual Synchrony and the 'Place of Women' in Ancient Egypt (Oriental Institute Museum Hieratic Ostracon 13512)', in D. P. Silverman (ed.), *Festschrift for Professor Ed. Wente* (Philadelphia, 1996). I am grateful to Dr Wilfong for sending me a copy of his article before it went to press.

CHILDREN AND PARENTS

12. **A Widower Cares for his Children:** P Turin 1880 (Turin Strike Papyrus) v. 5, 2–6, 16 = *RAD* 47, 15–48, 13. Discussed in Janssen/Janssen, *Growing up*, 17; William F. Edgerton, 'The Strikes in Ramses III's Twenty-Ninth Year', *JNES* 10 (1951), 142–3.

13. **A Son Supports his Father:** O Glasgow D.1925.71. Transcription and translation in A. G. McDowell, *Hieratic Ostraca in the Hunterian Museum, Glasgow* (Oxford, 1992), pls. VIII–IX.

14. **Bad Children Are Disinherited:** Will of Naunakhte = Papyri Ashmolean Museum, Oxford 1945.95 and 1945.97. Transcription, translation and commentary in Černý, 'The Will of Naunakhte and the Related Documents', *JEA* 31 (1945), 29–53 and pls. VIII–XII; also published in K*RI* VI. 237–40. Translation and commentary in Allam, *HOP* 268–74 (no. 262).

SUPPORT OF WOMEN

15. **Women Help Each Other:** (A): O DeM 117; (B): O DeM 132; also published in K*RI* III. 558. Translations in Wente, *Letters*, 156–7 (nos. 228 and 232). See also Sweeney, 'Women's Correspondence from Deir el-Medineh', Sesto Congresso Internazionale di Egittologia: Atti, vol. 2 (Turin, 1993), 523–9.

16. **A Man Makes Demands on his In-Laws:** *HO* 70, 2 = O Prague 1826. Translations in Wente, *Letters*, 147–8 (no. 200); Allam, *HOP* 246 (no. 249).

17. **A Woman Goes Back to her Parents:** *HO* 23, 4 = O Petrie 61. Translation and commentary in Allam, *HOP* 242–3 (no. 243); McDowell, *Jurisdiction*, 123–4.

18. **Charity after a Divorce:** O University College, London 19614. Allam, *HOP* Plates, 74–5. Translation and commentary in Allam, *HOP* 253–4 (no. 256); discussion by Janssen in *Gleanings*, 109–15.

19. **Women Doing Men's Jobs:** Pap. Geneva D 191 = Černý, *LRL* 57–60 (no. 37). Translation in Wente, *Letters*, 174–5 (no. 290).

20. A Woman Who Did not Need A Man: *HO* 56, 1 = O Nash 6. Translation and commentary in Allam, *HOP* 222–3 (no. 222).

ADULTERY

C. J. Eyre, 'Crime and Adultery in Ancient Egypt', *JEA* 70 (1984), 92–105.

21. Accusations against Officials: P Salt 124 r. 2, 1–4. Primary publication by J. Černý, 'Papyrus Salt 124 (Brit. Mus. 10055)', *JEA* 15 (1929), 243–58 and pls. XLII–XLVI. Translation and commentary in Allam, *HOP* 281–7 (no. 266).

22. The Wealthy Seducer: P DeM 27; also published in *KRI* V. 578–9. Translation and commentary in Allam, *HOP* 301–2 (no. 272). Discussion by Janssen in *Gleanings*, 116–23.

23. An Unfaithful Wife: O DeM 439. Translation and discussion in Allam, *HOP* 124 (no. 110); J. F. Borghouts, 'Monthu and Matrimonial Squabbles', *RdʼE* 33 (1981), 11–22; Wente, *Letters*, 148 (no. 202).

24. A Census: Stato Civile, unpublished. Černý, NB 15.64–79; 17.18–19. Cf. Valbelle, *Ouvriers*, 56–61.

Chapter 2: Daily Life

HEALTH CARE

John F. Nunn, *Ancient Egyptian Medicine* (London, 1996).

25. The Village Doctor: *HO* 83–4 = O British Museum 5634ʳ; also published in *KRI* III. 515–25. Jac. J. Janssen, 'Absence from Work by the Necropolis Workmen of Thebes', *SAK* 8 (1980), 127–52.

26. Filling a Prescription: O University College London 3. *KRI* VII. 214. Wente, *Letters*, 142 (no. 186).

27. A Blind Workman Asks Help from His Son: O Berlin P 11247. Published in *Hieratische Papyrus aus den Königliche Museen zu Berlin*, vol. 3 (Leipzig, 1911), pls. 35–35a; also published in *KRI* III. 532–3. Translation in Wente, *Letters*, 142 (no. 185). C. A. Keller, 'Royal Painters: Deir el-Medina in Dynasty XIX', in Edward Bleiberg and Rita Freed (eds.), *Fragments of a Shattered Visage*, Monographs of the Institute of Egyptian Art and Archaeology, 1 (Memphis, 1991), 50–86, at 56. Ebers no. 371: Walter Wreszinski, *Der Papyrus Ebers* (Leipzig, 1913), 105.

28. A Request for Medicine Gone Astray: O Gard 177. *KRI* VII. 305.

29. Qen-her-khepesh-efʼs Medical Papyrus: P Chester Beatty VI r. 4,1–6,6. Published in Gardiner, *HPBM* 3rd, pls. 30–2, especially 30–1. Translation and commentary: Frans Jonckheere, *Le Papyrus médical Chester Beatty*.

La Médecine Égyptienne no. 2 (Brussels, 1947), esp. 19–25; Thierry Bardinet, *Les Papyrus médicaux de l'Égypte pharaonique* (Paris, 1995), 455–61, esp. 456–7. I would like to thank Tony Randall and Sally Crawford for their help with the translation of this text.

30. Medical Collection on an Ostracon: O DeM 1091. Translation and commentary: F. Jonkheere, *CdE* 29 no. 57 (1954), 48–50; Bardinet, *Les Papyrus médicaux*, 479 (with translations of other medical texts on ostraca).

LAUNDRY

Rosalind Hall, *Egyptian Textiles* (Aylesbury, 1986), 48–56.

31. The Village Laundry List: O DeM 258; also published in *KRI* III. 571–2. See Janssen, *Prices*, 258.

32. Dropping off at the Cleaners: O DeM 30; also published in *KRI* I. 363.

WATER

Jac. J. Janssen, 'The Water Supply of a Desert Village', *Medelhavsmuseet Bulletin* 14 (1979), 9–15; Barry J. Kemp *et al.*, *Amarna Reports* I. EES Occasional Publications, 1 (London, 1984), 60–80. See also Selke Eichler, 'Untersuchungen zu den Wasserträgern von Deir-el-Medineh', I *SAK* 17 (1990), 135–75, and II *SAK* 18 (1991), 173–205. Schafik Allam, 'À propos de l'approvisionnement en eau de la colonie ouvrière de Deir el-Médîneh', in Bernadette Menu (ed.), *Les Problèmes institutionnels de l'eau en Égypte ancienne et dans l'Antiquité méditerranéenne*. Bd'E 110 (Cairo, 1994), 1–15.

33. Water for Every Household: O Medelhavsmuseet (Stockholm) 14126. Janssen, 'Water Supply', *Medelhavsmuseet Bulletin* 14 (1979), 9–15; also published in *KRI* VII. 196–7.

34. Delivery Shortfalls: O DeM 60; also published in *KRI* III. 563. Helck, *Materialien*, 845.

35. Attempts to Dig a Well: (A) O DeM 92; also published in *KRI* V. 460. **(B)** P Turin 1923 (+ fragments) r. 2–8 = *KRI* VI. 368. The passage is written in red.

Translation and discussion of both passages: Raphael Ventura, 'On the Location of the Administrative Outpost of the Community of Workmen in Western Thebes', *JEA* 73 (1987), 149–60.

THE WEATHER

36. Rain: Jaroslav Černý and A. A. Sadek, *Graffiti de la Montagne Thébaine*, iv. *Transcriptions et Indices* (Cairo, 1970–3). **(A)** Graffito 3012. **(B)** Graffito 2868; also published in *KRI* VI. 250. **(C)** Graffito 1736; also published in *KRI* VI. 203.

THE HOUSE

37. Household Repairs: O Varille 13. *KRI* VII. 238. Janssen, *Prices*, 394–6.

38. House Inventory: O Cairo 25670. Wente, *Letters*, 138 (no. 170); Allam, *HOP* 67–8 (no. 34).

THE TOMB

39. Tomb Improvements: O BM 5624. A. Blackman, 'Oracles in Ancient Egypt', *JEA* 12 (1926), 176–85, pls. xxxiv–xlii; also published in *KRI* V. 475–6. Allam, *HOP* 43–5 (no. 20); Jac. J. Janssen, 'The Rules of Legal Proceeding in the Community of Necropolis Workmen at Deir el-Medîna', *BiOr* 32 (1975), 293; McDowell, *Jurisdiction*, 131–2.

40. Paying for the Decoration: O DeM 198ᵛ; also published in *KRI* IV. 230. Janssen in *Gleanings*, 118.

41. A Tomb Inventory: O Vienna 1 + O IFAO 628. L. M. J. Zonhoven, 'The Inspection of a Tomb at Deir el-Medîna (O. Wien Aeg. 1)', *JEA* 65 (1979), 89–98; also published in *KRI* V. 504–5. Valbelle, *Ouvriers*, 299.

42. Tomb Furniture: Headrest BM 63783. *KRI* VII. 200.

43. A Tomb is Reassigned: O Madrid 16,234. *KRI* VII. 335–6. See Zonhoven, *JEA* 65 (1979), 98 n. 80. On the coffin: Bruyère, *Rapport (1928)*, 99, fig. 57 [1], and p. 112; cf. Černý, *Community*, 154 n. 2.

44. Burial: Graffito in the chapel of Tomb 291. B. Bruyère and Ch. Kuentz, *La Tombe de Nakht-Min et la tombe d'Ari-Nefer*. MIFAO LIV (Cairo, 1926), 56–62 and 76; pls. vi and ix. Translation in Černý, *Community*, 373. On Tomb 1338 as the possible tomb of Amen-nakhte and descendants, see ibid. 349–50.

ECONOMICS

ECONOMIC EXCHANGE

45. Sale of an Ox: O Turin 57456.

46. The shopping list: (A) *HO* 54, 4 = O Černý 19; also published in *KRI* III. 533–4. Translation and commentary, Janssen, *Prices*, 510; Keller, 'Royal Painters', 59; Allam, *HOP* 72–3 (no. 39). (B) O DeM 125; also published in *KRI* III. 543. Allam, *HOP* 96 (no. 65).

47. The Middleman: *HO* 45, 1 = O Petrie 14; also published in *KRI* V. 524. Translation and commentary: Helck, *Materialien*, 499; Allam *HOP* 230–2 (no. 230).

48. Credit: Jac. J. Janssen, 'Debts and Credit in the New Kingdom', *JEA* 80 (1994), 129–36. (A) O Gard 162. *KRI* VII. 309–10. Janssen, op. cit. 131.

(B) *HO* 28, 1 = O Petrie 51; also published in *KRI* VI. 869–70. Discussed by Janssen, op. cit. 129–30.

49. **Gift Giving:** O DeM 643; also published in *KRI* V. 602–3. See Jac. J. Janssen, 'Gift Giving in Ancient Egypt as an Economic Feature', *JEA* 68 (1982), 253–8.

PRODUCTION FOR TRADE

50. **The Carpenter's Bill:** O DeM 146; also published in *KRI* VI. 664.

51. **Commission for Painting:** O DeM 419; also published in *KRI* VI. 156. Wente, *Letters*, 166 (no. 276).

52. **Co-operation between Carpenters and Painters:** O Berlin P 12343. *Hier. Pap.* III, pl. 34; also published in *KRI* VI. 164–5. The same individuals appear also in *HO* 60, 5, which also records the payments for decoration: see Janssen, *Prices*, 534–5.

53. **Price Setting:** *HO* 22, 2 = O Gard 3; also published in *KRI* V. 584–5.

54. **The Superiors Commandeer Work:** O Cairo 25516^v 26–8; also published in *KRI* IV. 387.

55. **The Marketplace:** O Brooklyn Acc No 37.1880 E^v 1–7. *KRI* VII. 310–11. Translation and commentary: Janssen, *De Markt op de Oever*, 14.

THE DONKEY BUSINESS

56. **Donkey Rental:** O DeM 1068^r col. II; also published in *KRI* VI. 250.

57. **Breaking the Lease:** O DeM 624.

58. **Borrowing:** O DeM 582; also published in *KRI* V. 575–6. Helck, *Materialien*, 502; Allam, *HOP* 138–9 (no. 131).

59. **Guarantee of Quiet Enjoyment:** O Turin 57173; also published in *KRI* V. 457. Allam, *HOP* 249–50 (no. 252).

60. **Why the Guarantee Was Necessary:** O Gard 165^r. Allam, *HOP* 183–4, pls. 44–5 (no. 183); also published in *KRI* III. 548–50. For an extract from the *verso* of this text, see 'Law' No. 133, below.

61. **Borrower Responsible for Deaths:** O Berlin P 1121. *Hier. Pap.* III, pl. 35; also published in *KRI* V. 524–5. Helck, *Materialien*, 500; Allam, *HOP* 26–7 (no. 5); M. Malanine, 'Notes juridiques (A propos de l'ouvrage de E. Seidl)', *BIFAO* 46 (1947), 118–22; S. Eichler, 'Untersuchungen zu den Wasserträgern von Deir-el-Medineh II', *SAK* 18 (1991), 179–80.

62. **A Loophole:** O DeM 305; also published in *KRI* V. 556. Helck, *Materialien*, 498.

Chapter 3: Religion

THE OFFICIAL CULTS

Mario Tosi, 'Popular Cults at Deir el-Medina', in Anna Maria Donadoni Roveri (ed.), *Egyptian Civilization: Religious Beliefs* (Milan, 1988), 162–77. Amenophis I: Jaroslav Černý, 'Le Culte d'Amenophis Ier chez les ouvriers de la nécropole thébaine', *BIFAO* 27 (1927), 159–203.

63. The Ritual of Amenophis I: P Cairo 58030 (top half) + Turin CGT 54042 with duplicate Cat. 1876 (= Pleyte-Rossi, 27–8) and Suppl. 10125. The extracts translated are T XII, 4–11 and T XVIII, 12–14. Ernesta Bacchi, *Il Rituale di Amenhotpe I*. Pubblicazioni Egittologiche del R. Museo di Torino VI (Turin, 1942), 17–19 and 42. Translation and discussion in Harold H. Nelson, 'Certain Reliefs at Karnak and Medinet Habu and the Ritual of Amenophis I', *JNES* 8 (1949), 201–32 and 310–48, esp. 208–12 and 310–13; translation and discussion of parallel version of P Chester-Beatty IX in Gardiner, *HPBM* 3rd, 1. 78–106.

64. A New Cult Statue for Ramesses VI: P Turin 1879 v. *KRI* VI. 335–7. Translation and discussion, Willem Hovestreydt, 'A Letter to the King Relating to the Foundation of a Statue (P. Turin 1879 vso.)', *Lingua Aegyptia* 5 (1997), 107–21, incorporating two newly identified fragments; Helck, *Materialien*, 197–8.

65. The Priests: O Cairo J. 59464; J. Černý, 'Le Culte de Amenophis Ier chez les ouvriers de la nécropole thébaine', *BIFAO* 35 (1935), 43.

66. Local Festivals: Festivals of Amenophis I: (A) O Cairo 25559 r.; also published in *KRI* VI. 104. **(B)** O Cairo 25234. Černý, *BIFAO* 27, (1927), 183–4; also published in *KRI* VI. 370.

67. Great Festivals: The Festival of the Valley: O Cairo 25265, II, 1–2. Černý NB 101, 23; see also Černý, *BIFAO* 27 (1927), 186 n. 1. Erhart Graefe, 'Talfest', *LÄ* VI. 187–9; Siegfried Schott, *Das Schöne Fest vom Wüstentale*. Akademie der Wissenschaften und der Literatur in Mainz, Abhandlungen der Geistes- und Sozialwissenschaftlichen Klasse, Jahrgang 1952. No. 11 (Wiesbaden, 1953).

68. Preparations for the festival: (A) O DeM 127; also published in *KRI* III. 557. Wente, *Letters*, 139 (no. 172). **(B)** O DeM 551. Wente, *Letters*, 139 (no. 173).

69. Music for the Cult: O Cairo 25752. Wente, *Letters*, 140 (no. 180).

PERSONAL PIETY

70. Stelae: O DeM 246; also published in *KRI* V. 566. Translation and commentary in van Walsem, in *Gleanings*, 193–5; Wente, *Letters*, 139 (no. 246).

71. **The Mercy of Meresger:** Stela Turin 50058; also published in *KRI* III. 772–3. Many translations, including Assman, *Hymnen und Gebete*, 354–5 (no. 149); B. Gunn, 'The Religion of the Poor in Ancient Egypt', *JEA* 3 (1916), 86–7.

72. **Living near to God:** Stela British Museum EA 278. M. L. Bierbrier, *Hieroglyphic Texts from Egyptian Stelae, etc.*, 10 (London, 1982), 37–8 and pl. 86; also published in *KRI* VI. 275–6. Translation in Assman, *Hymnen und Gebete*, 359–60 (no. 155); partial translation in J. Černý, *JEA* 31 (1945), 45–7.

On the cave above the temple of Hathor and its use as a sanatorium, see Marek Marciniak, 'Un texte inédit de Deir el-Bahri', *BIFAO* 81 (1981), 283–91 and pls. xxxiii–iv; on the cave-sanctuaries of Meresger and Ptah and the probable provenance of our stela, see Bernard Bruyère, *Mert Seger à Deir el Médineh*. MIFAO LVIII (Cairo, 1930), 23–31.

73. **Manifestations of God:** J. F. Borghouts, 'Divine Intervention in Ancient Egypt and its Manifestation (*b3w*)', in *Gleanings*, 1–70. (A) Stela Turin 50044; also published in *KRI* III. 795. Borghouts in *Gleanings*, 6. (B) O Gard 166. Allam, HOP 184–5 and pl. 46 (no. 184); also published in *KRI* III. 550. Translation and commentary: Borghouts in *Gleanings*, 4–5.

74. **Manipulating the Power of a God:** O DeM 251. Borghouts in *Gleanings*, 15–19; Wente, *Letters*, 141 (no. 182).

MINOR GODS: BES AND TA-WERET

Ta-Weret: Rolf Gundlach, 'Thoeris', *LÄ* VI. 494–7; Valbelle, *Ouvriers*, 316. Sanctuaries: *PM* I/2, 690; Ann H. Bomann, *The Private Chapel in Ancient Egypt* (London and New York, 1991), 69–70; E. S. Bogoslovsky, 'Monuments and Documents from Deir el-Medîna in the Museums of the USSR' (in Russian), *VDI* 4 (122) (1972), 65–89 (Eng. summary pp. 88–9), at 75–85 and 89 and pl. 8; Bes: Hartwig Altenmüller, 'Bes', *LÄ* I. 720–4; Bruyère, *Rapport (1934–1935)* pt. 3, 93–108; J. F. Romano, 'The Origin of The Bes-Image', *BES* 2 (1980), 39–56.

75. **Praise for Ta-Weret:** Pushkin Museum of Fine Arts (Moscow), no. I.1a.4867 a–b. Bogoslovsky, *VDI* 4 (122), 1972, 75–85 and 89, and pl. 8; J. J. Clère, 'Un mot pour "marriage" en égyptien de l'époque ramesside', *Rd'E* 20 (1968), 171–5; also published in *KRI* III. 753–4.

THE DEAD

76. **An 'Able Spirit of Re' Stela:** Stela Turin N. 50020; see Robert Demarée, *The 3ḫ iḳr n Rꜥ-Stelae*. Egyptologische Uitgaven 3 (Leiden, 1983), 47–9 and pl. v (A 15). On the *akhu* in general, see this same volume. The extract from the Instructions of Any is P Bulaq IV 8, 20–9, 3; see Georges

Posener, 'Les ʿafārīt dans l'ancienne Égypte', *MDAIK* 37 (1981), 393–401 (including a transcription of the text); Demarée, op. cit. 269–70.

77. **A Letter to a Deceased Wife:** *HO* 80 = O Louvre 698 v. 12–22. Translations: Wente, *Letters*, 217–19 (no. 353); P. J. Frandsen, 'The Letter to Ikhtay's Coffin: O. Louvre Inv. No. 698', in *Village Voices*, 31–49; Černý, *Community*, 369–70.

There is an extensive bibliography on letters to the dead. The basic edition of most letters is Alan H. Gardiner and Kurt Sethe, *Egyptian Letters to the Dead, Mainly from the Old and Middle Kingdoms* (London, 1928); see also the review by B. Gunn in *JEA* 16 (1930), 147–55. For more bibliography, see Frandsen, op. cit. 31 n. 3; and John Baines, 'Practical Religion and Piety', *JEA* 73 (1987), 86–8.

ORACLES

For a general description of oracles at Deir el-Medina, see J. Černý, 'Egyptian Oracles', in R. A. Parker, *A Saite Oracle Papyrus from Thebes in the Brooklyn Museum [Papyrus Brooklyn 47.218.3]* (Providence, RI, 1962), 35–48. On the opening in the floor of the chapel of Amenophis I, see A. H. Bomann, *The Private Chapel in Ancient Egypt* (London and New York, 1991), 73.

78. **Questions Addressed to Oracles:** (*a*) O IFAO 561; (*b*) O IFAO 502; (*c*) O IFAO 556; (*d*) O IFAO 884; (*e*) O Gard; (*f*) O IFAO 995; (*g*) O IFAO 680; (*h*) O IFAO 854; (*i*) O IFAO 996; (*j*) O IFAO 875, O IFAO 879, O IFAO 1004, O IFAO 1005.

a, b, c in J. Černý, 'Questions adressées aux oracles', *BIFAO* 35 (1935), 41–58, pls. I–IV;

g in J. Černý, 'Nouvelle série de questions adressées aux oracles', *BIFAO* 41 (1942), 13–24, pls. I–III;

d, e, f, h, i, j in J. Černý, 'Troisième série de questions adressées aux oracles', *BIFAO* 72 (1972), 49–69, pls. XV–XXV. See also Černý in Parker, *Saite Oracle Papyrus*, 46.

79. **Request for an Oracle:** P Nevill. J. Barns, 'The Nevill Papyrus: A Late Ramesside Letter to an Oracle', *JEA* 35 (1949), 69–71; Wente, *Letters*, 219 (no. 355).

80. **Striking a Bargain with the God:** *HO* 50, 2 = O Gardiner 310; also published in K*RI* III. 797. Wente, *Letters*, 219 (no. 354); Allam, HOP 190–1.

81. **Dreams:** P Chester Beatty III, r. 5,13–6,2 and 7, 10–7, 25. Gardiner, *HPBM* 3rd, pls. 6–7. Translation and commentary, ibid. 7–23.

82. **Calendar of Lucky and Unlucky Days:** Papyrus Cairo Jd'E 86637ʳ III, 1–IV, 4. Abd el-Mohsen Bakir, *The Cairo Calendar No. 86637* (Cairo,

1966), pls. III, I–IV, 4; translation, pp. 13–14; further transcription, translation, and commentary in Christian Leitz, *Tagewählerei: Das Buch* ḥзt nḥḥ pḥ.wy ḏt *und verwandte Texte*. Ägyptologische Abhandlungen, vol. 55 (Wiesbaden, 1994), 11–18. On the use made of such calendars, Rosemarie Drenkhan, 'Zur Anwendung der "Tagewählkalender" ', *MDAIK* 28 (1972), 85–94.

83. The Wise Woman: Bernadette Letellier, 'La Destinée de deux enfants, un ostracon ramesside inédit', *Livre du Centenaire de l'IFAO (1880–1980)*. MIFAO 104 (Cairo, 1980), 127–33 and pl. IX; also published in K*RI* VII. 257–8. Wente, *Letters*, 141–2 (no. 184). On the Wise Woman, see Borghouts in *Gleanings*, 25–7.

MAGIC

Joris F. Borghouts, 'Magical Practices among the Villagers', in Leonard H. Lesko (ed.), *Pharaoh's Workers* (Ithaca and London, 1994), 119–30; J. F. Borghouts, *Ancient Egyptian Magical Texts*. Religious Texts Translation Series NISABA, vol. 9 (Leiden, 1978); J. F. Borghouts, 'Magie', in *LÄ* III. 1137–51.

84. A Spell against Nightmares: P Chester Beatty III r. 10, 10–19; Borghouts, *Magical Texts*, 3–4 (no. 7).

85. A Spell against an Enemy: O Armytage 6–9; Alan W. Shorter, 'A Magical Ostracon', *JEA* 22 (1936), 165–8; Borghouts, *Magical Texts*, 1–2 (no. 3).

86. The Scorpion-Charmer: P Ch. Beatty XI r. 4, 7–8, restored with help of P Turin 1933. Gardiner, *HPBM* 3rd, pl. 65. Translation, Frédérique Von Känel, *Les Prêtres-ouâb de Sekhmet et les conjurateurs de Serket*. Bibliothèque de l'École des Hautes Études, Section des Sciences Religieuses, vol. 87 (Paris, 1984), 183–4.

On scorpion-charmers in general, see Von Känel, op. cit. 284–98; Serge Sauneron, *Un traité égyptien d'ophiologie. Papyrus du Brooklyn Museum N°s 47.218.48 et 85*. Publications de l'Institut Français d'Archéologie Orientale, Bibliothèque Générale, vol. 11 (Cairo, 1989), 198–206.

87. Sharing a Magical Spell: P Geneva MAH 15274[v] II. Adhémar Massart, 'The Egyptian Geneva Papyrus MAH 15274', *MDAIK* 15 (1957), pl. XXXVIII; translation and commentary: ibid. 182. On access to magical texts at Deir el-Medina, see R. K. Ritner, 'O. Gardiner 363: A Spell against Night Terrors', *JARCE* 27 (1990), 40–1.

88. A Myth: P Chester Beatty XI r. 1, 5–3, 12, completed by P Turin 1993. Gardiner, *HPBM* 3rd, pls. 64–5. Borghouts, *Magical Texts*, 51–5 (no. 84); the same spell is known from at least three further texts from Deir el-Medina, ibid. 122 notes to no. 84.

THE AFTERLIFE

89. Shabti of Setau: Bruyère, *Rapport (1933–1934)*, 98–9; Černý, *Community*, 50–1. On shabtis in general, Hans Schneider, *Shabtis*, pt. 1: *An Introduction to the History of the Ancient Egyptian Funerary Statuettes. Collections of the National Museum of Antiquities at Leiden*, II pt. 1. (Leiden, 1977) (the shabtis of Setau are discussed on p. 291); at Deir el-Medina, Dominique Valbelle, *Ouchebtis de Deir el-Médineh*. DFIFAO XV (Cairo, 1972).

90. The Book of the Dead: Ernesto Schiaparelli, *Relazione sui Lavori della Missione Archeologica Italiana in Egitto (Anni 1903–1920)*, vol. 2, *La Tomba Intatta dell'Architetto Cha nella necropoli di Tebe* (Turin, 1927), 56 (spell 109a). See Thomas George Allen, *The Book of the Dead or Going Forth by Day*. Studies in Ancient Oriental Civilization, no. 37 (Chicago, 1974), 86; Thomas George Allen, *The Egyptian Book of the Dead: Documents in the Oriental Institute Museum at the University of Chicago*. The University of Chicago, Oriental Institute Publications, vol. 82 (Chicago, 1960), 183–4. Raymond O. Faulkner, *The Ancient Egyptian Book of the Dead* (London, revised edition 1985), 102.

91. Pyramidion of Tuterbay and his son Paser: Bruyère, *Rapport (1933–1934)*, 27–31, pls. VIII–IX. Agnes Rammant-Peeters, *Les Pyramidions égyptiens du nouvel empire*. Orientalia Lovaniensia Analecta 11 (Leuven, 1983), 73–4 and 162 (Doc. 68).

92. The Song of the Harper: Tomb 359 of the chief workman In-her-khau, Bruyère, *Rapport* (1930), pl. XXIII. Translation and discussion in Miriam Lichtheim, 'The Songs of the Harpers', *JNES* 4 (1945), 178–212 and pls. I–VII, esp. pp. 201–2; translation in Siegfried Schott, *Altägyptische Liebeslieder* (Zurich, 1950), 135–6 (no. 98); John L. Foster, *Echoes of Egyptian Voices*. Oklahoma Series in Classical Culture 12 (Norman, Okla., and London, 1992), 80–1.

Chapter 4: Education

INTRODUCTION

Janssen/Janssen, *Growing Up*, ch. 6, 'The Schoolboy', 67–89.

93. Colophons: (A) O DeM 1106, 3–5. See G. Posener, *Rd'E* 7 (1950), 75–6. (B) O DeM 1014 II, 6–7.

94. A Call to Lessons: O DeM 438: see Hans-W. Fischer-Elfert, 'Vermischtes II', *GM* 135 (1993), 32–4; Wente, *Letters*, 166 (no. 275).

95. The Curriculum: Annie Gasse in *Village Voices*, 53.

96. A Grammatical Paradigm: *HO* 8, 7 = O Petrie 28. On paradigms, see Alan H. Gardiner, *Ancient Egyptian Onomastica*, Text, vol. 1 (Oxford, 1947), 4 n. 2.

97. A Name List: O DeM 1410. Cf. Pascal Vernus, 'Namensbildung', *LÄ* IV. 333–7.

LITERATURE

98. A Private Library: On the discovery of the archive, Georges Posener in Jaroslav Černý, *Papyrus Hiératiques Deir el-Medinéh*, vol. 1 [*N^os I–XVII*]. DFIFAO 8 (Cairo, 1978), vii–viii. On the history of the archive, P. W. Pestman, 'Who Were the Owners, in the "Community of Workmen", of the Chester Beatty Papyri', in *Gleanings*, 155–72.

99. The Amen-nakhte Family Archive: P Brit. Mus. 10326 r. 19–v. 1. Černý, *LRL* 18,12–19,2 (no. 9). Translation: Wente, *LRL* 37–42; Wente, *Letters*, 190–2 (no. 313).

100. Collecting Texts: O Berlin 10628 = *Hier. Pap.* III, pl. 39; also published in *KRI* V. 564. Wente, *Letters*, 165–6 (no. 273); Allam, HOP 27 (no. 6).

INSTRUCTION TEXTS

101. P Chester Beatty IV: (A) P Chester Beatty IV v. 2,5–3,11; Gardiner, *HPBM* 3rd, pls. 18–19. Translations: ibid. 38–9; Lichtheim, *Ancient Egyptian Literature*, 2. 175–8; Brunner, *Altägyptische Weisheit*, 224–6; R. B. Parkinson, *Voices from Ancient Egypt* (London, 1991), 148–50 (no. 12). (B) Pap. Chester Beatty IV 6,3–6,9. Text in Gardiner, *HPBM* 3rd, pls. 20–20A. Translation, ibid. 43; Brunner, *Altägyptische Weisheit*, 229 (no. 12).

102. *Instruction of Amen-nakhte*: The most complete of the seven copies—all on ostraca—is O BM 41541. Original publication: G. Posener, 'Exorde de l'instruction éducative d'Amennakhte (Recherches Littéraires, V)', *Rd'E* 10 (1955), 61–72. Most recently, S. Bickel and B. Mathieu, 'L'Écrivain Amennakht et son *Enseignement*', *BIFAO* 93 (1993), 31–51 with 8 plates.

103. Instruction of Hori: *HO* 6, 1 = O Gardiner 2. Hans-W. Fischer-Elfert, *Literarische Ostraka der Ramessidenzeit in übersetzung* (Wiesbaden, 1986), 1–4. Bickel and Mathieu, *BIFAO* 93 (1993), 49–51.

104. The Fate of the Unmindful Son: 8 ostraca (O Turin 57436 r.; *HO* 3, 3 r.; O Cairo 25770 r.; O DeM 1036, 1254, 1255, 1256, 1599). G. Posener, 'Ostraca inédits du Musée de Turin (Recherches Littéraires III)', *Rd'E* 8 (1951), 175–9.

105. Thou Shalt Not . . . : *HO* I = O Petrie 11. Translations in Brunner, *Altägyptische Weisheit*, 215–7 (no. 11); Miriam Lichtheim, *Late Egyptian*

Wisdom Literature in the International Context. Orbis Biblicus et Orientalis 52 (Göttingen, 1983), 7–9.

SATIRICAL LETTERS

106. **Amen-nakhte's letter:** *HO* 38, 1 = O Gard 25ᵛ; also published in K*RI* V. 646–7. Translation and commentary: G. Posener, *Rd'E* 16 (1964), 40–1; Bickel and Mathieu, *BIFAO* 93 (1993), 40–1.

107. **Menna's Letter:** *HO* LXXVIII–LXXIX = O Oriental Inst. Chicago 12074; also published in K*RI* VI. 215–17. Brunner, *Altägyptische Weisheit*, 399–402 (no. 32); William Kelly Simpson, 'Allusions to *The Shipwrecked Sailor* and *The Eloquent Peasant* in a Ramesside Text', *JAOS* 78 (1958), 50–1; R. B. Parkinson, *The Tale of the Eloquent Peasant* (Oxford, 1991), pp. xxix–xxx; John L. Foster, 'Oriental Institute Ostracon #12074: "Menna's Lament" or "Letter to a Wayward Son"', *JSSEA* 14 (1984), 88–99; id., *Echoes of Egyptian Voices* (Norman, Okla., and London, 1992), 56–8.

STORIES

108. *The Blinding of Truth*: P Chester Beatty II = Pap. Brit. Mus. 10682; the extract translates 4,5–6,7. Gardiner, *HPBM* 3rd, pls. 1–4. Translations and commentary, Gardiner, *HPBM* 3rd, 2–6; Lichtheim, *Ancient Egyptian Literature*, 2. 211–14, with references to further translations and discussions.

109. *Khonsu-em-heb and the Ghost*: Publication, with translation and commentary: Jürgen von Beckerath, 'Zur Geschichte von Chonsemhab und dem Geist', *ZÄS* 119 (1992), 90–107. For English translation, see esp. Edward F. Wente in William Kelly Simpson, *The Literature of Ancient Egypt* (2nd edn., New Haven and London, 1973), 137–41.

110. **Love Songs:** O DeM 1266 + O Cairo 25218. G. Posener, *Catalogue des ostraca hiératiques littéraires de Deir el Medinéh*, *DFIFAO* 18 (3) (Cairo, 1972), pls. 74–9. Translation and commentary: Michael V. Fox, *The Song of Songs and the Ancient Egyptian Love Songs* (Madison, Wis., 1985), 29–44 (includes hieroglyphic transcription on pp. 383–9). For the history of Chester Beatty I, see Pestman in *Gleanings*, 161–2.

PRAISE OF CITIES

Miriam Lichtheim, 'The Praise of Cities in the Literature of the Egyptian New Kingdom,' in Stanley M. Burstein and Louis A. Okin (eds.), *Panhellenica* (Fs. Truesdell S. Brown) (Lawrence, Kan., 1980), 15–23.

111. **Longing for Thebes:** *HO* 8, 3 = O Petrie 39. Assmann, *Hymnen und Gebete*, 386 (no. 185).

112. **Amen-nakhte's praise of Thebes:** *HO* 38, 1 = O Gard 25ʳ; also published in K*RI* V. 646–7. Translation and commentary: Bickel and

Mathieu, *BIFAO* 93 (1993), 38–40; Assmann, *Hymnen und Gebete*, 385 (no. 183); Černý, *Community*, 348. Lichtheim, in *Panhellenica* (as above), 21.

HYMNS

113. Hymn on the Coronation of Ramesses IV: O Turin 57001[']; also published in K*RI* VI. 68–9. Most recent translation by Bickel and Mathieu in *BIFAO* 93 (1993), 41–3. See also Assman, *Hymnen und Gebete*, 498–9 (no. 241).

On Ramesses IV: C. A. Keller, 'Speculations Concerning Interconnections between the Royal Policy and Reputation of Ramesses IV', in David P. Silverman (ed.), *For his Ka: Essays Offered in Memory of Klaus Baer*. Studies in Ancient Oriental Civilization, no. 55 (Chicago, 1994), 145–57.

114. Hymn of Transfiguration by Pa-nefer: O Turin 57003. On hymns of transfiguration, see Jan Assman, 'Verklärung', *LÄ* VI. 998–1006. I would like to thank Ludwig Morenz who identified the genre for me.

115. Praise of Amen by the Scribe Amen-mose: O Mich 82 = pl. 28.

116. Appeal to Amen by Pagefy: *HO* 7, 3 = O Petrie 6; also published in K*RI* VI. 270–1.

117. Hymn to the Sun by Hor-Min: *HO* 96, 2 = O Gard 319.

HISTORY

A. McDowell, 'Awareness of the Past in Deir el-Medîna', in *Village Voices*, 95–109.

118. King List: O Cairo 25646; also published in K*RI* II. 700. For discussion, see Allan K. Philips, 'Horemheb, Founder of the XIXth Dynasty? O. Cairo 25646 Reconsidered', *Orientalia* 46 (1977), 116–21; McDowell in *Village Voices*, 96.

119. Historical Fiction: Pap. Turin 1940 + 1941. Published and translated by Giuseppe Botti, 'A Fragment of the Story of a Military Expedition of Thutmosis III to Syria (P. Turin 1940–1941)', *JEA* 41 (1955), 64–71 and pls. XVI–XVIII. See also Thomas von der Way, *Die Textüberlieferung Ramses' II. zur Qadeš-Schlacht*. HÄB 22 (Hildesheim, 1984), 186–8.

Chapter 5: Law

PRINCIPLES OF JUDGEMENT

120. Justice: O Mich 47 = pl. 50. Translation and commentary: Allam, *HOP* 212–3 (no. 215); K*RI* III. 514–15.

121. The Litigant's Prayer: O Borchardt. Georges Posener, 'Amon juge du pauvre', *Beiträge zur ägyptischen Bauforschung und Altertumskunde*, 12. (Fs. Herbert Ricke) (1971), 59–63. Assman, *Hymnen und Gebete*, 387–8 (no. 187); Allam, *HOP* 42–3 (no. 19).

122. **Laws and Precedent:** P Boulaq X^r. Jac. J. Janssen and P. W. Pestman, 'Burial and Inheritance in the Community of the Necropolis Workmen at Thebes (Pap. Bulaq X and O. Petrie 16)', *JESHO* 11 (1968), 137–70; also published in K*RI* V. 449–51.

THE AUTHORITIES AND THE COURT

123. **Women on the Court:** *HO* 71, 3 r. = O Gard 150; also published in K*RI* V. 527. Allam, *HOP* 181 (no. 180).

124. **The Use of Witnesses:** O DeM 56; also published in K*RI* V. 502. Allam, *HOP* 82–3 (no. 47).

ENFORCEMENT OF THE VERDICT

125. **Penalty for Non-Compliance:** O DeM 564; also published in K*RI* V. 451. Allam, *HOP* 133 (no. 124).

126. **Reluctant Enforcement:** *HO* 49, 1 = O Gard 53; also published in K*RI* V. 484. Allam, *HOP* 158–9 (no. 155).

127. **The Bailiff:** P Turin 1976 = Bakir, *Epistolography*, pls. 25–6 and pl. XXXII; also published in K*RI* VI. 598–9. Allam, *HOP* 317–18; Wente, *Letters*, 137–8 (no. 169).

THE ORACLE

128. **The Oracle in Action:** *HO* 16, 4 = O Petrie 21; also published in K*RI* V. 518–9. R. J. Demarée ' "Remove your Stela" (O. Petrie 21 = *Hier. Ostr.* 16, 4)', in *Gleanings*, 101–8; Allam, *HOP* 237–8 (no. 236).

129. **Enforcement: The Oracle:** O DeM 133. McDowell, *Jurisdiction*, 137.

PROPERTY

130. **Official Property:** *HO* 43, 4 = O Gard 23; also published in K*RI* VI. 663. Allam, *HOP* 153–4 (no. 149).

131. **Private Property:** O DeM 586; also published in K*RI* V. 583. Allam, *HOP* 139–40 (no. 132).

132. **Land Sale:** O DeM 593; also published in K*RI* VI. 374. Allam, *HOP* 142 (no. 135).

133. **Land outside the Village:** O Gard 165^v. Allam, *HOP* 183–4, pls. 44–5 (no. 183); also published in K*RI* III. 548–50. For land use by the workmen in general, see Andrea McDowell, 'Agricultural Activity by the Workmen of Deir el-Medina', *JEA* 78 (1992), 195–206.

134. **A Ruined Chapel** . . . . : O BM 5625. Aylward M. Blackman, 'Oracles in Ancient Egypt', *JEA* 12 (1926), 176–90, pls. xxxiv–xlii, esp. pp. 181–3, pls. xxxv–xxxvi; also published in K*RI* VI. 252–3. Allam, *HOP* 46–7 (no. 21).

135. **An Easement:** O Cairo 25555 + additional fragment (Černý NB 101.117–18); also published in K*RI* V. 456–7 (minor errors in transcription). Allam, *HOP* 59–61 (no. 29).

136. **Equity:** Ashmolean Museum HO 655. Andrea G. McDowell, 'An Incised Hieratic Ostracon (Ashmolean HO 655)', *JEA* 81 (1995), 220–5 and pl. xx.

CONTRACTS

137. **Dunning the Dead:** O Touche H.2. K*RI* VII. 232–3.

TORTS

138. **The Oracle Names the Thief:** *HO* 27, 3 = O Gard 4; also published in K*RI* VI. 142. Allam, *HOP* 151–2 (no. 147).

139. **The Perplexed Victim:** (*a*) O IFAO 598; (*b*) O IFAO 563 (*c*) O Brussels, Musées Royaux du Cinquantenaire, E 317; (*d*) O IFAO 852 (*e*) O IFAO 999; (*f*) O IFAO 868; (*g*) O IFAO 501 (*h*) O IFAO 941; (*i*) O IFAO 870.
    a, b, g in Černý, *BIFAO* 35 (1935), 41–58; *BIFAO* 41 (1942), 13–24; *c, d, e, f, h, i* in Černý, *BIFAO* 72 (1972), 49–69, pls. xv–xxv. See also McDowell, *Jurisdiction*, 133–4.

140. **Compensation:** O Oriental Institute 110 (provisional number). J. Černý, 'Restitution of, and Penalty Attaching to, Stolen Property in Ramesside Times', *JEA* 23 (1937), 186–9; also published in K*RI* VII. 319.

141. **Incarceration as Punishment?:** O Turin 57455ʳ. Translation and commentary: McDowell, *Jurisdiction*, 231–2.

142. **Slander:** O Cairo 25556; also published in K*RI* IV. 302–3. Allam, *HOP* 61–3 (no. 30); A. McDowell, 'Een schijnproces in het Egyptische strafrecht?', *Phoenix* 33: 2 (1987), 17–22; McDowell, *Jurisdiction*, 251–3.

CRIME

143. **Assault:** (A) Geneva Papyrus MAH 15247 v. III, 1–3. Adhémar Massart, *MDAIK* 15 (Fs. Hermann Junker) (1957), p. 183 and pl. 38; also published in K*RI* VI. 144. (B) P Turin 1977, 1–4 = Bakir, *Epistolography*, pls. 26–7 and xxxiii, Allam, *HOP* 318–19 (no. 279); McDowell, *Jurisdiction*, 227.

144. **'The Theft of Copper is the Abomination of this Village':** *HO* 46, 2 = O Nash 1; also published in K*RI* IV. 315–17. Allam, *HOP* 214–17 (no. 217).

145. Theft of State Property: *HO* 47, 1 = O Nash 2; also published in *KRI* IV. 317–19. Allam, *HOP* 217–19.

146. Reporting Crime: P Salt 124 r. 1, 1–4; 2, 5–18, v. 2, 1–7. J. Černý, 'Papyrus Salt 124 (Brit. Mus. 10055)', *JEA* 15 (1929), 243–58 and pls. XLII–XLVI; also published in *KRI* IV. 408–14.

147. The Duty to Report: P Turin 1880 (Turin Strike Papyrus) = *RAD* 57,6–58,6: Edgerton, *JNES* 10 (1951), 141. Paul J. Frandsen, 'Editing Reality: The Turin Strike Papyrus', in Sarah Israelit-Groll (ed.), *Studies in Egyptology Presented to Miriam Lichtheim*, vol. 1 (Jerusalem, 1990), 166–99, esp. 193–6.

148. The Place of Examination: (A) O Turin 57556; also published in *KRI* VII. 293. (B) O Turin 57031ʳ 1–2; also published in *KRI* V. 502–3. On the riverbank and the Place of Examination, see McDowell, *Jurisdiction*, 219–23.

149. Punishments: O Berlin 12654, Allam, *HOP* 35–8, pls. 12–15 (no. 15); also published in *KRI* VI. 344–5. Jac. J. Janssen, 'The Mission of the Scribe Pesiūr (O. Berlin 12654)', in *Gleanings*, 133–47.

THE GREAT TOMB ROBBERIES

150. The Initial Report: P Abbott 5,8–6,24. Peet, *The Great Tomb Robberies*, pls. III–IV. Translation and discussion, ibid. 28–45.

151. Workmen Arrested and Interrogated: (A) Giornale dell'anno 17-B *recto* VIII, 2–11 = P Turin Cat. 2029 plus many further pieces. Primary publication: Giuseppe Botti and T. Eric Peet, *Il Giornale della Necropoli di Tebe* (Turin, 1928), pl. 24; also published in *KRI* VI. 579. Translation: Botti and Peet, op. cit. 26. Partial translation and commentary, Peet, *The Great Tomb Robberies*, 77. (B) Gioronale dell'anno 17-C 1–7. Primary publication: Botti and Peet, op. cit. pl. 49; also published in *KRI* VI. 598.

152. Rough Company: P Mayer B, 7–14. T. Eric Peet, *The Mayer Papyri A & B* (London, 1920), unnumbered plate at end of volume. Transcription also in *KRI* VI. 515–16. Translation: Peet, *Mayer Papyri A&B*, 20. On the signs of pillaging in the tomb of Ramesses VI, see Cyril Aldred, 'More Light on the Ramesside Tomb Robberies', in John Ruffle, G. A. Gaballa, and Kenneth A. Kitchen (eds.), *Glimpses of Ancient Egypt: Studies in Honour of H. W. Fairman* (Warminster, 1979), 92–9.

Chapter 6: Work on the Tomb

INTRODUCTION

E. S. Bogoslovsky, 'Hundred Egyptian Draughtsmen', *ZÄS* 107 (1980), 91–3; Cathleen A. Keller, 'Royal Painters: Deir el-Medina in Dynasty XIX', in

Fragments of a Shattered Visage, E. Bleiberg and R. Freed (eds.), Monographs of the Institute of Egyptian Art and Archaeology, 1 (Memphis, 1991), 50–86; Maya Müller, 'Zum Werkfahren an thebanischen Grabwänden des Neuen Reiches', *SAK* 13 (1986), 149–64, pls. 13–18.

153. Plan of the Tombs of Ramesses IV: P Turin Cat. 1885ʳ. H. Carter and A. H. Gardiner, 'The Tomb of Ramesses IV and the Turin Plan of a Royal Tomb', *JEA* 4 (1917), 130–58 and pls. xxix–xxx; text in *KRI* VI. 58–60. For other tomb plans, see J. Černý, *Valley of the Kings*. Bd'E 61 (Cairo, 1973), 23–35; C. N. Reeves, 'Two Architectural Drawings from the Valley of the Kings', *Cd'E* 61 (1986), 43–9.

ACCESSION OF A NEW KING AND THE CHOICE OF A TOMB SITE

154. The Death of Sety II and Accession of Siptah: O Cairo 25515 v. II,21–III,9; IV,6–V,2.

155. Announcement of the Accession of Ramesses VI: *HO* 68, 1 = O British Museum 50722 + O Cairo 25726; also published in *KRI* VI. 364. Translation: Černý, *Valley of the Kings*, 16.

156. Choosing the Tomb Site for Ramesses IV: O DeM 45, rt. 15–17; also published in *KRI* VI, 119–21. Translation: Černý, *Valley of the Kings*, 17.

THE WORK IN PROGRESS

157. The Lighting of the Work: (A) O Cairo 25820 v. (called *recto* on the facsimile); also published in *KRI* VI. 661. The lighting of the work in general is discussed by Černý, *Valley of the Kings*, 43–54. **(B)** O Cairo J.72454 (Černý NB 106, 5) completed by O Cairo 25545.

CHISELS FOR THE STONECUTTERS

158. Chisels are Issued to the Gang: O Cairo 25509, r. I,15–20; also published in *KRI* IV. 299–301.

159. Blunted Chisels are Collected to be Reforged: P Geneva MAH 15274 v. I,1–6. Adhémar Massart, 'The Egyptian Geneva Papyrus MAH 15274', *MDAIK* 15 (1957), 172–85 and pls. xxiv–xxxviii, esp. pp. 181–2 and pl. xxxviii; also published in *KRI* VI. 144.

GYPSUM FOR PLASTERING THE WALLS

160. Preparing the Raw Gypsum: Giuseppe Botti and T. Eric Peet, *Il Giornale della Necropoli di Tebe* (Turin, 1928), 31–2 and pl. 31 (Giornale dell'anno 17-Bᵛ 3 [1–8]); also published in *KRI* VI. 583. On the properties of gypsum and on its use by the workmen, see A. Lucas, *Ancient Egyptian*

Materials and Industries, 4th edn. revised and enlarged by J. R. Harris (London, 1962), 6–7 and 76–9; Černý, *Valley of the Kings*, 35–42.

161. **The Plasterers' Progress:** Graffito in tomb of Ramesses IX. M. E. Lefébure, *Les Hypogées royaux de Thèbes*. Mém. Miss. III(1) (Paris, 1889), pl. 9 fig. 6A; Félix Guilmant, *Le Tombeau de Ramesès IX*. MIFAO 15 (Cairo, 1907), pl. LXIV r. Transcription and translation, Černý, *Valley of the Kings*, 41.

162. **Running out of Gypsum:** O DeM 437. Translated in Wente, *Letters*, 134 (no. 159).

PAINTING THE TOMB

163. **Pigments Issued to a Painter:** (A) O Strasbourg H.41. *KRI* VII. 195,1–6. On Egyptian pigments, see J. R. Harris, *Lexicographical Studies in Ancient Egyptian Minerals* (Berlin, 1961), 141–62; Lucas, *Ancient Materials and Industries*, 4th edn. 338–66. (B) O Cairo 25247 v. 1–7 and 15; edge 1–3. *KRI* VII. 334–5.

164. **A Painter Asks for Help with his Work:** P. Ashmolean 1958.112. C. J. Eyre, 'A Draughtsman's Letter from Thebes', *SAK* 11 (1984), 195–207; also published in *KRI* VII. 339–40. Translated in Wente, *Letters*, 134 (no. 158).

165. **The Pigments are Exhausted:** O Toronto A. 11, v. 1–13; Alan H. Gardiner, Herbert Thompson, and J. G. Milne, *Theban Ostraca* (London, 1913), 16 k–m; also published in *KRI* III. 43–4. Translated in Wente, *Letters*, 46–7 (no. 49).

MONITORING PROGRESS

166. **Measuring the Stonecutters' Progress:** O Cairo 25536 r.

167. **Progress Reports:** O Oriental Inst. Chicago 16991. E. F. Wente, 'A Letter of Complaint to the Vizier To', *JNES* 20 (1961), 252–7; also published in *KRI* V. 559–60. Translated in Wente, *Letters*, 50–1 (no. 56).

168. **A Vizier's Answer:** O DeM 114; also published in *KRI* III. 45–6. Translated in Wente, *Letters*, 47–8 (no. 51).

169. **An Attendance List:** O Cairo 25785; also published in *KRI* IV. 234–5. On attendance lists in general, see Jac. J. Janssen, 'Absence from Work by the Necropolis Workmen of Thebes', *SAK* 8 (1980), 127–53.

FINAL PREPARATIONS FOR THE BURIAL

170. **Transporting the Funeral Equipment for Ramesses IV:** P Turin 2044 r. 1,3–11. *KRI* VI. 340,12–341,2; Valbelles, *Ouvriers*, 36 n. 1 and 199–200.

171. **Preparing to Install the Funerary Equipment:** O Turin 57366. Jac. J. Janssen, 'Gear for the Tombs (O Turin 57366 and O BM 50733 + O Petrie 30)', *Rd'E* 43 (1992), 107–22.

172. **Installing the Funerary Equipment:** P Turin 2002 r. III, 10–25; IV, 14–21; Pleyte-Rossi, 104,10–105,25 and 107,14–21. The first section is also to be found in Allam, *HOP* Plates, 132–3; *KRI* VI. 244,12–245,9. The whole is transcribed in Černý, MS. 3.724–7 (Griffith Institute, Oxford). See Valbelle, *Ouvriers*, 36 n. 2, 200; Černý, *Community*, 11–12; Raphael Ventura, *Living in a City of the Dead*. Orbis Biblicus et Orientalis 69 (Göttingen, 1986), 32.

173. **Final Preparations for the Burial of Merneptah:** O Cairo 25504 r. II, 6–10; also published in *KRI* IV. 155–8. Discussed by Jac. J. Janssen, *Rd'E* 43 (1992), 108; Valbelle, *Ouvriers*, 177–8; Wolfgang Helck, *Verwaltung des Mittleren und Neuen Reichs* (Leiden, 1958), 325–6.

THE BURIAL

174. **The Burial of Ramesses III:** O DeM 40, r. 1–2 and 15; also published in *KRI* VI. 106–7.

175. **Ramesses V is Buried:** O Cairo 25254. *KRI* VI. 343. J. Černý, in I. E. S. Edwards, C. J. Gadd, N. G. L. Hammond, and E. Sollberger (eds.), *The Cambridge Ancient History*, 3rd edn., vol. 2, pt. 2 (Cambridge, 1975), 612; id., *Valley of the Kings*, 34. On the mummy of Ramesses V, see G. Elliot Smith, *The Royal Mummies*, Cairo Cat. Gén. nos. 61051–100 (Cairo, 1912), 90–2. On the family relationship between Ramesses V and Ramesses VI, see Edward F. Wente in James E. Harris and Edward F. Wente, eds. *An X-Ray Atlas of the Royal Mummies* (Chicago and London, 1980), 266–8. On the place and time of Ramesses V's burial, see, e.g. C. N. Reeves, *Valley of the Kings* (London and New York, 1990), 117.

176. **Libyan Nomads Reach Thebes:** P Turin 2071 r. 1–v. 1. *KRI* VI. 637–8; Allam, *HOP* Plates, 122–7. Discussion by B. Haring, in *Village Voices*, 74.

177. **Mobilizing Defences:** P Louvre 3169. *KRI* VI. 523. Translation: K. A. Kitchen in Anthony Leahy (ed.), *Libya and Egypt: c.1300–750 BC* (London, 1990), 22–3; Wente, *Letters*, 53 (no. 61). See also Haring, in *Village Voices*, 77.

178. **Civil War:** P Turin 2044 v. 2,8–3,6 *KRI* VI. 340–3. Translation: Černý, *Community*, 277–8; Černý, *CAH* 3rd edn., 2: 2. 612–13.

THE WORKMEN

179. **List of New Appointments:** O Cairo 25581; also published in *KRI* IV. 151–2. On the date, see Černý, *Community*, 183.

180. **Career Worries:** O IFAO [693]. Černý NB 104.79.

181. **Buying a Promotion:** O Cairo 25800; also published in K*RI* VI. 257.

182. **Mass Job Cuts:** O Berlin 12654. Allam, *HOP* Plates, 12–15; translation and commentary in ibid. 35–8; also published in K*RI* VI. 344–5. Translation and further discussion by Jac. J. Janssen, 'The Mission of the Scribe Pesiūr (O. Berlin 12654)', in *Gleanings*, 133–47.

SUPPLIES AND RATIONS

183. **A Ration Distribution:** O Cairo 25608 r.

184. **Official Corruption:** *HO* 34, 4 = O Leipzig 2; also published in K*RI* V. 467–8. Allam, *HOP* 199–200.

185. **A Personal Favour from the King:** Stela British Museum 588. British Museum, *Hieroglyphic Texts from Egyptian Stelae, etc.* Pt. 10, ed. M. L. Bierbrier (London, 1982), 24–5, pl. 57; also published in K*RI* VI. 83–4. Translation and discussion: Jac. J. Janssen, 'An Unusual Donation Stela of the Twentieth Dynasty', *JEA* 49 (1963), 64–70.

186. **Maidservants for the Gang:** Černý, *LRL* 50,13–51,3. Translation in Wente, *Letters*, 197–8 (no. 319); Wente, *LRL* 65–7.

DEMONSTRATIONS

187. **The Turin Strike Papyrus:** P Turin 1880 (Turin Strike Papyrus) = *RAD* 56, 8–57, 4; William F. Edgerton, 'The Strikes in Ramses III's Twenty-ninth Year', *JNES* 10 (1951), 137–45. Paul J. Frandsen, 'Editing Reality: The Turin Strike Papyrus', in Sarah Israelit-Groll (ed.), *Studies in Egyptology Presented to Miriam Lichtheim*, vol. 1 (Jerusalem, 1990), 166–99, esp. 189–92.

188. **The Shortfalls in the Rations:** O Turin 57072, 2–13; also published in K*RI* V. 535–6. Jac. J. Janssen, 'Background Information on the Strikes of Year 29 of Ramesses III', *OrAnt* 18 (1979), 301–8.

189. **Torchlight Demonstrations:** (A) O Varille 39 r. 10–15 = K*RI* VI. 300–2. See also Frandsen in *Studies in Egyptology*, 182–3. (B) O DeM 44 r. 18–22; also published in K*RI* VI. 116–18. On both texts and torch-carrying in general, see Jac. J. Janssen, 'Carrying Torches', in Terence DuQuesne (ed.), *Hermes Aegyptiacus: Egyptological Studies for BH Stricker. Discussions in Egyptology* Special Number 2 (Oxford, 1995), 115–21.

190. **An Oracle about Rations:** O IFAO [556]. Černý NB 104.29.

Epilogue

For a general discussion of the last years of the gang of the Necropolis, see Valbelle, *Ouvriers*, 219–26.

191. **The Gang is Scattered:** Pap. Berlin 10494. Černý, *LRL* 23–4 (no. 12). Translation and commentary: Wente, *LRL*, 44–5; Wente, *Letters*, 176–7 (no. 292).

192. **New Duties:** Pap. Phillips. Černý, *LRL* 28–30 (no. 15). Translation and commentary: Wente, *LRL*, 47–8; Wente, *Letters* 196–7 (no. 318).

193. **Visits to the Old Haunts:** (A) Graffito 714, in red. Spiegelberg, *Graffiti*, 57; *KRI* V. 849. (B) Graffito 1393. Jaroslav Černý, *Graffiti Hiéroglyphic et Hiératiques de la Nécropole Thébaine*. DFIFAO 9 (Cairo, 1956), 27. (C) Graffito 51. Spiegelberg, *Graffiti*, 7. Cf. the correction of the date by Černý, *Community*, 372 n. 4.

THE ROYAL TOMBS STAND OPEN

194. **Graffito in the Tomb of Ramesses II:** Spiegelberg, *Graffiti*, 93, IV.

195. **In the Tomb of Ramesses VI:** Spiegelberg, *Graffiti*, 92, II. C. A. Keller, 'How Many Draughtsmen Named Amenhotep? A Study of Some Deir el-Medina Painters', *JARCE* 21 (1984), 124.

196. **Reburying the Kings of Old:** Gaston Maspero, *Les Momies Royales de Déir el-Bahari*. Mémoires . . . de la Mission Archéologique Française au Caire, vol. 1, fasc. 4 (Cairo, 1889), 563–4. Translation in James Henry Breasted, *Ancient Records of Egypt* IV (New York, 1906, reissued 1962), § 640; Černý, *Community*, 372–3. The texts documenting the reburials of the New Kingdom pharaohs are discussed by Kenneth A. Kitchen, *Third Intermediate Period in Egypt* (1973), pp. 257–8, 262, 277–8; see also Valbelle, *Ouvriers*, 226.

197. **The Last Two Captains of the Gang:** J. Černý, 'Studies in the Chronology of the Twenty-First Dynasty', *JEA* 32 (1946), 26–7, and *Community*, 124 and 312–13. Maspero, *Les Momies Royales*, 522, recollated by Černý for his *JEA* transcription.

Glossary

***akh*-spirit**   spirit of a dead person who has special powers to influence events in this world and the next

Ba   the 'soul' or non-physical aspect of the individual

Amen   chief god of the New Kingdom

Amenophis   the deified Amenhotep I; this variant spelling is used here merely to differentiate the deified aspect of the king from his historical self

Amenhotep I   first king of the New Kingdom and founder of the village

barley   the grain used for brewing beer

cubit   unit of length of 52.5 cm. Divided into 7 'palms', of 4 'fingers' each

deben   unit of weight of 91 grams. Used especially for measuring copper

Deir el-Bahri   the bay in the cliffs of West Thebes which forms the setting for the funerary temples of the founder of the Middle Kingdom, Mentuhotep, and of Queen Hatshepsut

dual king   a title formed from the two most common words for 'king', which correspond to Upper and Lower Egypt and other aspects of kingship

emmer   the grain used for making bread

Enclosure of the Necropolis   administrative headquarters of the gang, situated to the north of the village

ennead   the first nine gods of creation, including the creator god Atum and his immediate offspring

finger   unit of length, $\frac{1}{4}$ of a palm.

god's father   a type of priest

Great Pit   (also called Grand Puits) a deep pit which was intended to serve as a well but which remained dry and was later filled with rubbish, including many ostraca

hin   unit of volume, 0.48 litres. Used especially for fluids

inundation   first four-month season of the year, after summer and before winter

ka   the creative life force of the individual

lector priest   literally 'he who carries the ritual-book'; a priest specialized in ritual

l.p.h.   'life, prosperity and health!'; good wishes expressed every time the king's name or that of the deified pharaoh Amenophis I is mentioned

Khonsu   god, son of Amen and Mut; member of the Theban triad

Medinet Habu   funerary temple of Ramesses III to the south-east of the village. The workmen moved to this temple when they abandoned Deir el-Medina at the end of the Twentieth Dynasty.

Meresger   goddess of the Theban necropolis, often depicted as a cobra

Mut   goddess, consort of Amen, member of the Theban triad

Necropolis   name of the administrative department concerned with work on the royal tomb

necropolis   the physical area in which are found the tombs of the kings and nobles

oipe   unit of volume equivalent to $\frac{1}{4}$ sack, thus 19.22 litres

ostracon   potsherd or flake of limestone used as a writing surface

palm   unit of length, $\frac{1}{7}$ of a cubit

Pre   variant writing of the name of the god Re

Ramesseum   funerary temple of Ramesses II, to the north-east of the village

sack   unit of volume of 76.88 litres, equivalent to 4 *oipe*. Used especially for measuring grain.

shabti   funerary figurine intended to serve the deceased in the Afterlife

sniw   unit of weight of varying amount but approximately $\frac{1}{10}$ of a *deben*, thus about 9 grams. Used especially for weighing silver.

summer   third and final four-month season of the year, after winter and before inundation

Ta-Weret   household goddess associated with childbirth, usually depicted as a pregnant hippopotamus

temenos   sacred precinct surrounding a temple or chapel

Turin Strike Papyrus   journal kept by the scribe Amen-nakhte of the strikes and other events of year 29 Ramesses III

verse points   points inserted above a line of text to mark a pause as an aid to reading

vizier   chief administrative officer of Egypt

wab-**priest**   literally, 'a pure one'; a general term for priest

winter   second four-month season of the year, after inundation and before summer

Index of Texts

(References in **bold** are to text nos.)

Index of Names

General Index